CHEYNE PUBLICATIONS
Unit 1, Willoughby Mews,
Wix's Lane,
London SW4 OHQ

GW00598158

Editor Simon Scrutton

The contents of this book are believed correct at the time of printing. Nevertheless, the publisher can accept no responsibility for errors or omissions or changes in the details given.

ISBN ISBN 0-9527409-1-5

Typeset by: INDEVISUAL DESIGN 01273 478059

Printed by APR 01825 761626

First published March 1999

Establishments are independently researched and inspected. Inspections are anonymous and carried out by our team of inspectors. The guide is independent in its editorial selection and does not accept advertising, payment or hospitality from listed establishments.

The idea of this book is to show you that the best food will cost you only a little more than its "factory-produced" alternative, and also where you can buy it.

> *It will certainly be less expensive than convenience foods!*

> *You only live once, which would you rather fill your body with?*

> *All that is needed is time and enthusiasm !*

Contents

How to use this book

All shops recommended by this guide are clearly listed in alphabetical order, giving it's opening time, nearest tube or rail station and buses that pass nearby.

Each one has been given it's own number. If you wish to find a certain product in a shop near you, look it up in the index to the rear of the book and it will list the shop numbers stocking the item; shops having a particularly wide selection of this product or making this item a speciality have their number marked with a * in this index.

Shops have also been divided into their relevant postal areas. Find these in the listings starting on page 166.

For background information on products and their producers turn to page 136 and read "Tips when buying and names to seek out"

Shops included in this book are all of a high standard. A few are exceptional, both in the variety of goods offered and in the service they provide, these have been awarded a ★ by their entry; some other outlets, while not quite coming up to ★ level in the products they offer, still give outstanding service and advice, these have been awarded an **S.**

A full list of these shops is on page 8

For standards to remain high, we would welcome justified criticism of any shop. These can be written on the forms on page 217. Likewise, if we have inadvertently missed any shops you feel are of an exceptional standard, or a new one opens near you, please let us know.

We hope this book makes your life a little easier, and eating the recommended products gives you added pleasure.

About the author

Simon Scrutton was Chef/proprietor of Byrons Restaurant in Eastbourne for over 20 years; where every effort was made to procure organic vegetables, local wild mushrooms and beautifully fresh fish from the local boats.

This culminated in winning Restaurant of the Year for Great Britain in one of Egon Ronay's prestigious guides.

Until moving to London, he broadcast each week as the food and wine expert of Invicta, Ocean Wave and Southern Sound Radio.

He has since been working as a restaurant and hotel inspector for one of the major national guides, and is also a partner in Mario and Simon Pasta and Mediterranean Sauce Company.

AWARDS

STARS ★

Given for the range of products offered, their freshness and quality, plus the manner in which they are served.

Aberdeen Sea Products, Unit 2, Toulmin St, SE1

Algerian Coffee Stores, 52 Old Compton St, W1

Allen & Co. 117 Mount St, W1

Amato Patisserie, 14 Old Compton St, W1

Max Angle, 1 Kennington Lane, SE 11

R.S Ashby, 4/5 Leadenhall Market, EC3

Ashdown, 23/25 Leadenhall Market, EC3

Barstow & Barr, 24 Liverpool St, N1

Billingsgate Market, North Quay West India Dock, E14

Blagden Fishmongers, 65 Paddington St. W1

Bluebird, 350 King's Road, SW3

Box's of Fulham, 110 Wandsworth Bridge Rd, SW6

Brown's, 37-39 Chalbert Street, NW8

Bumblebee, 30/32 & 33 Brecknock Rd. N7

Bushwacker Wholefoods, 132 King St. W6

Butlers Wharf Gastrodome, Shad Thames, SE1

Café Mezzo, 100 Wardour Street, W1

The Camden Coffee Shop, 11 Delancey Street, NW1

Cecil & Co. 393 Liverpool St. N1

Chalmers & Gray, 67 Notting Hill Gate, W11

The Cheese Block, 69 Lordship Lane, SE22

The Cheeseboard, 26 Royal Hill, Greenwich, SE10

& Clarke's, 122 Kensington Church Street, W8

Condon Fishmongers, 363 Wandsworth Road, SW8

Cope's of Bromley, 6 Widmore Road, Bromley, Kent

Da Rocco, 67 Highbury Park, N5

De Baere, 5 William St. SW1

De Gustibus, 53 Blandford Street, W1

Fortnum & Mason, 181 Piccadilly, W1

Fresco Fish, 60 Seven Sisters Rd. N7

La Fromagerie, 30 Highbury Park, N5

Frank Godfrey, 7 Highbury Park, N5

Golborne Fisheries, 75 Golborne Rd, W10

Good Harvest, 14 Newport Place, WC2

Graham's, 134 East End Road, N2

Hand Made Food, 40 Tranquil Vale, SE3

Harrods, Knightsbridge, SW1

Steve Hatt, 88-90 Essex Road, N1

The House of Albert Roux, 229 Ebury Street, SW1

Hamish Johnston, 48 Northcote Road, SW11

Harvey Nichols, Knightsbridge, SW1

The Hive, 53 Webb's Road, SW11

Jarvis & Sons, 56 Coombe Road, Norbiton, Surrey

Jeroboams, 24 Bute Street, SW7

Konditor & Cook, 22 Cornwall Road, SE1

C.Lidgate, 110 Holland Park Avenue, SW7

Limoncello, 402 St.John Street, EC1

Machen Brothers, 44 Turnham Green Terrace, W4 (0181-994 2646)

Maison Blanc, 102 Holland Park Avenue, W11

W. Martyn, 135 Muswell Hill Broadway, N10

Mise-en-Place, 21 Battersea Rise, SW11

Monmouth Coffee Company, 27 Monmouth Street, WC2

Neal's Yard Dairy, 17 Short's Gardens, Covent Garden, WC2

The Oil Merchant, 47 Ashchurch Grove, W12

Oz Fish Gallery and Prawn Bar, 95 Ballards Lane, N3

Planet Organic, 42 Westbourne Grove, W2 (0171-221 7171)

Porterford, 6 Bow Lane, EC4

Portwine, 24 Earlham Street, WC2

Walter Purkis & Sons, 52 Muswell Hill Broadway, N10

Randalls, 113 Wandsworth Bridge Road, SW6

The Real Cheeseshop, 62 Barnes High Street, SW13

Rippon Cheese Stores, 26 Upper Tachbrook Street, SW1

Sesame Health Foods, 128 Regent's Park Road, NW1

Scott & Son, 94 High Road, East Finchley, N2

Stenton, 55 Aldensley Road, W6

The Tea House, 15 Neal Street, Covent Garden, WC2

The Teddington Cheese, 42 Station Rd, Teddington, Surrey

Vivian's, 2 Worple Way, Richmond, Surrey

Wembley Exotics, 133-135 Ealing Road, Alperton, W10

Wild Oats Wholefoods, 210 Westbourne Grove, W11

SERVICE AWARDS

Given to shops perhaps not offering the widest range of goods, but none the less largely making up for this by giving excellent service and advice.

Marked with an **S**

Adamou & Sons, 124-126 Chiswick High Road, W4

Andreas, 18 Lordship Lane, East Dulwich, SE22

Eastern Grocers, 53 Hanbury Street, E1

Andreas Michli & Sons, 33 Salisbury Road, N4

W.J.Miller, 14 Stratford Road, W8

M. Moen & Sons, 17 The Pavement, SW4

Piacenza Delicatessen, 2 Brixton Road, SW9

Southfield Fruiterers, 253 Wimbledon Park Road, SW18

Sri Thai, 56 Shepherd's Bush Road, W6

L.Terroni & Sons, 138-140 Clerkenwell Rd, EC1

Valentina, 210 Upper Richmond Road West, SW14

The Village Pantry, 133 Pitshanger Lane, Ealing, W5

1   ABERDEEN SEA PRODUCTS ★

Unit 2, Toulmin Street, SE1 1PP
Tel: 0171-407 0247

Open: Mon-Thur 6am-1pm; Fri 6am-2pm; Sat 6am-10.30am
Closed: Sun & Bank Holidays

The strange opening hours here denote the fact that this is a main supplier to restaurants and other London fish shops, obtaining supplies straight from the coast overnight. Because of this, many restaurant items can usually be bought to try at home, including their excellent gravadlax, swordfish and tuna steaks, sea-bass (both wild and individually-sized farmed) and wild salmon; plus live eels, octopus and pike if ordered.
Tube: Borough   Buses: 35, 40, 133, 344, P3

2   A & C Co. CONTINENTAL GROCERIES

3 Atlantic Road. SW9 8HX
Tel: 0171-733 3766

Open: Mon-Sat 8am-8pm
Closed: Sun & Bank Holidays

Useful little shop, with many Portuguese specialities, efficiently run by the Cardoso's. They also sell a diversification of foods of what is now described as Mediterranean; this includes items such as Greek pilavuna bread, home-made taramasalata and houmous, fresh herbs plus a good range of pulses and spices. They make their own Caldo Verde (very thinly sliced green cabbage for Portuguese soup).
Tube & Rail: Brixton   Buses: 2, 3, 45, 109, 118, 133, 159, 196, 250

3   ACKERMANS ★

9 Goldhurst Terrace, NW6 3HX
Tel: 0171-624 2742

Open: Mon-Fri 9.30am-6pm; Sat 9.30am-5pm
Closed: Sun & Bank Holidays

This delightful little shop, just off the Finchley Road, sells what is probably London's best home-grown chocolate. What started as a small business about 50 years ago now sends hand-made chocolates all around the world; and indeed supply many of our other recommended chocolatiers. They can also be bought straight from the shop.
Tube: Swiss Cottage; Rail South Hampstead Buses: 13, 31, 82, 268, C12

Tip:

For a delicious condiment try Nanami Togarashi - this is a blend of chili pepper mixed with dried seaweed, sesame seeds and orange peel. A little livens up fried eggs like nothing else. It's cheaply available in small glass jars from Japanese grocers and the larger food halls.

4   ADAMOU & SONS

124-126 Chiswick High Road, W4 1PU
Tel: 0181-994 0752

Open: Mon-Sat 8am-7.30pm; Sun & Bank Holidays 8am-2pm
Closed: 25 & 26 Dec

Self-service grocer/greengrocer run by the Adamou family stocking a diverse range of products coming from as far afield as the Mediterranean and far-east. So everything from a good selection of dried pasta and olive oil, to curry paste and Thai basics. Their wide selection of fruit and vegetables makes an attractive pavement display. Friendly service; and helpful cooking advice.

Tube: Turnham Green   Buses: 27, 237, 267, 391, H91

5   ADA'S (formerly Criterion Ices)

118 Sydenham Road, SE26 5JX
Tel: 0181-776 6747

Open: Mon-Sat 9.30am-6pm; Sun 11am-6pm
Closed: 25 & 26 Dec

Turn left coming out of the railway station to find this ice cream parlour housed in Ada's Café. The ice cream here is available by the small tub or in bulk containers, and although no longer made on the premises since the change of ownership, is made with double cream in Suffolk - standards remain high.

Rail: Sydenham   Buses: 194, 202, 352, 450

6   ALEXANDER & KNIGHT

18 Barnes High Street, SW13 9LW
Tel: 0181-876 12972

Open: Tue, Thur & Fri 8am-5pm; Weds 8am-1pm; Sat 8am-4pm
Closed: Sun & Mon

Good local fishmonger, generally stocking tuna fish and fresh squid as well as more traditional items.

Rail: Barnes Bridge (5 minutes)   Bus: 209

7   ALGERIAN COFFEE STORES ★

52 Old Compton St. W1V 6PB
Tel: 0171-437 2480

Open: Mon-Sat 9am-7pm
Closed: Sun & Bank Holidays

Excellent little shop, whose windows bulge with every conceivable type of domestic coffee maker. Inside little has changed since the turn of the century; their claim to be a haven to all those bored with standard items is easily justified, the walls being covered with shelving holding their stocks of over 50 varieties. The choice of teas and tisanes is even more expansive, with every conceivable region and flavour on offer. Other useful items offered are ground roasted figs, vanilla pods, marron glacé, real maple syrup and a selection of Valrhona chocolate. A mail order service operates, plus a free deliver service for the W1 area for orders of over 25lbs.

Tube: Leicester Square/Piccadilly Circus

Buses:12, 14, 19, 22, 38, 94

8   ALLEN & CO. ★

117 Mount Street. W1Y 6HX
Tel: 0171-499 5831

Open: Mon-Fri 5am-4pm; Sat 6am-1pm

Closed: Sun & Bank Holidays

Very popular as a supplier to some of the capitals most prestigious restaurants, hence the early opening. This is one of London's best butchers and game dealers; you will find fresh foie gras and ducks legs (used by restaurants in confit). Grass-fed beef from Scotland, free-range pork and excellent lamb from the West Country. The range of game is enormous, if you are searching for something unusual, some snipe say, this is a good starting point! Free local delivery.

Tube: Green Park (5 minutes)   Buses:2, 8, 9, 10, 14, 16, 19, 22, 36, 38, 73, 74, 82, 137, 137a (all 5 minutes)

9   ALWADI ALAKHDAR

36 Upper Berkeley Street, W1H 7PG
Tel: 0171-402 7385

Open: Sun-Sat 8am-10pm

Closed: Bank Holidays

Lebanese supermarket, just off Edgware Road, stocking a wide range of Arab groceries. The chilled counter displays kebabs, falafel and stuffed vine leaves; while the window is crammed with a good selection of sweetmeats and sticky pastries.

Tube: Edgware Road (5 minutes)

Buses: 6, 7, 15, 16, 16a, 23, 36, 98

10   AMALFI DELICATESSEN

240 St. Paul's Road, Highbury, N1 2LJ
Tel: 0171-359 4398

Open: Mon-Sat 9am-7pm

Closed: Sun & Bank Holidays

This excellent Italian delicatessen has been run by Mrs Fattorusso since 1977. Offerings include all the necessities including fresh pasta, antipasti and well-sourced olive oils. Good ice cream from Marine Ices (q.v).

Rail: Highbury & Islington/Canonbury   Buses: 19, 30, 277

11 AMANDINE PATISSERIE
122 Wandsworth Bridge Road, SW6 2TF
Tel: 0171-371 8871

Open: Mon-Sun 7.30am-6pm
Closed: 25, 26 Dec & 1 Jan

Popular patisserie/café selling good quality baguettes, croissants, pain au chocolats etc. This stretch of Wandsworth Bridge Road also offers excellent fish (Box's), meat (Randall's) and a useful little deli (Eaton's); the combined quality of which beats any known supermarket - and all from one parking/bus stop!

Tube: Fulham Broadway (15 minutes)   Buses: 28, 295, C4

12 AMATO PATISSERIE ★
14 Old Compton Street, W1V 5PE
Tel: 0171 734 5733

Open: Mon-Sat 8am-10pm; Sun & Bank Holidays 10am-8pm
Closed: 25, 26 Dec & 1 Jan

Excellent patisserie/café whose window is so tempting for the sweet of tooth it is hard to pass by. Cakes are of the highest standard and are offered whole or by the slice. Good croissants.

Tube: Leicester Square   Buses: 12, 14, 19, 22, 38, 94

13 AMBRA
59a/61 Abbey Road, NW8 9DA
Tel: 0171-328 8692

Open: Mon-Sat 9am-10pm ; Sun 10am-10pm
Closed: Bank Holidays

Useful delicatessen/café, also selling a few interesting vegetables.

Tube: St. John's Wood   Buses: 139

14 AMICI DELICATESSEN
78 High Road, East Finchley N2 9PN
Tel: 0181-444 2932

Open: Mon-Fri 9am-7pm; Sat 8.30am-7pm
Closed: Sun & Bank Holidays

Italian delicatessen and tiny café just by the East End Road/Fortis Green junction. An impressive selection of dried pasta (mainly De Cecco) and a good range of olive oils plus all the basics to produce an Italian meal, make this a useful stop off.

Tube: East Finchley   Buses: 102, 143, 263

**Please use the forms at the back of this book
to recommend your own favourite shops**

15   ANDREAS DELICATESSEN

18 Lordship Lane, SE22 8HN
Tel: 0181-299 2214

Open: Mon-Fri 8.30am-9pm; Sat 8am-10pm; Sun & Bank Holidays
10am-10pm
Closed: 25, 26 Dec & 1 Jan

The Malekos family have run this friendly Cypriot grocer/greengrocer
since 1984. Popular items include Greek cakes and their excellent home-
made houmus and taramasalata, whose are made without preservatives.
They have a policy that if it's Greek, and they haven't got it, they can get it!
Rail: East Dulwich Buses: 37, 40, 176, 185, 484

16   ANDREAS FISH BAR

445 Green Lanes, N4 1HA
Tel: 0181-347 5310

Open: Mon-Thur 8.30am-8.30pm; Fri & Sat 8.30am-9.30pm; Sun 8.30am-
7.30pm
Closed: Bank Holidays

A window display offers a good selection of interesting fish here,
including a few exotics; and the shop certainly fills a need in this fish-
starved area. The wet fish section is combined with a fish and chip shop,
which on our visit was not of the same high standard.
Rail: Harringay Green Lanes   Buses: 29, 141, 171a, 922

17   MAX ANGLE ★

1 Kennington Lane, SE11 4RG
Tel: 0171-735 1931

Open: Tue, Thur, Sat & Sun 8am-4pm; Wed 8am-1pm; Fri 8am-5pm
Closed: Mon & Bank Holidays

Tony Bradley's excellent fish shop next to The Lobster Pot restaurant fills
a real need in this area, and has been run with great enthusiasm since he
took it over in 1995. Beautifully displayed fish might include fresh tuna
and swordfish, sea bass and turbot; all of which can be bought by the
piece. Undyed kippers and smoked haddock, rock oysters, crabs and
lobsters are other treats. Bronze turkeys can be ordered at Christmas.
Tube: Elephant & Castle/Kennington Buses: 3, 109, 159, 322

18   ANTEPLILER

47 Green Lanes, N4 1AG
Tel: 0181-809 1003

Open: Mon-Sun 9am-9pm Closed: 25 & 26 Dec

Excellent Middle-Eastern baker/pattiserie, well-known for its baklava and
eastern sweetmeats.
Rail: Harringay Green Lanes   Buses: 29, 141, 171a

19   APPLE N' ORANGE
20 Old Dover Road, SE3 7BT
Tel: 0181-858 1307

Open: Mon-Sat 8am-5.30pm (Fri till 6pm)
Closed: Sun & Bank Holidays
Greengrocer in the same parade as G.G. Sparkes the butcher (q.v)
offering a good selection plus value for traditional fruit and vegetables,
in a otherwise expensive area.
Rail: Westcombe Park (10 minutes)   Buses: 53, 54, 108, 286

20   APPLEWOLD FARM SHOP
206 Portobello Road, W11 1LA
Tel: 0171-229 5282

Sadly now closed!

21   ARCHIE FOOD STORE
14 Moscow Road, W2 4BT
Tel: 0171-229 2275

Open: Mon-Sun 8am-8pm
Closed: Bank Holidays
Little middle-eastern grocer/greengrocer selling a good selection of
pulses and dried fruit; plus a selection of fresh fruit (often including
fresh dates and pomegranates) and vegetables.
Tube: Bayswater   Buses: 70

22   ARIGATO
48 Brewer Street, WIR 3FG
Tel: 0171-287 1722

Open: Mon-Sat 9am-9pm; Sun 11am-8pm;
Closed: Bank Holidays
Useful in the area, this shop has a selection of mainly packeted or frozen
Japanese goods. These include the excellent Nanami Togararashi
seasoning, wasabi horseradish, noodles plus whole mackerel and
octopus from the freezer. Take-away sushi counter.
Tube: Leicester Square/Piccadilly Circus   Buses: 12, 14, 19, 22, 38 , 94

23   ARKWRIGHTS
20 Barnes High Street, SW13 9LW
Tel: 0181-878 1520

Open: Mon noon-6pm; Tue-Fri 9am-6pm; Sat 9am-5.30pm
Closed: Sun & Bank Holidays
Popular little shop selling excellent sausages, in various modern flavours,
and hamburgers (of rissole proportions) - all made on the premises.
Rail: Barnes Bridge (5 minutes)   Bus: 209

24 R.S. ASHBY

4/5 Leadenhall Market, EC3V 1LR
Tel: 0171-626 3871

Open: Mon-Fri 5am-4pm; Fri 5am-5pm
Closed: Sun & Bank Holidays

Established for over half a century this excellent butcher has some of the best meat available; including Buccleuch Scottish beef, lamb from Wales and Scotland and mutton from Ireland - all from known herds. These are backed up by excellent bacon and ham from Denhay, good home-made sausages, interesting charcuterie, Bronze turkeys at Christmas and a large selection of cheese. Game in season, often includes pheasant supremes, useful for a quick meal. A range of dishes such as chicken korma or chicken with coriander and lemon is available to cook at home.

Tube: Bank/Monument   Buses: 8, 22a, 22b, 25, 26, 35, 47, 48, 149

25 ASHDOWN ★

23/25 Leadenhall Market, EC3V 1LR
Tel: 0171-626 1949

Open: Mon-Thur 6am-3.30pm; Fri 6am-4pm
Closed: Sat, Sun & Bank Holidays

Excellent fishmonger, in the elegant Leadenhall Arcade, with it's own up market restaurant above. Luxury items such as sea-bass, halibut, turbot and scallops are everyday items. While native oysters, wild salmon, pike and a large selection of game are available in season. Excellent smoked salmon comes in London and Scottish cures and their own fish cakes are delicious if a little expensive. Oysters and lobsters are held in sea water tanks in the basement, while eels, crayfish, and langoustines can be procured with a little notice. Fresh geese and Bronze turkeys at Christmas.

Tube: Bank/Monument   Buses: 8, 22a, 22b, 25, 26, 35, 47, 48, 149

26 JANE ASHER PARTY CAKES

22/24 Cale Street, SW3 3QV
Tel: 0171-584 6177

Open: Mon-Sat 9.30am-5.30pm
Closed: Sun & Bank Holidays

Cake shop owned by the eponymous actress and cookery writer. Cakes can be personalised into various exciting shapes, but for this service a minimum of one weeks notice is required; but stock items are available and the standards are high.

Tube: South Kensington (10 minutes)
Buses: 11, 14, 19, 22, 49, 211, 319, 345, 349

27 ATARI-YA FOOD

595 High Road, No2rth Finchley, N12 0DY
Tel: 0181-446 6669
Branch @ 7 Station Parade, Noel Road, W3 (0181-896 1552)

Open: Tue-Fri 10am-6.30pm; Sat & Sun 10am-7pm
Closed: Mon & Bank Holidays

Japanese fishmonger offering wet fish for cooking, fish for the preparation of sushi plus a counter of beautifully prepared sushi; possibly including squid, octopus and sea-urchin. A few basic Japanese groceries are also stocked.

Tube: West Finchley (10 mins)   Bus: 263

28 ATHENIAN GROCERY

16a Moscow Road, W2 4BT
Tel: 0171-229 6280

Open: Mon-Fri 8.30am-5.30pm; Sat & Sun 8.30am-1.30pm; Bank Holidays 10am-1pm
Closed: 25 & 26 Dec

Excellent Greek corner shop, selling everything from fresh fruit and vegetables, to pulses and dried fruit.

Tube: Bayswater   Bus: 70

29 AU GOURMET GREC

124 Northfield Avenue, W13 9RT
Tel: 0181-579 2722

Open: Tue, Thur & Fri 9.30am-6pm; Weds 9.30am-1.30pm; Sat 9am-5pm;
Closed: Sun, Mon & Bank Holidays

Popular Greek and East European grocer with a good delicatessen section. Excellent Ukrainian rye bread from The Kolos Bakery of Bradford.

Tube: Northfields   Buses: E2, E3

30 AUSTRIAN SAUSAGE CENTRE

10a Belmont Street, NW1 8HH
Tel: 0171-267 5412

Open: Mon-Fri 7am-5pm; Sat 7am-1pm
Closed: Sun & Bank Holidays

In an industrial estate just off the Chalk Farm Road, the entrance of this shop hides behind a door covered in hanging plastic strips. A wide variety of cooked meat, plus sausages from Poland and Germany and Austria are on offer.

Tube: Chalk Farm   Buses: 31, 168, C11, C12

31 AZIZ BABA DELI PASTAHANESI
47 Newington Green, N16 9PX
Tel: 0171-359 2338

Open: Mon-Sun 8.30am-9pm
Closed: Bank Holidays

Excellent Turkish bakery and good value traiteur. Expect to find home-made stuffed aubergines and vine leaves as well as traditional salads.

Rail: Canonbury (5 mins)   Buses: 73, 171a

32 THE BAGATELLE BOUTIQUE
44 Harrington Road, SW7 3NB
Tel: 0171-581 1551

Open: Mon-Sat 8am-8pm; Sun 8am-6pm
Closed Christmas Day

Although basically a splendid French bakery and patisserie in the heart of West London, Bagatelle, under the direction of Monsieur Lesellier, offers so much more. A good range of charcuterie (including many excellent patés and terrines), backed up by a selection of carefully kept French cheese; plus traiteur dishes - 3 starters, main courses, salads and vegetables on offer each day; and a larger permanent choice which can be ordered; plus useful items such as smoked salmon, fresh foie gras and caviar as temptations. They are one of London's largest suppliers of bread and pastries to the restaurant trade, using 100% French flour. We the public benefit from this - delicious croissants, baguettes, rustic and flavoured bread plus a selection of cakes and pastries. The fact they are practically open the year round, makes them doubly useful.

South Kensington (5 minutes)   Buses: 49, 70, 74

33 BAKER & SPICE
46 Walton Street, SW3 1RB
Tel: 0171-589 4734

Open: Mon-Sat 7am-7pm; Sun 8.30am-2pm
Closed: Bank Holidays

Useful little shop run by Gail Stephenson and Philippe Dade, supplying good bread and cakes plus traiteur dishes and a few cheeses. Disappointing powdery meringues.

Tube: South Kensington (5 mins)   Buses: 14, 49, 345

34 BALHAM MARKET
Hildreth Street, SW12

Open: Mon, Tue, Weds, Fri & Sat 9.30am-5pm; Thur 9.30am-1pm
Closed: Sun & Bank Holidays

Situated in a pedestrian street between Bedford Hill and Balham High Street this little market has a good selection of fruit and vegetables, including two stalls specialising in Afro-Caribbean products. Local shops supply halal meat and interesting fish.

Tube: Balham   Buses: 155, 315, 355

35   BALHAM WHOLE FOOD SHOP

8 Bedford Hill, SW12 9RG
Tel: 0181-673 4842

Open: Mon, Wed, Fri & Sat 9.30am-6pm; Tue & Thur 9.30am-7pm
Closed: Sun, Bank Holidays & Lunch each day 1-2.30pm

Good little health-food shop just off Balham High Road, jam-packed with carefully chosen products from around the world. Martin Pitt eggs.

Rail/Tube: Balham   Buses: 155, 315, 355

36   B & J FISHERIES

147a Kilburn High Road, NW6 7HT
Tel: 0171-624 0356
Branch @ 35 Craven Park Road, NW10 (0181-963 0722)

Open: Tue-Sat 8.30am-5.30pm; Sat 8.30am-5pm
Closed: Sun, Mon & Bank Holidays

Excellent display of gleaming fresh fish at this popular little fish shop.

Rail: Kilburn High Road; Tube: Kilburn Park
Buses: 16, 16A, 28, 31, 32, 98, 206

37   B & M SEAFOODS & THE PURE MEAT CO.

258 Kentish Town Road, NW5 2AA
Tel: 0171-485 0346

Open: Tue-Sat 9am-6pm
Closed: Sun, Mon & Bank Holidays

Bob Birchenall has been supplying Kentish Town and it's environs with his fresh fish and excellently sourced meat, game and poultry since 1987.

Tube: Kentish Town   Buses: 134, 135, 214, C2, C11

38   BARRETT'S

40 England's Lane, NW3 4UE
Tel: 0171-722 1131

Open: Mon-Sat 8.30am-5.30pm
Closed: Sun & Bank Holidays

Good traditional butcher, particularly well known for it's excellent Scottish beef.

Tube: Chalk Farm   Buses: 31, 168, C11, C12,
     Tip:
For easy Party nibbles try St. Michael Premium Snack Mix for about £1-20 for a 90g bag from Marks & Spencer. It resembles an up market, but very much more subtle version of Bombay mix, and tastes good as well.

40 BARROW BOAR

Fosters Farm, South Barrow, Yeovil, Somerset, BA22 7LN
Tel: 01963 440315

The Dauncey's introduced Wild Boar to their family farm in 1984, and have seen it's popularity rise ever since. Animals are reared naturally, foraging in open pasture with oak coppices. Their diet, although supplemented by potatoes and beet, is much as it would have been in the wild. The business has expanded and now also supplies rare meats from around the world, including bison, alligator and locusts - which are meant to be excellent stir-fried!

Mail Order Only

41 BARSTOW & BARR ★

24 Liverpool Road, N1 OPU
Tel: 0171-359 4222
Branch @ 32-34 Earl's Court Road, W8 6EJ (0171-937 8004)

Open: Tue-Fri 10am-10pm; Mon noon-10pm; Sat 9am-6pm;
Sun 10-30-2.30pm. Closed: Bank Holidays

The Barr's excellent cheese shop, near the junction with Upper Street, is among London's best. The British Isles and France are the main events, with about 120 varieties to choose from. Knowledgeable and friendly advice is always at hand. Good free-range eggs from Ireland are a bonus.

Tube: Angel   Buses: 4, 19, 30, 38, 43, 73, 153

42 BATTERSEA HIGH STREET MARKET

Battersea High Street, SW11

Open: Mon-Sat 9.30am-4.30pm
Closed: Sun & Bank Holidays

Old-fashioned fruit and vegetable market offering very competitive prices, particularly near closing time on Saturday night, when serious bargains are to be had.

Rail: Clapham Junction   Buses: 44, 49, 319, 344, 345

43 G.H. BAXTER

330 Greenford Avenue, Hanwell, W7 3DA
Tel: 0181-578 1728

Open: Mon-Sat 6.30am-5.30pm; Sun 8am-1pm
Closed: Bank Holidays

This good quality butcher, run by the Wright family for nearly 100 years, stocks free-range chickens and pork as well as top quality grass-reared beef and lamb. Their connections with the catering trade provide the bonus of Sunday opening.

Rail: South Greenford/Castle Bar Park (10 minutes)   Buses: 41, E3

44 BELSIZE VILLAGE DELICATESSEN

39 Belsize Lane, NW3 5AS
Tel: 0171-794 4258

Open: Mon-Fri 8.30am-7pm; Sat 8.30am-6pm; Sun 9am-2pm
Closed: Bank Holidays

Find this popular delicatessen set in the cluster of useful shops that
surrounds the junction with Belsize Crescent. Traiteur and salad dishes
are the heart of the operation, and are good; a summer visit brought
gaspacho, chicken provencale, spare ribs in barbecue sauce, salmon
fishcakes and stuffed aubergines from among the offerings. Standard deli
items are all in evidence, charcuterie and cheeses being strong suits,
particularly the French variety of the later, which arrives directly from
France on Thursdays.

Tube: Swiss Cottage (10 minutes)   Buses: none within 5 minutes walk

45 BERWICK STREET MARKET

Berwick Street & Rupert Street, W1

Open: Mon-Sat 9am-5pm
Closed: Sun & Bank Holidays

Excellent market with a delightful old-fashioned atmosphere.
Competition appears to be strong particularly among the fruit and
vegetable stalls - some of which stock fresh herbs and up market
produce, all at bargain prices. Fish stalls often have exotics and usually
fresh carp as well. Well worth a visit in it's own right, and you can also
pick up probably London's best sausages from Simply Sausages (qv).

Tube: Piccadilly   Buses: 3, 6, 7, 8, 10, 12, 13, 14, 15, 19, 22, 23, 25,
38, 53, 55, 73, 88, 94, 98, 139, 159, 176, X53

46 BEST FRUIT FARE

77 The Broadway, Southall, Middx. UB1 1LA
Tel: 0181-574 6596

Open: Mon -Sun 7am-8pm
Closed: 25 & 26 Dec

Good Asian greengrocer. Useful opening hours.

Rail: Southall   Buses: 95, 105, 120, 195, 207, 607, E5, H32

47 BETHNAL GREEN ROAD MARKET

Bethnal Green Road, E2

Open: Mon, Tue, Weds, Fri & Sat 8.30am-5.30pm; Thur 8.30am-12.30am
Closed: Sun & Bank Holidays

Market between Vallance Road and Wilmot Street selling good value
fruit, vegetables, fish and meat.

Tube: Bethnal Green   Buses: 8 , 106, 253, D6

48 R.A. BEVAN & SONS
136 Richmond Road,
Kingston-upon-Thames, Surrey, KT2 5EZ
Tel: 0181-546 0783

Open: Mon 8.30am-5pm; Tue, Thur & Fri 8.30am-5.30pm;
Weds 8.30am-1pm: Sat 8am-4pm
Closed: Sun & Bank Holidays
Family butcher selling top quality meat, from carefully chosen sources,
plus a selection of home-cooked meats.
Rail: Kingston Buses: 65, 415

49 BEVERLY HILLS BAKERY
3 Egerton Terrace, SW3 2BX
Tel: 0171-584 4401

Open: Mon-Sun 7.30am-6.30pm
Closed: Bank Holidays
Popular American-style bakery selling traditional items such as muffins
(in various interesting flavours) and pecan pie, all made on the premises
from natural ingredients. Baskets of muffins, mini-croissants and cookies
are available; starting from £25 for 27 pieces - including delivery to a
London address.
Tube: South Kensington Buses: 14, 74, C1

50 BIBENDUM CRUSTACEA
Michelin House, 81 Fulham Road, SW3 6RD
Tel: 0171-589 0864

Open: Mon-Sat 9.30am-7pm; Sun 9.30-3pm; Bank Holidays 9.30-7pm
Closed: 25, 26 Dec & 1 Jan
This elaborate fish stall is located under the covered forecourt of the
splendid Michelin building. As the name implies crustaceans are the
main event; but a range of white fish, often including brill, turbot, tuna
and halibut are stocked. The generous opening hours make this an
excellent source of goodies for those surprise guests.
Tube: South Kensington (5 minutes)   Buses: 14, 49, 345,

51 BIFULCO
182 Cricklewood Lane, NW2 2DX
Tel: 0181-452 2674

Open: Mon-Fri 7am-5.30pm; Sat 7am-1pm
Closed: Sun & Bank Holidays
Good butcher just off Hendon Way selling grass-fed Scottish beef, and
other carefully sourced items including Bronze turkeys. Free delivery.
Rail: Cricklewood (10 mins)   Buses: 13, 28, 82, 139, 245, 260

52   BIGGLES

66 Marylebone Lane, W1M 5FF
Tel: 0171-224 5937

Open: Tue-Fri 9.30am-6pm; Mon & Sat 9.30am-4.30pm
Closed: Sun & Bank Holidays

Colin Bailey has run this specialist sausage shop, tucked away just north of Wigmore Street, since 1989. He produces over 50 varieties as diverse as traditional Cumberland's to Kangaroo, all in natural skins with no mechanically recovered meat or artificial colourants used.

Tube: Bond Street (5 mins)   Buses: 3, 7, 8, 10, 12, 16a, 25 , 53, 55, 73, 88, 98, 113, 137, 137a, 176, X53

53   BIG MARKET RETAIL

192 Ealing Road, Alperton, HAO 4SS
Tel: 0181-903 5927

Open: Mon-Sun 8am-8pm
Closed: 25 Dec

Find good value fruit and vegetables from the Indian sub-continent at this self-service greengrocers - opposite the all night Wembley Exotics(q.v); to make sure of an absolute bargain there is also the equally competitive Santa Fruits across the road. Almost give-away prices are to be found at all these shops, tomatoes at 15p a pound on a recent visit!

Tube: Alperton   Buses: 79, 83, 224, 297

54   BILLINGSGATE MARKET ★

Billingsgate Road, North Quay West India Dock,
Isle of Dogs, E14

Open: Tue-Sat 5am-8.30am
Closed: Sun, Mon & Bank Holidays

This world famous fish market is just as fascinating in it's new location. Every conceivable fish is available when in season; but don't expect bargains unless you buy in bulk or have an account.

Rail/DLR: West India Quay   Buses: 277, D6, D7, D8

55   BLAGDEN FISHMONGERS ★

65 Paddington Street, W1M 3RR
Tel: 0171-935 8321

Open: Mon 7.30am-4.30pm; Tue-Fri 7.30am-5pm; Sat 7.30am-1pm
Closed: Sun & Bank Holidays

Since it was established in the early '50s this has been one of London's best fishmongers. Very little has been frozen, apart from a selection of exotics, so supplies follow the seasons. Wild salmon, turbot, halibut, john dory and sea bass are all stocked when available. A wide range of game is also available in season, plus Bronze turkeys and geese at

Christmas. Friendly, helpful service is backed up by recipe sheets to help you cook different types of fish and game. Free local delivery.
Tube: Baker Street
Buses: 2, 13, 18, 27, 30, 74, 82, 113, 139, 159, 274

56 BLISS

428 St. John St. EC1V 4NJ
Tel: 0171-837 3720

Open: Mon-Fri 8am-7pm; Sat, Sun & Bank Holidays 9am-6pm
Closed: 25 & 26 Dec

Tim Jones runs this tiny baker/patisserie, which produces a range of excellent bread - possibly walnut, sunflower or sesame seed - as well as the more usual varieties; plus biscuits, quiches and delicious cakes. Their croissants, coming in a variety of flavours, are very popular. All these can be eaten in-house at their café at the back, accompanied by excellent coffee or tea.
Tube: Angel   Buses: 19, 38, 153, 171a

57 THE BLUEBIRD GASTRODROME ★

350 King's Road, SW3 5UU
Tel: 0171-559 1153/1222

Open: Mon-Sat 9am-late; Sun 11am-5pm
Closed: Bank Holidays

Sir Terence Conran's Bluebird venture is a gourmets delight, until the opening of Villandry (q.v), offering a range of first-class items not to be found under one roof in London. There are separate departments for meat, fish, fruit and vegetables, charcuterie and patisserie each sporting carefully sourced products. Bread of a high standard and comes from the in-house bakery; a large selection of traiteur dishes from the restaurant kitchens upstairs is also on display, many of these need a little finishing at home. A selection of vinegar and olive oil is on offer, some sold straight from barrels - so bring a bottle. Expect a full gastronomic education with seasonal fruit and vegetables alone listing such items such as lovage, sea kale, nettles , wild mushrooms and the promise of over 100 types of apple in the autumn. Prices are generally high, but bargains are always to be found among the vegetables, and on other items that perhaps need a little searching out (i.e 2 dozen snails with shells for just over £2). A telephone ordering system and delivery service operate (deliveries cost £3-50, but are free for purchases of over £75).
Tube: Sloane Square (15 minutes)
Buses: 11, 19, 22, 31, 49, 211, 319, 345

58 BON VIVANT DELICATESSEN

59 Nightingale Lane, SW12 8ST
Tel: 0181-675 6314

Open: Mon-Fri 8.30am-8pm; Sat 8.30-7pm; Sun 9.30am-12.30pm
Closed: Bank Holidays

Excellent delicatessen run with enthusiasm by Simon Robertson since 1986. Good selection of cheese, particularly the best of English; bacon from Denhay and Slack's, and eggs to accompany it from Martin Pitt; Saturday tends to be the best wild mushroom day. Good home-made traiteur dishes from the deep freeze and toffee from Penrith.

Tube: Clapham South   Bus: G1

59 L. BOOTH of St. Pauls

3 St.Andrews Hill, EC4V 5BY
Tel: 0171-236 5486

Open: Mon-Fri 7am-6pm; Sat 7am-noon
Closed: Sun & Bank Holidays

Interesting grocer/greengrocer run by Tony Booth. As well as day to day necessities, exotic fruit and vegetables, he is a major supplier of wild mushrooms to the catering trade; these and his other speciality - an almost a year-round supply of asparagus - make this a "destination" shop.

Tube: Blackfriars/St.Pauls   Buses: 4, 11, 15, 17, 23, 25, 26, 76, 172

60 BOROUGH MARKET

West side of Borough High Street, SE1

Open: Mon-Sat 5.30am-10pm
Closed: Sun & Bank Holidays

Really a wholesale market, hence the hours, and possibly London's oldest. Fantastic displays of fruit and vegetables, and with a little persuasion some of the stalls will sell in domestic quantities.

Tube/Rail: London Bridge   Buses: 21, 35, 40, 48, 133, 344, N21

61 BOX'S OF FULHAM ★

110 Wandsworth Bridge Road, SW6 2TF

Open:Tue-Sat 5am-6pm
Closed: Sun, Mon & Bank Holidays

Excellent fishmonger which is deservedly popular in the wholesale trade. Because of this the selection is wide and if not in stock, Donal Box will do his utmost to procure it for you. So expect to find sea bass, brill or turbot, Dover soles, tuna and swordfish steaks plus a good range of shellfish. First class "London" (mild) cure smoked salmon is produced on the premises; this is occasionally joined by their own kippers and Arbroath-style smokies. Bronze turkeys at Christmas.

Tube: Fulham Broadway (10 minutes)   Buses: 28, 295

62 BRIXTON MARKET
Electric Avenue, Pope's Road & Brixton Station Road, SW9

Open: Mon, Tue, Thur, Fri & Sat 8.30am-5.30pm; Wed 8.30am-1pm
Closed: Sun & Bank Holidays

Vibrant street market selling many African and Caribbean foodstuffs as well as the more familiar. It's an exciting place to shop, and prices are keen, particularly for fruit and veg. Saturday can be unpleasantly busy. Good cheap meat and fish shops abound, many with temporary names and no telephone listings. See Granville Arcade (q.v.).

Tube & Rail: Brixton   Buses: 2, 3, 35, 45, 109, 118, 133, 159, 196, 250

63 BRIXTON WHOLE FOODS ★
59 Atlantic Road, SW9 8PU
Tel: 0171-737 2210

Open: Mon & Fri 9.30am-6pm; Tue-Thur & Sat 9.30am-5.30pm
Closed: Sun & Bank Holidays

Excellent health-food shop surrounded by the bustle and excitement of Brixton Market. Excellent bread including some from The Village Bakery and The Celtic Baker. An enormous range of pulses, including organic Puy lentils; fruit juices; and specialist spices (these sold loose at bargain prices). Organic milk and soya milk plus a selection of yoghurt encompassing cow, goat, sheep and soya. If something is not stocked they take great pride in trying to obtain it.

Tube/Rail: Brixton   Buses: 2, 3, 35, 45, 109, 118, 133, 159, 196, 250

64 BROADWAY MARKET
Upper Tooting Road, SW17

Open: Mon, Tue, Thur, Fri & Sat 9.30am-5pm; Weds 9am-1pm
Closed: Sun & Bank Holidays

Undercover market just north of the tube station. A few good fruit and vegetables stalls, plus a fish stall with a few exotics. Meat here is more geared to price than quality.

Tube: Tooting Broadway   Buses: 155, 219, 355

65 BROTHERHOOD'S
38 Replingham Road, SW18 5LR
Tel: 0181-874 2138

Open: Mon-Fri 8.30am-8pm; Sat 9am-6pm; Sun 9am-3pm
Closed: Bank Holidays

A good selection of carefully chosen charcuterie, olive oil and Neal's Yard (q.v) cheeses make this delicatessen deservedly popular with the residents of Southfields.

Tube:Southfields   Buses: 39, 156

66 BROWN'S ★

37-39 Charlbert Street, NW8 6JN
Tel: 0171-722 8237

Open: Mon-Sat 7.45am-5.30pm
Closed: Sun & Bank Holidays
One of London's best fishmongers; always a good selection of fish and shellfish, and usually lobsters and crabs. Delivery service.
Tube: St. John's Wood   Buses: 274

67 B's

167 Draycott Avenue, SW3 3AJ
Tel: 0171-581 0676

Open: Mon-Fri 7am-7pm; Sat 7am-4pm. Closed: Sun & Bank Holidays
A useful grocer/greengrocer/deli selling everything from fresh herbs to tinned cassoulet.
Tube: South Kensington Buses: 14, 49, 345

68 BUCKINGHAM BUTCHERS

63 Blythe Road, W14 OHP
Tel: 0171- 603 5170

Open: Mon, Tue, Wed & Fri 8.30am-5.30pm; Thur 8.30am-noon;
Sat 8.30am-5pm
Closed: Sun & Bank Holidays
Small butcher offering personal service, good meat and Martin Pitt eggs.
Tube: Olympia (10 minutes)   Buses: 9, 9a, 10, 27, 28, 391 (5 minutes)

69 BUMBLEBEE ★

30, 32 & 33 Brecknock Road, N7 ODD
Tel: 0171-607 1936

Open: Mon-Sat 9.30am-6.30pm (Thurs till 8.00pm)
Closed: Sun & Bank Holidays
An impressive set of three shops, near the junction with Leighton Road, between them selling everything from carefully chosen groceries, health foods and organic vegetables, to British farmhouse cheese, dairy products and Martin Pitt eggs. A few healthy looking take-away dishes are on offer at No. 32. Worth a visit! No.33 is across the road.
Tube: Tufnell Park (10 minutes)   Buses: 10, C12

70 BUNCES

10 Broadway Parade, N8 9DE
Tel: 0181-340 5542

Open: Mon-Sat 8.30am-7pm; Sun 10am-4pmClosed: Bank Holidays
This popular delicatessen/traiteur has been run by the Foradaris family since 1990. Expect to find a good selection of charcuterie, a large range

of fresh pasta, hard to find items like rice paper and mostarda di frutta and tempting Belgian chocolates. Moussaka and stifado set the style for traiteur items, and are good value.

Rail: Crouch End & Hornsey (10 minutes)   Buses: 41, 91, W5

71   BUSHWACKER WHOLE FOODS ★
132 King Street, Hammersmith, W6 OQU
Tel: 0181-748 2061

Open: Mon 10am-6.30pm; Tue-Thur 10am-6pm; Fri 9.30am-6pm; Sat 9.30am-6.30pm
Closed: Sun & Bank Holidays

Chris and Sunita Shipton's excellent shop can be found opposite Hammersmith Town Hall, and draws in discerning vegetarians from miles around. No effort has been spared seeking out speciality bread, butter, coffee, eggs, preserves, milk, yoghurts and pulses - many organic; plus a range of chocolate for diabetics.

Tube: Hammersmith   Buses: 27, 190, 266, 267, 391, H91

72   BUTCHER & EDMONDS ★
1, 2 & 3 Grand Avenue, Leadenhall Market, EC3V 1LR
Tel: 0171-626 5816

Open: Mon-Fri 6.30am-4pm. Closed: Sat, Sun & Bank Holidays

Specialist game dealer, in the delightful Leadenhall Arcade, having one of the widest selections in London. Thursday and Friday bring the best selection, but telephone first as supplies vary with the weather. Their meat is also of good quality and includes French chickens, Bronze turkeys and excellent haggis at Christmas and Aberdeen Angus beef. Gulls eggs are available in season (end of April and all May).

Tube: Monument/Bank   Buses: 8, 22a, 22b, 25, 26, 35, 47, 48, 149

73   BUTE STREET BOUCHERIE
19 Bute Street, SW7 3EY
Tel: 0171-581 0210

Open: Mon-Fri 7.30am-6pm; Sat 7.30am-5pm
Closed: Sun & Bank Holidays

Martin Croucher's butchers is very popular with the strong local French population; and panders to their need with boudins, French ducks and occasionally fresh foie gras. Some organic meat.

Tube: South Kensington Buses: 14, 49, 70, 74, 345, C1

DID YOU KNOW? After the Indian sub-continent, Britain consumes more spices and exotic fruit per capita than any other country. If you think this figure can't include you, look at the ingredients listed on a brown sauce bottle, these will include garlic, dates, tamarinds and many spices!

74   BUTLERS WHARF GASTRODROME ★

Sir Terence Conran's original "Gastrodrome" (now joined by The
Bluebird [q.v]) consists of four restaurants, each with its own individual
style of cooking, an excellent wine merchant (attached to Le Pont de La
Tour restaurant), and the two food-shops below.

OILS AND SPICE SHOP

36e Shad Thames, SE1 2YE
Tel: 0171-403 3434
Open: 12 noon-6pm Closed: 25, 26 Dec & 1 Jan
The location of this shop is most appropriate for it was here that the
British East India Company unloaded its precious spice cargoes in
days gone by. Over 50 different spices are now offered, and a selection
of oils from all over the world. These include estate-bottled olive oil
from Italy and first-pressing oils from France, Portugal, Spain and
Greece; also nut and seed oils - including pistachio and pumpkin.

LE PONT DE LA TOUR FOOD STORE

36d Shad Thames, SE1 2YE
Tel: 0171-403 4030
Open: Mon-Fri 9am-8.30pm; Sat & Sun 10am-6pm
Closed: 25, 26 Dec & 1 Jan
Described by Sir Terence as "a delicatessen selling daily-baked bread
by our own bakery and specialist items that people with an
appreciation for food and wine might like". This aim has certainly
been achieved, for as well as the enormous range of excellent bread -
10 varieties at any time, and a alternating range of nearly 50; any of
which can be ordered with 24 hours notice - the shop is crammed
with goodies ranging from top-quality fresh fish and crustacia to
charcuterie, cheese and deli items. Delicious fresh soup is available
throughout the day, and sandwiches are made to order.
Tube: London Bridge/Tower Hill (10 minutes)   Buses: 42, 47, 78

75   CAFE MEZZO ★

100 Wardour Street, W1Y 3LE
Tel: 0171-314 4060
Open: Mon-Sat 8.30am; Sun & Bank Holidays 10am-10-30pm
Closed: 25 & 26 Dec
Attached to the well-known restaurant complex of the same name this
excellent café/patisserie is the equal of any other in Soho. A window full
of cakes and fresh fruit tarts shows just some of what is on offer, and
unlike many patisseries everything tastes as delicious as it looks!
Tube: Piccadilly/Oxford Circus/Tottenham Court Road
Buses: 8, 10, 14, 19, 22, 38, 73

76 THE CAMDEN COFFEE SHOP ★

11 Delancey Street, NW1 7NW
Tel: 0171-387 4080

Open: Mon & Wed 9.30am-5pm; Tue, Fri & Sat 9.30am-6pm;
Thur 9.30-3pm. Closed: Sun & Bank Holidays

The choice is restricted to eight varieties at George Hajiconstantinou's excellent little coffee shop; this ensures that the beans, which are all roasted on the premises, are in peak condition. Bargain prices and excellent service.

Tube: Camden Town
Buses: 24, 27, 29, 31, 134, 135, 168, 214, 253, 274, C2

77 I. CAMISA & SON

61 Old Compton St. W1V 5PN
Tel: 0171-437 7610

Open: Mon-Fri 8.30am-5.55pm; Sat 8am-5.55pm
Closed: Sun & Bank Holidays

This busy Italian delicatessen, crammed full of goodies, has been run by the same family since the mid '70s. Good range of Italian cheese, charcuterie, olives plus fresh and dried pasta is backed up by home-made sauces and char-grilled vegetables.

Tube: Piccadilly Circus/Leicester Square
Buses: 14, 19, 22, 24, 29, 94, 38, 176, 229

78 CARLUCCIO'S

28a Neal Street, WC2H 9PS
Tel: 0171-240 1487

Open: Mon-Thur 11am-7pm;Fri 7 Sat 10am-6pm
Closed: Sun & Bank Holidays

Italian delicatessen run by the Carluccio family, of television fame. All the standards are available here at a price, plus traiteur dishes and their speciality - wild mushrooms. Delivery service for central London.

Tube: Covent Garden   Buses: 14, 19, 24, 29, 38, 176

79 CARMELLI BAKERIES

128 Golders Green Road, NW11 8MB
Tel: 0181-455 3063

Open: Mon-Wed 7am-midnight; Thur 7am-all night; Fri till 3pm; Sat 7pm-Mon 1am
Closed: Jewish religious holidays, including Passover

Impressive modern kosher bakery specialising in bagels, which are particularly popular late at night. Flavours include poppy seed, onion, sesame and cinnamon. Everything is made on the premises, including the cream cheese for their cheesecakes. A tempting display of pastries is hard to resist. Wedding cakes are a speciality.

Tube: Golders Green (5 minutes)

Buses: 83, 183, 210, 240, H2, H3

80   T.H. CARR
139 Pitshangar Lane, W5 1RH
Tel: 0181-997 5639

Open: Mon 9am-1pm; Tues, Thur & Fri 8am-5.30pm; Weds 8am-1pm; Sat 8am-4pm

Closed: Sun, Bank Holidays & Tues after; & 2 weeks in September.

Popular fishmonger run since 1982 by the Saunders family, Mr Saunders has just finished a long stint as Chairman of The London Fish & Poultry Association, so he really knows his job. The selection is not enormous but always gleamingly fresh, and still might include Sea bass, tuna and Dover sole. Exotics, fresh clams and the like can be procured with a little notice. Game in season, plus geese and Bronze turkeys at Christmas.

Tube/Rail: Ealing Broadway (15 minutes)   Buses: E2, E9

81   CARR TAYLOR
Westfield, Hastings, East Sussex, TN35 4SG
Tel: 01424 752501

A vineyard that is, as far as we know, Britain's only vertjus producer. This is supplied by mail order. £14-25 for six bottles at the time of writing, vertjus is made from crushed and strained unripe grapes, but is not acidic like vinegar - having more of a sherry quality.

Mail Order Only

82   THE CATCH
760 Fulham Road, SW6 5SH
Tel: 0171-736 1523

Open: Tue-Fri 8.30am-5.30pm; Sat 8.30am-4pm

Closed: Sun, Mon & Bank Holidays

Tiny fishmongers run with great enthusiasm; the simple window display may only show a little of what's available; as most will be refrigerated. The end of the week brings an impressive choice.

Tube: Parsons Green/Putney Bridge (10 minutes)   Buses:14, C4

83   CAVIAR KASPIA
18 Bruton Place, W1X 7AA
Tel: 0171-493 2612

Open: Mon-Sat 10am-11pm.

Closed: Sun & Bank Holidays

Since opening in 1987 this shop, tucked away off Berkeley Square, has been one of London's best sources of caviar. All types are stocked, as

well as pre-prepared blinis to impress your friends.
Tube: Green Park/Bond Street.   Bus: 8

84   CECIL & CO ★

393 Liverpool Road, N1 1NP
Tel: 0171-700 6757

Open: Mon 8am-noon; Tue-Fri 8am-2pm; 8am-10.30am
Closed: Sun & Bank Holidays

Fishmonger specialising in supplying the wholesale trade, hence the
strange opening hours. Because of this the range offered is more extensive
than other local establishments. Weather permitting fish includes sea bass,
brill, halibut and turbot. Undyed kippers, Arbroath smokies, fresh crabs,
and oysters are normal stock items; as are a range of exotics and tuna and
swordfish steaks. It's one of London's few fish shops to regularly stock live
eels. James Knight of Mayfair (q.v) is under the same ownership.
Tube/Rail: Highbury & Islington   Buses: 19, 30, 153, 271, 277

85   CERES WHOLE FOODS

427a Upper Richmond Road West,
East Sheen, Surrey, SW14 7PJ
Tel: 0181-878 7403

Open: Mon-Sat 9am-5.30pm
Closed: Sun & Bank Holidays

Small health food shop opposite Waitrose. Despite it's size all the usual
requirements are stocked plus the luxury of Martin Pitt eggs.
Rail: Mortlake (10 minutes)   Buses: 33, 337

86   CHALMERS & GRAY ★

67 Notting Hill Gate, W11 3JS
Tel: 0171-221 6177

Open: Mon-Fri 8am-6pm; Sat 8am-5pm
Closed: Sun & Bank Holidays

The fish is beautifully presented and the selection wide at this popular
shop close to the tube station, which ranks amongst London's best fish
shops. Prices are firm, but more than reasonable for the service and
quality offered. John Gray is only too willing to order special items such
as carp or pike which are not normally stocked. Free delivery service for
the West End.
Tube: Notting Hill Gate. Buses: 12, 27, 28, 31, 52, 52a, 70, 94, 302

Please use the forms at the back of this book
to recommend your own favourite shops

87 CHAPEL MARKET, N1
Between Penton Street and Liverpool Road

Open: Tue, Wed, Fri & Sat 9am-5pm; Thur & Sun 9am-12.30pm
Closed: Mondays & Bank Holidays
Good value market for everyday food items of all kinds, but nothing
exotic except Barstow & Barr's cheese (qv) nearby.
Tube: Angel   Buses: 4, 19, 30, 38, 43, 73, 153

88 CHARBONNEL ET WALKER
1 Royal Arcade, 28 Old Bond Street, W1X 4BT
Tel: 0171-491 0939
Branch @ 20 Royal Exchange, EC3 (0171-283 5843)

Open: Mon-Fri 9am-6pm; Sat 10am-5pm
Closed: Sun & Bank Holidays
Madame Charbonnel and Mrs Walker started this chocolate shop in 1875.
While standards remain high and the products beautifully presented, prices
are high, for those that can afford them they make excellent presents.
Tube: Green Park   Buses: 9, 14, 19, 22, 38

89 CHARLES
46 Elizabeth Street, SW1W 9PA
Tel: 0171-730 3321

Open: Mon-Fri 8am-5.30pm; Sat 8am-1pm
Closed: Sun & Bank Holidays
Good quality butcher/fishmonger also selling game in season. Useful
source of caviar and fresh foie gras.
Tube: Sloane Square/Victoria   Bus: C1

90 THE CHEESE BLOCK ★
69 Lordship Lane, SE22 8EP
Tel: 0181-299 3636

Open: Mon-Fri 9am-7pm; Sat 9am-6pm; Sun 10am-1pm
Closed: Bank Holidays
Excellent cheese shop near the north end of Lordship Lane. Everything is
carefully labelled to help you chose, and quality is high. Generally over
200 cheeses are stocked at any one time.
Rail: East Dulwich (5 minutes)   Buses: 40, 176, 185, P13

91 THE CHEESEBOARD ★
26 Royal Hill, Greenwich, SE10 8RT
Tel: 0181-305 0401

Open: Mon-Wed 9am-5pm;Thur 9am-1pm;Fri 9am-5.30pm;Sat 8.30am-5pm
Closed: Sun & Bank Holidays
Excellent cheese shop, tucked up this little road, run with great

enthusiasm since 1984 by Michael Jones. Over 150 types of cheese are stocked from over ten countries (many unpasteurised), plus butter of an equally high standard. A selection of carefully chosen bread includes some from The Village Bakery, Cumbria. Mail order, often with next day delivery. A visit can be combined with Dring Brothers Butchers (almost next door). The new Docklands Light Railway extension (to open in 1999?) will open up excellent shops like these to many more people.

Rail: Greenwich (or DLR, then foot-tunnel under river)

Buses: 53, 53X, 180, 199

92   CHEESES

13 Fortis Green Road, N10 3HP
Tel: 0181-444 9141

Open: Mon-Thur 10am-5.30pm; Fri 10am-6pm; Sat 9.30am-6pm
Closed: Sun & Bank Holidays

Good little cheese shop specialising in French regional and British farmhouse cheeses. Knowledgeable staff.

Tube: East Finchley (5 minutes)   Buses: 102, 143, 263

93   CHELSEA CATERING CO

305 Fulham Road, SW10 9QH
Tel: 0171-351 0538

Open: Mon-Sat 8am-9pm Closed: Sun & Bank Holidays

Good delicatessen/traiteur which also operates an outside catering arm, hence the name. Excellent hams, include Denhay and their own cures; British cheeses include Denhay Cheddar, Ticklemore and Mrs Kirkham's Lancashire; and a treasure trove of goodies that include patés, biscuits, condiments and pastries.

Tube: Fulham Broadway (10 mins)   Buses: 14, 211(going east), 345

94   THE CHELSEA FISHERY

10 Cale Street, SW3 3QU
Tel: 0171-589 9432

Open: Tue-Sat 8.30am-4pm (Thur till 3pm)
Closed: Sun, Mon & Bank Holidays

Useful small fishmonger on Chelsea Green, not a vast selection but the fish always looks gleamingly fresh.

Tube: South Kensington (10 minutes)   Buses: 11, 14, 19, 211, 345, 349

95   THE CHOCOLATE CLUB

Unit 9, St. Pancras Commercial Centre, 63 Pratt St. NW1 OBY
Tel: 0171-267 5375

Under the chairmanship of Peter Sheppard chocloholics are sent a catalogue full of temptations and a regular news letter. Only the very best chocolate, from around the world, is offered, including unusual

seasonal items e.g Ackerman's truffle-filled Easter eggs. A gift service includes a hand-written card, and beautiful packaging. Membership of the club is free, but necessitates an initial £10 order.
Mail Order Only

96   THE CHOCOLATE SOCIETY
36 Elizabeth Street, SW1W 9NZ
Tel: 0171-259 9222
Open: Mon noon-6pm; Tues, Weds & Fri 9am-6pm; Thur 9am-7pm;
Sat 10am-5pm
Closed: Sun & Bank Holidays
Chocolate shop doubling as a café (selling very good hot chocolate supplied by Valrhona); also a very good source of cooking chocolate. Presents are a speciality, and a delivery service operates.
Tube: Sloane Square/Victoria (10 minutes)   Bus: C1

97   CHORAK
122 High Road, East Finchley, N2 9ED
Tel: 0181-442 0370
Open: Mon-Sat 8.30am-6pm
Closed: Sun & Bank Holidays
You can often see the bread being baked and apple tarts emerging from the ovens at this useful baker/café near the junction of Fortis Green. Chola, ciabatta and Irish soda bread are all baked on the premises; plus good Danish and other pastries.
Tube: East Finchley   Buses: 102, 143, 263

98   CHOUMBERT ROAD & RYE LANE MARKET
Rye Lane, Peckham, SE15
Open: Mon-Fri 9am-5pm
Closed: Sat, Sun & Bank Holidays
Excellent market, just off Rye Lane south of the railway station, especially for those seeking Caribbean and Asian food; you'll find fruit, vegetables, fish and meat here - some of it quite unusual.
Rail: Peckham Rye   Buses: 12, 37, 63, 78, 312, P3, P12, P13

99   CHRISP STREET MARKET
Market Square, Chrisp Street, E14
Open: Mon-Sat 9.30am-4pm
Closed: Sun & Bank Holidays
Undercover market offering good fruit and vegetables here (including exotics), particularly nearer the weekend.
Rail/DLR: All Saints/Devons Road   Buses: 309, D8

100 CHUANGLEE ORIENTAL SUPERMARKET
98 Streatham High Road, SW16 1BS
Tel: 0181-677 4033

Open: Sun-Sat 9am-7pm
Closed: 25 Dec

Useful shop, near the corner of Norfolk House Road, describing itself as
a suppler of Chinese-Japanese-Malaysian-Phillipino and Thai groceries
and seafood. Whilst this is true, goods are either preserved in jars or
deep-frozen, and some prices are high - 1lb frozen North Atlantic prawns
for £4·95 on an inspection visit - more than twice the price charged by
most fishmongers and supermarkets!
Rail: Streatham Hill
Buses: 57, 60, 109, 118, 133, 159, 201, 250, P13

101 CHURCH STREET MARKET
Church Street, NW8

Open: Tue-Sat 9am-5pm. Closed: Sun, Mon & Bank Holidays
The food section of this interesting market stretches from Edgware Road
to Lisson Grove. Good fruit and vegetables, cheap meat plus dried fruit
and nuts.
Tube: Edgware Road   Buses: 6, 7, 8, 15, 16, 16a, 23, 36, 98

102 CIACCIO
5 Warwick Way, SW1V 1QU
Tel: 0171-828 1342
Branch @ 17 Strutton Ground, SW1

Open: Mon-Fri 10am-7pm; Sat 9.30am-6pm
Closed: Sun & Bank Holidays
Situated near the eastern end of Warwick Way, this little shop is the outlet
for one of London's best fresh pasta producers. Both cooked and uncooked
varieties are sold here, plus a variety of home-made sauces, the former
can be eaten on site or taken away. The selection is limited, but by
planning ahead, a phone call can have a multitude of flavours waiting for
you the next day. Gorgonzola ravioli is a personal favourite of ours.
Tube: Pimlico/Victoria   Buses: 2, 24, 36, 185

103 CITY MEATS
421 King's Road, SW10
Tel: 0171-352 9894

Open: 8.30am-6pm. Closed: Sun & Bank Holidays
Useful butcher selling excellent albongidas (Spanish meat balls), black-
legged French free-range chickens plus a few good quality delicatessen items.
Tube: Fulham Broadway (15 minutes)
Buses: 11, 14, 22, 31, 211 (west-bound)

104 & CLARKE'S ★

122 Kensington Church Street, W8 4BH
Tel: 0171-229 2190

Open: Mon-Fri 8am-8pm; Sat 9am-4pm. Closed: Sun & Bank Holidays
A treasure trove of a shop next to Sally Clarke's famous restaurant.
Although bakery is their main claim to fame here - they bake twenty five
types of excellent bread (such as rosemary & raisin and oatmeal honeypot)
and supply to many shops in London to list here - all the periphery items
are made and chosen with equal care. Biscuits, cakes (their chocolate
cake is delicious) and shortbread, made on the premises; their own jam
and marmalade; preserved and fresh vegetables; a range of some of the
best butter; flour - from chestnut to buckwheat; olive and nut oil to
tempt any gourmet, British cheese from Neal's Yard (q.v), Winters Dairy
ice cream and coffee from the Monmouth Coffee House (q.v).
Tube: Notting Hill Gate (5 minutes)   Buses: 27, 28, 31, 52, 70

105 CONDON FISHMONGERS ★

363 Wandsworth Road, SARI 2JJ
Tel: 0171-622 2934

Open: Mon 8.45am-noon; Tues, Weds & Fri 8.45am-5.30pm; Thur 8.45-
1pm; Sat 8.15am-4.30pm. Closed: Sun & Bank Holidays
Originally opened in 1902, this excellent fish shop has a loyal local
following, and is still run by the same family. A wide selection of white
fish, including some luxury items like sea bass and turbot is backed up
by marvellous smoked items that Ken Condon produces from his
smokery. These include haddock, bloaters, kippers and his popular
smoked salmon; the now rarely found red herrings can be produced by
special order. A system of loaning out fish kettles to the buyers of large
fish is a nice touch, and shows their commitment to service.
Tube: Vauxhall & Stockwell; Rail: Vauxhall   Buses: 77, 77a, 322

106 LE CONNAISSEUR

49 Charlbert Street, NW8 6JN
Tel: 0171-722 7070

Open: Mon-Fri 8am-6pm; Sat 8am-5pm; Sun 9am-1pm
Closed: 25, 26 Dec & 1 Jan
Tiny patisserie run by Josef Keppeln close to Regents Park. Particularly
delicious fruit flans & tarts.
Tube: St. John's Wood (5 minutes)   Buses: 274

107 COOKSLEY'S BUTCHERS

12 The Broadway, Mill Hill, NW7 3LL
Tel: 0181-959 1374

Open: Mon-Fri 8.30am-5pm; Sat 8.30am-4pm

Closed: Sun & Bank Holidays
Top-class free-range meat and poultry are the speciality of this excellent butchers run by Nigel Cooksley.
Rail: Mill Hill Broadway   Buses: 113, 114, 186, 240, 251, 302

108 COOL CHILE COMPANY

PO Box 5702, W11 2GS
Tel: 0171-229 9360

Progressive company run by Dodie Miller supplying chili of all types, plus items such as Mexican chocolate and ground corn for making tortillas. Their price list is helpful by marking chili strengths on a scale of 1-10 and describing their individual characters. Seeds are generally available in January, so you can grow your own. Prices are reasonable, and because of their weight, delivery cheap.Some products are available from Harvey Nichols, Garcia's (qv) and some Sainsbury's. *Mail Order*

109 THE COOLER

67 Stoke Newington Church Street, N16 OAR
Tel: 0171-275 7266

Open: Mon-Sat 9am-9pm; Sun 10am-3pm Closed: Bank Holidays
Good delicatessen/café in a much needed area. Well -sourced items, include soup from The Real Company of Northumberland and condiments from Wiltshire Tracklements. Interesting wines are a bonus.
Rail: Stoke Newington (5 minutes)   Bus: 73

110 COPE'S OF BROMLEY ★

6 Widmore Road, Bromley, Kent BR1 1RY
Tel: 0181-460 3343

Open: Mon-Sat 9am-6pm Closed: Sun & Bank Holidays
Geoffrey Cope has been running his excellent fishmongers since 1967, and the shop has acted as a magnet for fish lovers for many miles around. An impressive selection often includes fresh tuna, marlin and swordfish as well as more familiar varieties. He uses an old smokehouse to produce his own smoked salmon and has a good stock of game in season.
Rail: Bromley South   Buses: 208, 227, 402

111 COPE'S SEAFOOD COMPANY

700 Fulham Road, SW6 5SA
Tel: 0171-371 7300

Open: Tue-Sat 10am-8pmClosed: Sun, Mon & Bank Holidays
Good little fishmonger, run by the brother of the above; specialising in caviar, fresh crab, oysters, Dover sole and the top end of the market.
Tube: Parson's Green/Putney Bridge (10 minutes)   Buses: 14, C4

112 COPPIN BROTHERS

276 Mitcham Road, Tooting, SW17 9NT
Tel: 0181-672 6053

Open: Mon-Fri 8am-5pm; Sat 8am-5.30pm
Closed: Sun & Bank Holidays

This excellent butcher, run by the Coppin family for over 100 years, is like an oasis in this area; expect to find grass-reared beef and lamb, plus free-range pork and poultry.

Tube: Tooting Broadway
Buses: 44, 57, 77, 127, 133, 264, 270, 280, 355, G1

113 THE CORNER SHOP & OFF LICENCE

59 Wellesley Road, Chiswick, W4 3AR
Tel: 0181-994 7434

Open: Mon-Sat 11am-10pm; Sun noon-2pm & 7pm-10pm
Closed: Bank Holidays

Useful little shop, on the corner with Clarence Road, selling grocery basics and Martin Pitt eggs.

Rail/Tube:Gunnersbury (5 minutes)   Buses: 237, 267, 391 (5 minutes)

114 J.A. CORNEY

9 Halleswelle Parade, Finchley Road, NW11 0DL
Tel: 0181-455 9588
Branch @ 81 High Street, Edgware (0181-952 0302)

Open: Tue-Thur 8am-5pm; Fri 8am-4pm; Sat & Sun 8am-1pm
Closed: Mon & Bank Holidays

Good old-fashioned fishmonger with everything displayed on marble slabs. A good selection might include fresh-water bream (lasht) from Ireland, sea bass and wild salmon, as well as the more mundane. Turnover is fast, and the prices keen!

Tube: Golders Green (10 minutes)   Buses: 82, 102, 260

115 CORNISH FISH DIRECT

The Pilchard Works, Tolcarne, Newlyn, Cornwall, TR18 5QH
Tel: 01327 263438

An excellent service, allowing you to receive fish as fresh as that used by the top restaurants. Simply discuss your order with them, and it will be delivered to your doorstep by noon the following day, neatly packed and filleted if required. A speciality is their salted pilchards, and their list is due to expand to include fish from outside Cornwall such as wild salmon from the Rivers Torridge, Severn and Wye. The minimum order is £30 plus carriage, but you can always share with a friend or freeze the beautifully fresh fish that will arrive!

Home delivery only

116 CORNUCOPIA

64 St. Mary's Road, Ealing W5 5EX
Tel: 0181-579 9431

Open: Mon-Sat 9am-5pm Closed: Sun & Bank Holidays

Health food shop with a good range of pulses, cheese and the bonus of Martin Pitt eggs.

Tube: South Ealing   Bus: 65

117 COVENT GARDEN FISHMONGERS

37 Turnham Green Terrace, W4 1RG
Tel: 0181-995 9273

Open: Tue & Wed 4.30am-5.30pm; Fri 4.30am-5.45pm; Sat 4.30am-5pm
Closed: Mon, Sun & Bank Holidays

The Diamond family have been running their excellent fish retail and wholesaler (hence the extended hours) since 1978. The enormous range of fish and crustacea is beautifully displayed, and excellent advice is on hand from Phil who has also written his own book The Covent Garden Fish Book. Game in season plus a small selection of ready-made sushi.

Tube: Turnham Green   Buses: E3, H91, 27, 237, 267

118 CRESCENT FRUITERERS

62 Belsize Lane, NW3 5AR
Tel: 0171-435 9444

Open: Mon-Fri 7am-7pm; Sat 7am-6pm; Sun 7am-1pm
Closed: Bank Holidays

Traditional greengrocer opposite Belsize Village Delicatessen (q.v), with modest mark-ups for the area. Also sells a good selection of cut flowers

Tube: Swiss Cottage (10 mins)   Buses: none within 5 minutes walk

119 CULLEN PATISSERIE

108 Holland Park Avenue, W11 4UA
Tel: 0171-221 3598
Branch @ Unit 5, Lancer Square, 28a Kensington Church Street, W8 (0171-937 3252)

Open: Mon-Sat 8am-8pm; Sun 8am-7pm
Closed: Bank Holidays

Good café/patisserie. Rather overshadowed by the excellent , but more expensive, Maison Blanc nearby. In a normal area this shop would be a "find".

Tube: Holland Park   Buses: 49, 94, 295

Tip:

To stop salt becoming damp in your salt-mill and refusing to grind, add a few grains of uncooked rice to the mill; this will cure the problem.

120 CURNICK

170 Fulham Road, SW10 9PR
Tel: 0171-370 1191

Open: Mon-Fri 8am-5.30pm; Sat 8am-4pm. Closed: Sun & Bank Holidays
Traditional butcher selling high quality meat and specialising in grass-reared beef from Sussex. Game in season.
Tube: Fulham Broadway (10 minutes)
Buses: 14, 49, 211 (east-bound), 345

121 R.F. CUTTING

109 St. John's Hill, Battersea, SW11 1SY
Tel: 0171-228 3367

Open: Mon 8am-5.30pm; Tue-Thur 7am-5.30pm; Fri 7am-6pm; Sat 7am-5pm Closed: Sun & Bank Holidays
Useful little butcher/greengrocer. Good home-made sausages and Martin Pitt eggs.
Rail: Clapham Junction (5 minutes)
Buses: 37, 39, 77a, 156, 170, 295, 337, C3

122 DADU'S CASH & CARRY

190-198 Upper Tooting Road, SW17 7EW
Tel: 0181-672 4984

Open: Mon-Sat 9.30am-7pm; Sun & Bank Holidays 10am-4pm
Closed: 25 Dec
Rather basically decorated supermarket selling an excellent range of Indian groceries, many packaged for restaurants and large families, but extremely good value. If you have space for big bags of rice, pulses and spices, you can buy them here for the same price as you would often pay for packets many times smaller.
Tube: Tooting Broadway   Buses: 155, 219, 355

123 DAMAS GATE

81-85 Uxbridge Road, W12 8NR
Tel: 0181-743 5116

Open: Mon-Sun 7am-10pm. Closed: Bank Holidays
Useful grocer/greengrocer/halal butcher specialising in the products of the Middle East. A more comprehensive range of halal meat is on offer at Shaheer at No 79 (0181-740 0096)
Tube: Shepherd's Bush   Buses: 49, 94, 95, 207, 237, 260, 295, 607

124 DANDELION

120 Northcote Road, Battersea, SW11 6QU
Tel: 0171-350 0902

Open: Mon-Sat 9.30am-6pm Closed: Sun & Bank Holidays

Health food shop selling a good selection of organic pulses and rice. A few vegetables and salads are generally on offer, plus a comprehensive range of vitamin supplements. Martin Pitt eggs.

Rail: Clapham Junction   Buses: 319, G1

125 DANIEL'S BAGEL BAKERY

12-13 Hallswelle Parade, Finchley Road, NW11 0DL
Tel: 0181-455 5826

Open: Sun-Weds 7am-9pm; Thur 7am-10pm; Fri - summer 7am-6pm, winter 1/ hrs before sabbath
Closed: Sabbath; Jewish religious holidays, including Passover

Good kosher bakery, also selling top-quality home-made biscuits. A delicatessen section offers gefilte fish balls, latkes etc.

Tube: Golders Green (10 minutes)   Buses: 82, 102, 260

126 DA ROCCO ★

67 Highbury Park, N5 1UA
Tel: 0171-359 2670

Open: Mon-Sat 8am-7pmClosed: Sun & Bank Holidays

Find this shop, specialising in fresh pasta, on the corner of Lucerne Road. Particularly popular is their vegetable tortelloni and their ravioli which comes with lobster, crab or veal stuffings.

Rail: Drayton Park (5 minutes) Buses: 4, 19, 236

127 DAVIDS FOOD STORE

215 Belsize Road, NW6 4AA
Tel: 0171-328 2773

Open: Sun-Sat 9am-8pmClosed: Bank Holidays

Useful little local grocer, and a source for Martin Pitt's eggs.

Tube: Kilburn Park; Rail: Kilburn High Road   Buses: 16, 16a, 28, 31, 32

128 DE BAERE ★

5 William Street, SW1X 9HL
Tel: 0171-235 4040
Branches @ 24 Bute St. SW7 (0171-591 0606)
& 101 Notting Hill Gate, W11 (0171-792 8080)

Open: Mon-Sun 9am-9pm (Summer); 9am-7pm (Winter)
Closed: 25, 26 Dec & 1 Jan

First class Belgian café/patisserie run by Rik De Baere offering chocolates, cakes, biscuits and croissants of the highest standard. These are are made in-house at the companies bakery in Acton.

Tube: Knightsbridge   Buses: 9, 10, 14, 19, 22, 52, 74, 137, 137a

129 D & D SPECIALIST CHOCOLATES

Berrydale House, 5 Lawn Road, NW3 2XS
Tel: 0171-722 2866

Useful source of dairy-free and carab "chocolate", with novelty items, such as hollow animals (bears, elephants, monkeys and dogs) as well as filled chocolates and bars. They try to despatch orders within 24 hours.
Mail Order Only

130 DEEPAK CASH & CARRY

953 Garrett Lane, SW17 0LW
Tel: 0181-767 7819
Branch @ 193 Upper Tooting Road, SW17

Open: Mon-Sat 9am-7pm; Sun 10am-3.30pm Closed: 25 Dec
Grocer, at the southern end of Garrett Lane, specialising in goods from the Indian sub-continent. Everything you need is stocked here, but often in catering-sized containers.
Tube: Tooting Broadway Buses: 44, 77, 127, 133, 219, 264, 270, 280, G1

131 DE GUSTIBUS ★

53 Blandford Street, W1H 3AF
Tel: 0171-486 6608

Open: Mon-Fri 7.30am-4.30pm; Sat 9am-2pm
Closed: Sun & Bank Holidays
Excellent bread shop specialising in delicious sour-doughs. A main supplier to other shops and restaurants.
Tube: Baker Street & Marble Arch (10 minutes)
Buses:2, 13, 30, 74, 82, 113, 139, 159, 274

132 THE DELI AT COOKSBRIDGE

Station House, Cooksbridge, Nr. Lewes,
East Sussex, BN8 4SW   Tel: 01273 401287

Open: Mon-Sat 10am-7pm Closed: Sun & Bank Holidays
Our one and only inclusion outside London - this delicatessen/traiteur is run with great enthusiasm by two ex-chefs, and is on a railway station, so ideal for commuters. Offerings include excellent home-made sauces, ready meals (held in their deep freeze) and well-kept cheeses. A successful catering business is also run from the premises, so home-made cheesecakes, Christmas pudding and pavlovas can be ordered; plus hampers at two days notice.
Rail: Cooksbridge

Please use the forms at the back of this book
to recommend your own favourite shops

133 THE DELICATESSEN SHOP

23 South End Road, NW3 2PT
Tel: 0171-435 7315

Open: Mon-Fri 9.30am-7pm; Sat 9am-6pm
Closed: Sun & Bank Holidays

Find Sandra Cavaciuti's delicatessen opposite the railway station; she manages to cram a lot into a small space, at busy times just getting in and out can be a problem. Specialities are fresh pasta (which you can often see spinning out of the machine) plus accompanying sauces, cheese and a range of pre-prepared dishes such as pancakes stuffed with spinach and ricotta. Individually made sandwiches are popular, and unusually can be made out of anything you see in the shop.

Rail: Hampstead Heath; Tube: Belsize Park (10 mins)   Buses: 24, 168

134 DEPTFORD CODFATHER

47 Deptford High Street, SE8 4AD
Tel: 0181-692 3292

Open: Mon-Sat 8am-5pm
Closed: Sun & Bank Holidays

Good little fishmonger, set in this street full of market stalls (see Deptford High Street Market below). As well as native varieties a wide selection of exotics are stocked and are popular with the local West Indian community.

Rail: Deptford   Buses: 47, 53, 177, 225, X53

135 DEPTFORD HIGH STREET MARKET

Deptford High Street, SE8

Open: Mon-Sat 8.30am-4pm
Closed: Sun & Bank Holidays

There are good fruit and vegetable stalls at this market, which stretches south from the railway station, particularly those favoured by the ex-Caribbean community. The surrounding shops offer good support, particularly Halal Butchers (at no. 109) and a branch of Kennedy's Sausages (q.v - at no. 64). See also Deptford Codfather (above).

Rail: Deptford   Buses: 47, 53, 177, 225, X53

136 DEVONIA

53a Old Town, SW4 0JQ
Tel: 0171-622 7017

Open: Mon-Fri 10am-6pm; Sat 10am-1pm
Closed: Sun & Bank Holidays

Useful little delicatessen specialising in products from the West Country. A popular outside catering operation is based at the shop.

Tube: Clapham Common   Buses: 45, 88, 137, 345

137 DI LIETO BAKERY & DELICATESSEN

175 South Lambeth Road, SW8 1XW
Tel: 0171-735 1997

Open: Mon-Sat 9.30am-7pm; Sun 11am-3pm
Closed: Bank Holidays & 2 weeks in August?

Bakery specialising in Italian bread, all baked on the premises. A delicatessen section stocks all the basics.

Tube: Stockwell (5 minutes)   Buses: 2, 88

138 DILLO'S

50 Leverton Street, NW5
Tel: 0171-482 1709

Open: Mon-Tue & Thur-Sun 9.30am-8pm
Closed: Weds, 25 Dec & 1 Jan

Corner shop (with Ascham St.) selling useful basics and Martin Pitt eggs.

Tube: Kentish Town   Buses:134, 135, 214, C2

139 DOKAL

133-135 The Broadway, Southall, Middx. UB1 1LW
Tel: 0181-574 1647

Open: Mon-Sun 9am-8pm
Closed; 25 & 26 Dec

Indian grocer, stocking everything imaginable, run by the Dokal family since 1970.

Rail: Southall   Buses: 95, 105, 120, 195, 207, 607, E5, H32

140 A. DOVE & SON

71 Northcote Road, SW11 6PJ
Tel: 0171-223 5191

Open: Mon 8am-1pm; Tue-Sat 8am-6pm
Closed: Sun & Bank Holidays

Excellent family butcher in a street that's a haven for foodies. Free range pork, Welsh Black and Aberdeen Angus beef, free-range chickens. Various homemade pies (mainly variations on the excellent beef) are available from the freezer. Game in season. Bronze Turkeys and free range geese between Thanksgiving and Christmas.

Rail: Clapham Junction   Buses: 319, G1

141 DRING BROTHERS

22 Royal Hill, SE10 8AT
Tel: 0181-858 4032

Open: Mon-Fri 8am-5pm; Sat 7.30am-4pm
Closed: Sun & Bank Holidays

Popular traditional butcher selling carefully hung meat, that has been well-sourced. Bronze turkeys at Christmas. Almost next door to The Cheeseboard (q.v).

Rail: Greenwich (or DLR, then foot-tunnel under river)
Buses: 53, 53X, 180, 199

142 DRONE'S - THE GROCER

1 Pont Street, SW1X 9EJ
Tel: 0171-259 6188

Open: Mon-Sun 8.30am-10pm
Closed: Bank Holidays

Next door to the restaurant of the same name, this trendy delicatessen/traiteur sells good take-away dishes, chutneys and preserves, sauces and dried pasta (including phallic shapes). Prices reflect the area.

Tube: Sloane Square (10 mins)   Buses: 19, 22, 137, 137a, C1

143 DUGANS CHOCOLATES

149a Upper Street, N1 1RA
Tel: 0171-354 4666

Open: Mon-Sat 10am-6.30pm; Sun 11am-5.30pm
Closed: Bank Holidays

Good little chocolate shop run by Annie Dugan Webster, stocking excellent Belgian chocolates and seasonal novelties which make unusual presents. Proper aniseed balls are a bonus.

Tube: Angel   Buses: 4, 19, 30, 38, 43, X43

144 DUNN'S

6 The Broadway, Crouch End, N8 9SN
Tel: 0181-340 1614

Open: Mon-Sat 7.15am-6pm
Closed: Sun & Bank Holidays

Established in 1827, this good family baker produces bread suitable for vegetarians out of stone-ground wholemeal or unbleached flour. Wedding cakes are also a speciality.

Rail: Crouch Hill/Highgate (15 minutes)   Buses: 41, 91, W2, W7

145 EARLHAM STREET MARKET

Earlham Street, WC2

Open: Mon-Sat 9am-5pm
Closed: Sun & Bank Holidays

This little market between Shaftesbury Avenue and Monmouth Street has good fruit and vegetables at bargain prices; not worth a special trip, but useful if visiting The Monmouth Coffee Company (qv) round the corner.

Tube: Leicester Square   Buses: 14, 19, 24, 38, 176

146 EASTERN GROCERS

53 Hanbury Street, E1 5JP
Tel: 0171-377 1824

Open: Mon-Sun 9am-8.30pm. Closed: 25 Dec

Traditional Bangladeshy grocer/greengrocer/halal butcher. As well mountains of Asian provisions they have deep-freezes brimming with imported fish, most with mysterious names such as Climbing Perch, Silver Barb Fish, Ayre, Boal, and Hilsha. Whole frozen eels are a regular item. Helpful service.

Tube & Rail: Liverpool Street   Buses: 67

147 EAST STREET MARKET

East Street & Dawes Street, SE17

Open: Tue, Wed, Fri & Sat 8am-5pm; Thur & Sun 8am-2pm
Closed: Mon & Bank Holidays

Good fruit and vegetables are to be found at this buzzing market.

Tube: Elephant & Castle/Kennington
Buses: 12, 35, 40, 45, 68, 171, 176, 184, 345, P5

148 EATON CONTINENTAL

65 Eaton Terrace, SW1W 8TN
Tel: 0171-730 7914

Open: Mon-Sat 7.30am-7pm; Sun 7.30am-1pm; Bank Holidays 8am-1pm
Closed: 25 Dec

Simple corner shop (in this case with Chester Row), useful for basics. Martin Pitt eggs.

Tube: Sloane Square   Buses: C1

149 EATONS

128 Wandsworth Bridge Road, SW6 2UL
Tel: 0171-736 8344

Open: Mon-Fri 9am-7pm; Sat 9am-6pm. Closed: Sun & Bank Holidays

Local delicatessen/café with limited space; but everything has been carefully chosen, from Duskins apple juice to top-quality chutney and relishes.

Tube: Fulham Broadway (10 mins)   Buses: 28, 295, C4

150 ROBERT EDWARDS

19 Leopold Road, Wimbledon, SW19 7BB
Tel: 0181-946 5834

Open: Mon-Fri 7am-5pm; Sat 7am-1.30pm
Closed: Sun & Bank Holidays

Good traditional butcher, selling grass-reared Scottish beef, home-made sausages and some game in season.

Tube: Wimbledon Park (10 minutes)   Bus: 156

151 JAMES ELLIOTT

96 Essex Road, N1 8LU
Tel: 0171-226 3658

Open: Mon-Sat 6am-6pm
Closed: Sun & Bank Holidays

This southern stretch of Essex Road has good food shops (see Steve Hatt [q.v], plus more, almost up to guide standards); and this butcher is one of them. Carefully hung beef, free-range chickens, free-range pork and lamb from Devon. These are backed up by a few excellent cheeses and ice cream from Winters Dairy.

Tube: Angel (10 minutes); Rail: Essex Road   Buses: 38, 56, 73, 171a

152 S.A. ELLIOTT

261 Wimbledon Park Road, SW18
Now Sadly Closed

153 L'ETOILE DE SOUS

79 Golborne Road, W10 5NL
Tel: 0181-960 9769

Open: Mon-Sat 8am-8pm.
Closed: Sun & Bank Holidays

Patisserie specialising in authentic Moroccan pastries.

Tube: Ladbroke Grove/Westbourne Park   Buses: 23, 52, 70, 295, 302

154 L'EUROPA

78 Seven Sisters Road, N7 6AE
Tel: 0171-700 3132

Open: Mon-Sat 9am-6.30pm
Closed: Sun & Bank Holidays

Popular Italian delicatessen near the southern end of Seven Sisters Road. A good range of groceries is stocked, including a comprehensive charcuterie section and a vast choice of dried pasta.

Tube: Finsbury Park (10 minutes)   Buses: 253, 259, 279

155 EVERFRESH

207 Upper Tooting Road, SW17 7EW
Tel: 0181-672 7396

Open: Sun-Sat 8am-7pm
Closed: 25 & 26 Dec

Self-service greengrocer with an excellent selection of Asian fruit and vegetables.

Tube: Tooting Broadway   Buses: 155, 219, 355

156 FILERIC

57 Old Brompton Road, SW7 3JS
Tel: 0171-584 2967
Branch @ 12 Queenstown Road, SW8 (0171-720 4844)

Open: Mon-Sat 8am-8pm; Sun 9am-8pm
Closed: Bank Holidays

French café/delicatessen/patisserie, well patronised by the local ethnic community.

Tube: South Kensington   Buses: 14, 49, 345, C1

157 FINNS OF CHELSEA GREEN

4 Elystan Street, London SW3 3NS
Tel: 0171-225 0733/4

Open: Mon-Fri 8am-7pm; Sat 8am-2pm
Closed: Sun & Bank Holidays

Traiteur, run by Julia Bannister, preparing a comprehensive list of dishes on-site. These range from patés and terrines to boned and stuffed leg of lamb or basil and aubergine bake. A range of chutneys, dried mushrooms, natural fruit juices, cheese and teas is also available in the shop, plus excellent Penrith toffee and fudge. Their "at home" catering service is very popular

Tube: South Kensington (10 minutes)
Buses:11, 14, 19, 22, 49, 137, 211, 319

158 FISH & FOWL

145 Highgate Road, NW5 1LJ
Tel: 0171-284 4184

Open: Fri 9am-5.30pm; Sat 9am-6pm (see entry)
Closed: Sun & Bank Holidays

Despite its apparent limited opening hours, Adrian Rudolf's fish shop is one of the most useful in London. It's main raison d'étre is as a supplier to the restaurant trade, and the shop is open to the wholesale trade between Monday and Thursday in addition to the hours given above. Although there is no window display, the public are welcome to pop in for their requirements until 3.30pm - phone first! Most of the fish comes directly from the coast, cutting out the markets; as well as normal varieties he specialises in fresh tuna, swordfish, and imported exotics plus wild salmon when in season. His rock oysters are a particular bargain. The fowl include free-range chickens, excellent squab pigeons from Tuscany and an extensive selection of game in season.

Tube: Kentish Town/Rail: Gospel Oak   Buses: C2, C11, C12, 214

**Please use the forms at the back of this book
to recommend your own favourite shops**

159 THE FISH CENTRE

8 Stamford Hill, N16 6XZ
Tel: 0181-442 4412

Open: Tue-Thur 8am-5pm; Fri 8am-1pm; Sun 9am-1pm
Closed: All Sat & Jewish Holidays

This little fish shop close to the station changed hands shortly before we went to press (formerly being a branch of Stoller's q.v). Ambitious stocks of beautifully fresh fish were on display on our inspection visit - it deserves support.

Rail: Stoke Newington   Buses: 67, 76, 106, 149, 243

160 H. FORMAN & SON

6 Queen's Yard, Whitepost Lane, E9 5EW
Tel: 0181-985 0378

Open: Mon-Fri 7am-3pm; Sat 7am-9am
Closed: Sun & Bank Holidays

Established in 1905, and still run by the same family, the Forman's produce some of Britain's finest smoked fish. Their range includes swordfish, shark, marlin, tuna halibut, eel, sturgeon, trout and of course salmon. Some fresh fish is offered of the types used for smoking, plus caviar, gravadlax, Arbroath smokies and Craster kippers.

Tube: Stratford (10 minutes) Rail: Hackney Wick   Bus: 276

161 FORTNUM & MASON ★

181 Piccadilly, W1A 1ER
Tel: 0171-734 8040

Open: Mon-Sat 9.30am-6pm
Closed: Sun & Bank Holidays

This famous shop was established as a grocer by Hugh Mason, a St James' shopkeeper, and William Fortnum, a footman of Queen Anne's, in 1707. It has expanded it's interests greatly, but the ground floor is still devoted to food. Their range of tins and jars alone is enormous - many items being made specially for them. But their real strength lies in their excellent delicatessen and cheese counters. Great effort has been made here to search out the best sources - for example, butter and cream from Lane's in Kent; ham from Denhay, Mooreland Foods and Richard Woodall; smoked salmon from H. Forman (q.v) amongst others and Craster kippers. Their extensive selection of cheese includes the best generic types, all carefully chosen to follow the seasons - (e.g) award winning Stilton in November and December, and properly aged Parmesan. An excellent selection of bread includes many from De Gustibus (q.v). Hampers and finger food (for home entertaining) can be prepared by arrangement.

Tube: Piccadilly/Green Park   Buses: 9, 14, 19, 22, 38

162 FOX'S OF WANDSWORTH COMMON

14 Belle Vue Road, SW17 4DG
Tel: 0181-672 0987

Open: Mon-Fri 8.30am-8pm; Sat 8.30am-7pm; Sun 10am-4pm
Closed: Bank Holidays

Useful delicatessen stocking a bit of everything including excellent toffee from The Toffee Shop at Penrith. A popular sandwich bar takes up an area of the shop making a comprehensive selection of anything else difficult. A few seasonal fruit and vegetables are stocked.

Rail: Wandsworth Common   Buses: 319, G1

163 FOX'S SPICES

Masons Road, Stratford-upon-Avon, Warwickshire, CV37 9NF
Tel: 01789-266420

Useful source of ground spices and dried herbs. An interesting selection of Oriental and Indonesian seasoning mixes, including Thai green and red curry mixes, is also offered. Prices are reasonable, although there is a small charge for postage.

Mail Order Only

164 FRANCE FRESH FISH

99 Stroud Green Road, N4 3PX
Tel: 0171-263 9767

Open: Mon-Sat 9am-7pm
Closed: Sun & Bank Holidays

Good fishmonger for those seeking exotics from the Seychelles and the West Indies. More standard native varieties are also popular.

Tube: Finsbury Park   Buses: 210, W2, W3, W7

165 FRATELLI CAMISA

53 Charlotte Street, W1P 1LA
Tel: 0171-255 1240

Open: Mon-Wed, Fri & Sat 9am-6pm; Thur 9am-2pm
Closed: Sun & Bank Holidays

Delightful family-run Italian delicatessen selling everything from traditional salamis and Italian flour to home-made pasta and their accompanying sauces.

Tube: Piccadilly Circus   Buses: 3, 6, 7, 8, 10, 12, 13, 14, 15, 19, 22, 23, 25, 38, 53, 73, 88, 94, 98, 139, 159, 176, X53

166 FRATELLI DELICATESSEN

57 Park Road, Kingston, Surrey KT2 6DB
Tel: 0181-549 8021

Open: Mon-Fri 8.30am-6pm; Sat 8.30am-5pm

Closed: Sun & Bank Holidays
New owners Vignali Donatella and Mensano Antonio are maintaining high
standards at this Italian grocer. Comprehensive range of traiteur dishes.
Rail: Kingston   Buses: 57, 85, 213, 371, 501, 511, 521, K3, K5, K10

167 FREEDOWN FOOD CO.

Ash Farm, Stourpaine, Blandford, Dorset, DT11 8PW
Tel: 01258 456622

Supplier of exotic meats, including various cuts of kangaroo, wild boar,
ostrich, bison and emu. Crocodile tail meat (bone-in) is also available.
Meat is despatched on Wednesday evening to arrive on Thursday,
accompanied by some recipe ideas.
Mail Order Only

168 FREEMAN'S BUTCHERS

9 Topsfield Parade, Crouch End, N8 8PP
Tel: 0181-340 3100

Open: Mon-Sat 8am-6pm
Closed: Sun & Bank Holidays
Small but enthusiastic butcher specialising in free-range poultry, lamb,
pork and beef. A separate counter has a selection of organic meat. A few
charcuterie items and farmhouse cheeses are stocked, plus Martin Pitt eggs.
Rail: Crouch Hill (10 minutes)   Buses: 41, 91, W2, W5, W7

169 FRESCO FISH ★

60 Seven Sisters Road, N7 6AA
Tel: 0171-700 1939

Open: Tue-Thur 7am-6pm; Fri & Sat 7am-7pm
Closed: Sun, Mon, Bank Holidays & 2 weeks August
This first-class fishmonger, near the southern end of Seven Sisters Road, is
run by the Sophocli family. Good selection of exotics usually includes
kingfish, jackfish and snappers; native types are also available in abundance.
Tube: Finsbury Park (10 minutes)   Buses: 253, 259, 279,

170 THE FRESH FOOD CO.

326 Portobello Road, W10 5RU
Tel: 0181-969 0351

Supplier of organic fruit and vegetables, and Cornish fish; all delivered
to your door overnight. Home-produced crops are cut to order, so as
fresh as is possible. Send for their regularly changing price list, which
offers a wide selection of mixed "packages". As we go to press, the
minimum order is £25-95.
Home delivery only.

171 FRESHLANDS WHOLE FOODS

196 Old Street, EC1V 9FR
Tel: 0171-250 1708

Open: Mon-Fri 10.30am-6.30pm; Sat 10.30am-4.30pm
Closed: Sun & Bank Holidays

Long - established specialists in organic foods and dietary specialities (sugar/gluten/animal free products. An excellent range of bread, including some from the Village Bakery of Penrith, plus eggs from Martin Pitt. They have an extensive take-away section of vegetarian dishes and a fresh salad bar. Also stocked are aromatherapy oils and household items based on natural ingredients.

Tube: Old Street (Exit 6)   Buses: 55, 133, 143, 243

172 FRIENDS FOODS

83 Roman Road, E2 OQN
Tel: 0181-980 1843

Open: Mon, Wed, Thur & Sat 9.30am-6pm; Tue 10am-6pm; Fri 9.30am-7pm.
Closed: Sun & Bank Holidays

London Buddhist Centre Vegetarian whole food. Excellent bread from The Celtic Bakery, the best vegetarian cheese, good organic coffee, Martin Pitt eggs, tisines, pulses and organic fruit and vegetables.

Tube: Bethnal Green   Buses: 8, D6, 309

173 LA FROMAGERIE ★

30 Highbury Park, N5 2AA
Tel: 0171-359 7440

Open: Mon 10.30am-7.30pm; Tue-Sat 9.30am-7.30pm; Sun 10am-4.30pm
Closed: Bank Holidays

Patricia Michelson runs this excellent shop stocking nearly 200 cheeses, home-made quiches and vegetable tarts, plus French chocolate, olives, dried pasta, bread and croissants. At Christmas these are joined by Bernard Dufoux's excellent bomb-shaped chocolate cake, crammed with pistachios, citrus peel and gold leaf - rich but delicious! Free local delivery.

Rail: Drayton Park (5 minutes)   Buses: 4, 19, 236

174 FRY'S OF CHELSEA

14 Cale Street, SW3 3QU
Tel: 0171-589 0342

Open: Mon-Fri 5.30am-5pm; Sat 5.30am-1.30pm
Closed: Sun & Bank Holidays

Good local greengrocer run, by the Fry family, with an attractive pavement display of first class produce. A past winner of London's best greengrocer award. Their proper old-fashioned service includes delivery.

Tube: South Kensington (10 minutes)
Buses: 11, 14, 19, 22, 49, 137, 211, 319

175 FUDCO

184 Ealing Road, Alperton, HA0 4QD
Tel: 0181-902 4820

Open: Mon-Sun 9.30am-6.30pm. Closed: 25 Dec

Fascinating little shop crammed full of specialist flour, pulses, spices and nuts from the Indian sub-continent. You can often see the flour being milled at the back of the shop.

Tube/Rail: Wembley Central   Buses: 79, 83, 224, 297

176 FUNCHAL PATISSERIE

141 Stockwell Road, SW9 9TN
Tel: 0171-733 3134

Open: Mon-Sun 8am-8pm. Closed: Bank Holidays

Portuguese bakery with a good selection of bread and pastries, all made on the premises.

Tube: Brixton   Buses:18, 196, 250, 322, 345, P4

177 GALLO NERO DELICATESSEN

75 Stoke Newington High Street, N16 8EL
Tel: 0171-254 9770
Branch @ 45 Newington Green Road, N1 (0171-226 2002)

Open: Mon-Sat 8.30am-6.30pm. Closed: Sun & Bank Holidays

The Mori's have been running their little corner of Italy since 1974. All the standards are here; a good range of salami and ham, cheese plus fresh and dried pasta. Good Italian-style bread, and excellent draught unfiltered olive oil, so bring a bottle.

Rail: Stoke Newington   Buses: 67, 73, 76, 106, 149, 243

178 R. GARCIA & SONS

248-250 Portobello Road, W11 1LL
Tel: 0171-221 6119

Open: Mon-Sat 9am-6pm; Thur 9am-1.30pm.
Closed: Sun & Bank Holidays

Impressive Spanish grocer and delicatessen amid the bargains and excitement of Portobello Market. A good charcuterie section includes Morcilla (a type of Spanish black pudding with either rice or onions), salted pork ribs, good salamis and Serrano ham. A comprehensive selection of Spanish cheese include Manchego, Mahan, Cabrales and Tetilla all carefully kept. Turron "nougat" at Christmas. All the ingredients are here to produce a genuine Spanish meal and advice is on hand from the friendly staff.

Tube: Ladroke Grove (ten minutes)   Buses: 7, 23, 52, 70, 302

179 W.A. GARDNER

157 Arthur Road, SW19 8AD
Tel: 0181-946 2215

Open: Mon-Fri 8am-5.30pm; Sat 8am-3.30pm
Closed: for lunch between 1pm-2pm; Sun & Bank Holidays

Good butcher opposite Wimbledon Park Station. Well-hung Scotch beef,
free-range pork from Sussex, Bronze turkeys at Christmas and Martin Pitt
eggs.

Tube: Wimbledon Park   Buses: 156

180 LA GASTRONOMÍA

86 Park Hall Road, SE21 8BW Tel: 0181-766 0494
Branches @ 135 Half Moon Lane, Dulwich, SE24
(0171-274 1034)
& 18 Westow Hill, Crystal Palace, SE19 (0181-670 0717)

Open: Mon-Sat 8.30am-6.30pm
Closed: Sun & Bank Holidays

Excellent delicatessen traiteur specialising in Italian food and groceries.

Rail: West Dulwich   Buses: 3, 322

181 GASTRONOMIA ITALIA

8 Upper Tachbrook St, SW1V 1SH
Tel: 0171-834 2767

Open: Mon-Fri 9am-6pm; Sat 9am-5pm
Closed: Sun & Bank Holidays

Long established Italian delicatessen, run with enthusiasm by Mario
d'Annunzio. He offers a good selection of grocery products plus a few
Spanish and French cheeses.
His sandwiches are popular at lunchtime.

Tube: Victoria/Pimlico   Buses: 2, 36, 185

182 G. GAZZANO & SON

167-169 Farringdon Road, EC1R 3AL
Tel: 0171-837 1586

Open: Tue-Fri 8am-6pm (open Mon in Dec); Sat 8am-5pm; Sun 10.30-2pm
Closed: Bank Holidays

Family business established around the turn of the 1900's. Excellent
range of Italian products, fresh pasta, cooked meats, salami and
pancetta; fresh sauces, good range of Italian biscuits, cheese and char-
grilled vegetables.

Tube: Farringdon   Buses: 19, 38, 63, 221

183 GENNARO DELICATESSEN

23 Lewis Grove, SE13 6BG
Tel: 0181-852 1370

Open: Tue-Sat 9am-6pm

Closed: Sun, Mon & Bank Holidays

Popular delicatessen offering a wide range of good-quality dried pasta, Italian groceries and plenty of those delicious little luxuries that make a dinner party perfect.

Rail: Lewisham

Buses: 36, 47, 54, 75, 122, 136, 180, 185, 199, 208, 225, 380

184 GIACOBAZZI'S DELICATESSEN

150 Fleet Road, Hampstead, NW3 2QX
Tel: 0171-267 7222

Open: Mon-Fri 9.30am-7pm; Sat 9am-6pm

Closed: Sun & Bank Holidays; plus last week August & first 2 weeks Sept

Well-established Italian delicatessen, round the corner from The Royal Free Hospital, specialising in the area of North Eastern Italy. A range of traiteur dishes includes an excellent selection of home-made stuffed pasta, with interesting fillings such as artichoke, pumpkin and Gorgonzola; sauces to accompany these are also on offer, plus good char-grilled vegetables, salads and bread (most made in-house). Other items include top quality olive oil and vinegar, a fine range of Italian cheese, cakes and a selection of charcuterie.

Rail: Hampstead Heath; Tube: Belsize Park (5 minutes)

Buses: 24, 46, 168, 268, C11, C12

185 GIBBER OF HOLLOWAY

116-120 Seven Sisters Road, N7 6AE
Tel: 0171-607 5449

Open: Mon-Sat 8am-6pm

Closed: Sun & Bank Holidays

Bargain self-service greengrocer at the southern end of Seven Sisters Road. Prices rival most markets if you are able to buy in slightly larger quantities. A summer visit brought offerings of 10lb firm tomatoes for under £2, and 10 peaches or nectarines for £1. You can still buy single items if need be, but with prices like these you can afford to give things away! Good selection of Greek cheese.

Tube: Tube & Rail: Finsbury Park (10 minutes)   Buses: 253, 259, 279

Please use the forms at the back of this book
to recommend your own favourite shops

186 GIULIANO

43 The Broadway, Wimbledon, SW19 1QD
Tel: 0181-543 7366
Branch @ 1a Lacy Road, Putney, SW15 (0181-785 1741)

Open: Mon-Sat 9am-6pm

Closed: Sun & Bank Holidays

Useful Italian delicatessen opposite Wimbledon Station. Small range of fresh pasta, some made on the premises.

Tube & Rail: Wimbledon   Buses: 57, 93, 155

187 FRANK GODFREY ★

7 Highbury Park, N5 1QT
Tel: 0171-226 2425

Open: Mon-Sat 8am-6pm

Closed: Sun & Bank Holidays

Run by the Godfrey brothers, this excellent butcher specialises in Aberdeen Angus beef, lamb from the Orkney Islands, free-range pork from Sussex and their own excellent bacon and sausages. Unfortunately meat of this quality is not cheap, but the difference in flavour is transparent. Cottage Delight chutneys and their own Korma and Tikka Masala sauces are a popular sideline.

Tube: Highbury & Islington (10 minutes)   Buses: 4, 19, 236

188 GODIVA

150 Fenchurch Street, EC3M 6DB Tel: 0171-623 2287
Branches: Harrods, 87 Brompton Road, SW1 (0171-730 1234);
247 Regent Street, W1 (0171-495 2845);
Selfridges, 400 Oxford Street, W1 (0171-629 1234)

Open: Mon-Fri 9am-6pm

Closed: Sun & Bank Holidays

Supplier of good quality Belgian chocolates, designed and priced for the luxury market.

Tube: Bank Rail: Fenchurch Street   Buses: 40, 100, D1

189 GOLBORNE FISHERIES ★

75 Golborne Road, W10 5NP
Tel: 0181-960 3100

Open: Mon-Weds 7.30am-6pm; Thur-Sat 7.30am-8pm

Closed: Sun & Bank Holidays

One of London's best fishmongers, cramped full of exotica and more usual varieties, all gleamingly fresh. Worth a special trip.

Tube: Westbourne Park/Ladbroke Grove (5 minutes)

Buses: 23, 52, 70, 295, 302

190 GOLDEN GATE SUPERMARKET

14 Lisle St. WC2H 7PR
Tel: 0171-437 0014

Open: Mon-Sat 9am-8pm
Closed: Sun & Bank Holidays

This small shop is crammed full of all you need to make a perfect Chinese meal, including excellent fruit and vegetables and a few Thai ingredients such as lime leaves and lemon grass.

Tube: Leicester Square   Buses: 14, 19, 38

191 GOOD HARVEST FISH & MEAT MARKET ★

14 Newport Place, WC2H 7PR
Tel: 0171- 437 0712

Open: Mon-Sun 11am-7pm
Closed: 25 & 26 Dec

Live lobsters, crabs and sometimes carp; plus fresh eels, scallops, squid and a few of the firmer fish favoured by Chinese cooks. Abalone at weekends (about £15 per lb. but a little goes a long way. A few meats are stocked, but these are mainly Chinese exotics - ducks tongues etc. Service is friendly and nothing is too much trouble.

Tube: Leicester Square   Buses: 14, 19, 24, 29, 38, 176

192 GOODMAN'S GEESE

Walsgrove Farm, Great Witley, Worcester, Worcs, WR6 6JJ
Tel: 01299-896272

Excellent free-range geese for about £3 per lb (undrawn weight); and worth every penny. Give plenty of notice, as they sell out quickly.
Mail Order Only

193 GRAHAM'S ★

134 East End Road, N2 0RZ
Tel: 0181-883 6187

Open: Tue-Sat 8.30am-5.30pm; Sun 8.30am-1pm
Closed: Bank Holidays

Find this progressive little butcher in a modern parade of shops near the junction of Ossulton Way. Carefully sourced meat is all grass-reared, some being additive-free. Poultry from Suffolk Foods is organic. The summer brings home-made hamburgers and kebabs ready for the barbecue.

Tube: East Finchley (10 minutes)   Buses: 143

Tip:

To stop salt becoming damp in your salt-mill and refusing to grind, periodically add a few grains of uncooked rice to the mill; this will absorb any moisture and cure the problem.

194 GRANVILLE ARCADE
(Entrance in Pope's Road), Brixton Market, SW9

Open: Mon, Tue, Thur & Sat 8am-5.30pm; Wed 8am-1pm
Closed: Sun & Bank Holidays

Enter under the railway bridge in Pope's Road to explore this paradise of African and Caribbean food. There are too many stalls to mention by name - but fish fruit and vegetables are the strengths here, fresh meat the weakness. Expect to find about 50 varieties of fish, many strange and very colourful to the eye. Turn over is fast, so everything's very fresh. Exotic fruit and veg. might include mangoes, cassava, cho-cho, sugar cane, egusi and breadfruit.

Rail/Tube: Brixton   Buses: 2, 3, 35, 45, 109, 118, 133, 159, 196, 250

195 M&D GRODINSKI
223 Golders Green Road, NW11 9ES
Tel: 0181-458 1942

Open: Mon & Weds 6am-11pm; Tue 6am-9pm; Thur 6am-1am; Fri 6am-6pm
(or 45 minutes before Sabbath whichever is earlier);
Sun from after Sabbath-11pm.
Closed: Sat & Bank Holidays

Good kosher bakery, offering beautifully warm bread, biscuits and simple cakes - all on the premises.

Tube: Brent Cross (5 minutes)   Buses: 83, 183, 210, 240

196 GUNN'S
326 Norwood Road, SE27 9AF
Tel: 0181-670 0880

Open: Tue-Wed 9am-1pm; Thur-Fri 9am-5pm; Sat 9am-3pm
Closed: Sun, Mon & Bank Holidays

Good fishmonger run by the Gunn brothers, often stocking live eels.

Rail: Tulse Hill   Buses: 2, 68, 68a, 196, 315, 322, X68

197 HAELAN CENTRE
41 The Broadway, Crouch End, N8 8DT
Tel: 0181-340 4258

Open: Mon-Thur 9am-6pm; Fri 9am-6.30pm; Sat 9am-6pm; Sun 11am-3pm
Closed: Bank Holidays & the Sunday before Bank Holidays

This excellent health food shop has been run buy Nino Booth since 1971. Only vegetarian products are stocked, many of them organic; these include butter, coffee, cheese, eggs, dried fruit, olive oil and a first class range of pulses. Their comprehensive range of yogurts include cow's, goat's, sheep's and soya; again all organically produced. Books on herbal remedies and a homoepathic clinic operate upstairs.

Rail: Crouch Hill/Highgate (15 minutes)   Buses: 41, 91, W2, W7

198 HAMBLEDON HERBS

Court Farm, Milverton, Somerset, TA4 1NS
Tel: 01823 401205

Suppliers of a vast range of organic herbs and rare spices. Send for their interesting price list. *Mail Order Only*

199 HAMLINS OF KENSINGTON

3 Abingdon Road, W8 6AH
Tel: 0171-376 2191

Open: Mon-Fri 9.30am-6pm; Sat 9.30am-4pm
Closed: Sun & Bank Holidays

Good delicatessen/traiteur, very much geared to the latter. Prices are very reasonable for the quality on offer; the hamper menu starts at £13-30 a head (including the hire of a wicker hamper), while individual main courses kick off at £3-50. Delicatessen items include agood, selection of British and French cheeses; good bread and charcuterie items.

Tube: High Street Kensington (5 minutes)
Buses: 9, 9a, 10, 27, 28, 31, 49, C1

200 HAMPSTEAD BUTCHERS

17 Heath Street, NW3 6TR
Tel: 0171-435 3446

Open: Mon-Sat 8am-5.30pm
Closed: Sun & Bank Holidays

Popular butcher specialising in grass-reared animals and free-range chickens. Good selection of game in season.

Tube: Hampstead   Buses: 46, 268

201 HAMPSTEAD SEAFOODS

78 Hampstead High Street, NW3 1RE
Tel: 0171-435 3966

Open: Tue-Fri 7.30am-5pm; Sat 7.30am-4.30pm
Closed: Sun, Mon & Bank Holidays

Good little fishmonger tucked away in an alley holding The Hampstead Community Market (including a greengrocer and small delicatessen).

Tube: Hampstead   Buses: 46, 268

202 HAND MADE FOOD ★

40 Tranquil Vale, Blackheath, SE3 0BD
Tel: 0181-297 9966

Open: Mon-Fri 9am-6pm; Sat 9am-5.30pm
Closed: Sun & Bank Holidays

Classy shop specialising in excellent traiteur dishes at modest prices. Dishes vary by the day; but one visit brought baked salmon with fresh herbs, wild mushroom risotto cakes, Mediterranean stuffed aubergines and spinach, leek and feta filo pie among the offerings. The kitchen produces it's own patés and terrines, while the delicatessen section stocks Bay Tree chutneys and a selection of salami and cheeses. Hampers are a speciality and modestly priced, making a drive here worthwhile.

Rail: Blackheath   Buses: 13, 40, 44, 89, 108, 202

203 HARRODS ★

Knightsbridge, SW1X 7XL

Tel: 0171-730 1234

Open: Mon, Tue & Sat 10am-6pm; Wed, Thur & Fri 10am-7pm

Closed: Sun & Bank Holidays

With it's marvellous marble floors and tiled walls this is London's most glamorous food hall, and easily the most comprehensive, although many basic necessities are not available. Meat is carefully sourced, and includes excellent Devon lamb, grass-fed Aberdeen Angus, both white and Bronze turkeys from Homewood Partners at Christmas and a comprehensive selection of game in season. The fish and charcuterie departments are equally impressive. A splendid selection of bacon includes the delicious, but rarely found, sweet pickled variety. Over 300 types of cheese should satisfy the most demanding connoisseur. A specialist department deals in food for presents. First-class service goes without saying - there is a cost in all this however, as prices are not modest.

Tube: Knightsbridge   Buses: 910, 14, 19, 22, 52, 74, 137, 137a, C1

204 HARTS (VICTORIA) LTD

39 Tachbrook St, SW1V 2LZ

Tel: 0171-821 6341

Open: Mon-Sat 8am-5.30pm

Closed: Sun & Bank Holidays

Traditional butcher selling organic beef, lamb and pork as well as Peter Onion's excellent organic chickens.

Tube: Victoria   Buses: 2, 36, 185

205 HARVEY NICHOLS ★

Knightsbridge, SW1X 7RJ

Tel: 0171-235 5000

Open: Mon, Tue, Thur, Fri & Sat 10am-7pm; Weds 10am-8pm;

Sun noon-6pm

Closed: Bank Holidays

Find this treasure trove of a food hall perched on top of this department store adjacent to the Fifth Floor Café and Restaurant. Jars and packets of mainly own-label biscuits, jams, pasta (and accompanying sauces) and a selection of Japanese groceries are beautifully displayed on modern metal shelving. Good fresh fish, fruit and vegetables, and carefully sourced meat make this a one stop destination for those that can afford it. Standards are particularly high, and many of the items are packaged in such a way as to make them excellent presents.

Tube: Knightsbridge   Buses: 9, 10, 14, 19, 22, 52, 74, 137, 137a, C1

206 STEVE HATT FISHMONGER ★

88-90 Essex Road, Islington, N1 8LU
Tel: 0171-226 3963

Open: Tue-Sat 7am-5pm
Closed: Mon, Sun & Bank Holidays

Popular fish shop and game dealer which has been owned by the same family for over 100 years. As well as the usual staples, locals are supplied with sea-bass, wild salmon, lobster, oysters - all beautifully fresh, plus Sevruga and Beluga caviar for that special occasion. The autumn and winter bring a good selection of game, often including snipe and woodcock. Free-range turkeys at Christmas.

Tube: Angel Rail: Essex Road   Buses: 38, 56, 73, 171

207 HEAL FARM

Kings Nympton, Umberleigh, Devon, EX37 9TB
Tel: 01769 574341

First class farm, run for nearly 30 years by Anne Petch, producing pork and excellent pork products (including bacon) from rare breeds reared in natural and additive-free conditions. Their mail order service also supplies carefully reared beef and poultry from local farms. Delivery is charged at a standard £8-50, and for a large order (perhaps teaming up with friends) worth every penny. Their patés and rillettes are available from The Bluebird Gastrodrome (q.v). They are also one of the few suppliers of the unsurpassed Hereford "Trelough" ducks.
Mail Order Only

208 HEALTH & DIET CENTRE

151 Putney High Street, SW15 1SU
Tel: 0181-788 0944
Too many branches to mention here, see our listings near the back of this book

Open: Mon-Sat 9am-6pm
Closed: Sun & Bank Holidays, but enquire, as times and closing days vary with demand.

Find this health food shop fifty yards from the railway station, on the corner of Disraeli Road. Good selection of pulses, nuts and fruit juices and much more - including Martin Pitt eggs.

Tube: Putney Bridge (5 minutes) Rail: Putney   Buses: 14, 74, 85, 337

209 HENDON BAGEL BAKERY

55/57 Church Road, Hendon, NW4 4DU
Tel: 0181-203 6919

Open: Mon-Thur 7am-11pm; Fri 7am-6pm Sat; Sat 6pm-11pm Sun
(through the night) Closed: Jewish Religious Holidays
Excellent bagels, with fillings including from herring, salmon and tuna.
Parev (non-dairy cakes), plus a good assortment of cream cakes,
croissants and French pastries - the baker is from across the channel.
They have an expanding range of Kosher groceries.
Tube; Hendon Central (5 minutes)   Buses: 143, 183, 326

210 HEREFORD DUCK COMPANY

Trelough House, Wormbridge, Herefordshire, HR2 9DH
Tel: 01981 570767

An excellent breed of duck has been developed here - The Trelough - by
Barry Clark. Ducks wander in orchards of rare apple trees, are fed on a
mixture of natural grains and are reared without the need of an
automatic dose of antibiotcs. They have a marvellous flavour and are well
worth ordering. Jars of duck fat and confit are also available. If a London
outlet materializes you will read about it here first! *Mail order only*

211 H.R. HIGGINS (COFFEE MAN) LTD ★

79 Duke Street, W1M 6AS
Tel: 0171-491 8819

Open: Mon-Wed 8.45am-5.30pm; Thur & Fri 8.45am-6pm; Sat 10am-5pm
Closed: Sun & Bank Holidays
Established in 1942 around the corner in South Moulton Street, this
excellent coffee and tea emporium is still run by the family. Loyalty from
their country customers has dictated that mail order is now the larger
part of their business (postage is free for orders over 2.5Kg). A visit is an
interesting experience; its bonus being a collection of antique coffee-
making equipment.
Tube: Bond Street
Buses: 6, 7, 10, 12, 13, 15, 16a, 23, 73, 94, 98, 113, 135, 137, 137a, 139, 159

212 HIGHGATE BUTCHER

76 Highgate High Street, N6 5HX
Tel: 0181-340 9817

Open: Mon 7.30am-5pm; Tue-Fri 7.30am-5.45pm; Sat 7am-5pm
Closed: Sun & Bank Holidays
Small traditional butcher run by the Harper family. Grass-fed Scotch beef,
Welsh lamb, free-range chickens, home-cooked ham and their own
sausages in 16 flavours. Delivery for orders over £10.
Tube: Highgate (5 minutes)   Buses: 143, 210, 271

213 HILDRETH STREET MARKET
Hildreth Street, Balham, SW12

Open: Mon-Wed, Fri & Sat 9.30am-5pm; Thur 9.30am-2pm
Closed: Sun & Bank Holidays

Good value fruit and veg. here of all descriptions, and the surrounding shops offer a hotchpotch of interesting African and West Indian groceries. Balham Halal Meat Market on the corner of Balham High Road offers bargain meat including seldom found boiling hens.

Tube & Rail: Balham   Buses: 155, 315, 355

214 THE HIVE ★
93 Northcote Road, SW11 6PL
Tel: 0171-924 6233

Open: Mon-Sat 10am-6pm
Closed: Between 1pm-2pm for lunch; Sun & Bank Holidays

Now established at this new location (previously in Webbs Road) this excellent shop has London's largest selection of honey and honey products. These include honey fudge, candles and cosmetics. One wall of the shop is a working hive of 25, 000 bees (contained behind glass). The owner, James Harmill, also runs bee-keeping courses.

Rail: Clapham Junction (5 minutes)   Buses: 319, G1

215 HOLLY TREE FARM SHOP
Chester Road, Tabley, Knutsford, Cheshire WA16 OEU
Tel: 01565 651835

Karol Bailey rears excellent corn-fed/free-range geese on her farm and as well as her shop, runs a thriving mail order business.

Mail Order Only

216 HOO HING
North Circular Road, Park Royal, NW10
Tel: 0181-838 3388
Branch @ Eastway Commercial Centre, E9 (0181-533 2811)
& Bond Road (off Western Road), Mitcham (0181-6872 633)

Open: Mon-Fri 9am-7pm;
Sat & Bank Holidays 10am-7pm; Sun 11am-5pm
Closed: 25 & 26 Dec

Find this Chinese and Oriental supermarket on the drag north of Hanger Lane. Everything is stocked that the adventurous cook might need; ranging from fresh vegetables and tanks holding live crabs and lobsters to prepared sauces and endless rows of deep-frozen goodies.

Tube: Hanger Lane (10 minutes)   Buses: 112

217 THE HOUSE OF ALBERT ROUX ★

229 Ebury Street, SW1W 8UT
Tel: 0171- 730 3037

Open: Mon-Fri 7.30am-10.30pm; Sat 8am-3pm; Sun: 8am-3pm
Closed: Bank Holidays

Owned by one half of the famous Roux brothers this is an excellent source of luxury ingredients that can be so hard to find. Caviar, fresh foie gras, boudin blanc and duck confit to mention a few. More mundane groceries are also stocked, and great effort has been made to find the best generic types. Traiteur dishes, many delicious charcuterie items and an outside catering operation are sourced from kitchens on Wandsworth Road, but many dishes are available "off the shelf" (and priced per 100g) - these include plenty of choice for a complete meal, or perhaps a sauce to jazz up your own food. Not cheap, but everything is prepared to a very high standard. Temptation makes this a difficult shop to leave empty handed.

Tube: Victoria/Sloane Square (10 minutes)   Buses: 11, 211, 239

218 HUSSEY'S

64 Wapping Lane, E1 9RL
Tel: 0171-488 3686

Open: Mon-Fri 7am-6.15pm; Sat 6am-5pm
Closed: Sun & Bank Holidays

Efficiently run by the Hussey family since 1952, this is the best butcher for miles around. Top quality beef, lamb and pork is backed up by their own sausages and bacon sliced to order. Free delivery.

Tube: Wapping (peak hours only); Shadwell DLR   Buses: 100

219 HYAMS & COCKERTON

41-44 Southville, SW8
Tel: 0171-622 1167

Open: Mon-Sat 8.45am-noon
Closed: Sun & Bank Holidays

Wholesale greengrocers and fruiterers, tucked away behind New Covent Garden, who will willingly sell to the public if the buy in reasonable quantities. They are suppliers to some of London's top restaurants so stock everything from wild mushrooms and truffles (in season) to the more everyday produce. Cash is not encouraged unless you have the right change.

Tube: Stockwell   Buses: 77, 77a, 322

**Please use the forms at the back of this book
to recommend your own favourite shops**

220 IMPORTERS

180 High Street, Beckenham, Kent BR3
Tel: 0181-658 9049
Branches @ 76 Golders Green Road, NW11 (0181-455 8186)
& 3 The Green, W5 (0181-567 2981)

Open: Mon-Sat 9am-4pm
Closed: Sun & Bank Holidays

Shop selling a good range of coffee and tea. The coffee being roasted on the premises.

Rail: Beckenham Junction   Buses: 54, 351, 361, 367

221 INTERNATIONAL CHEESE CENTRE

21 Goodge Street, W1P 1FD
Tel: 0171-631 4191
Branches @
3b West Mall, Liverpool Street Station, EC2 (0171-628 6637)
& The Parade, Victoria Station, SW1 (0171-828 2886)

Open: Mon-Fri 9am-6.30pm; Sat 9.30am-6.30pm
Closed: Sun & Bank Holidays

Good cheese shops, covering a wide range as their name implies. Mini cheeses, smart packets of biscuits and jams make useful presents, making the station locations particularly handy.

Tube: Goodge Street   Buses: 10, 24, 29, 73, 134

222 INVERNESS STREET MARKET

Inverness Street, NW1

Open: Mon, Tue, Weds, Fri & Sat 9am-5pm; Thur 9am-1pm
Closed: Sun & Bank Holidays

Good-value fruit and veg.stalls at this little market just off Camden High Street, plus a cheese stall.

Tube: Camden Town.
Buses: 24, 27, 29, 31, 68, 134, 135, 168, 214, 253, 274, C2

223 THE ITALIAN FRUIT COMPANY

423 King's Road, SW10 0LR
Tel: 0171-354 5841

Open: Mon-Sat 8.30am-6pm
Closed: Sun & Bank Holidays

Small self-service greengrocer, in World's End, stocking traditional Italian vegetables as well as the more basic requirements. Treats vary from day to day, but might include baby globe artichokes, black cabbage, catalonia (asparagus chicory), broccoli ravi and wild mushrooms in season. They generally have a good range of potted herbs, these have been hardened-off, so are more robust than their supermarket equivalents, and will happily live in a window box or the garden.

Tube: Fulham Broadway (15 minutes)　　　Buses: 11, 22, 31, 211

224 JAMES'S CHEESE SHOP
188 High Street, Beckenham, Kent BR3 1EN
Tel: 0181-650 1411

Open: Mon, Tue, Thur, Fri & Sat 9am-5.30; Weds 9am-2pm
Closed: Sun & Bank Holidays

Useful shop selling a good selection of jam and honey as well as cheese.

Rail: Beckenham Junction　　　Buses: 54, 351, 361, 367

225 JAPAN CENTRE
212 Piccadilly, W1V 9LD
Tel: 0171-434 4218

Open: Mon-Sat 10am-7.30pm; Sun 10-6pm
Closed: 25 & 26 Dec

Find this useful supplier of Japanese food under the Travel Centre. All the basics are stocked as well as sushi lunch boxes.

Tube: Piccadilly Circus.

Buses: 3, 6, 9, 12, 13, 14, 15, 19, 22, 23, 24, 29, 38, 53, 88, 94, 139, 176

226 JARVIS & SONS ★
56 Coombe Road, Norbiton, Surrey, KT2 7AS
Tel: 0181-546 0989

Open: Mon & Tue 8am-3pm; Weds 8am-4pm; Thur, Fri & Sat 8am-5pm
Closed: Sun & Bank Holidays

Excellent fishmonger, poulterer and game dealer, offering a wide variety of beautifully displayed fish and seasonal game; deservedly drawing people in from all around the Kingston area.

Rail: Norbiton　　　Bus: K6

227 JAVA JAVA
26 Rupert Street, W1V 7FN
Tel: 0171-734 5821

Open: Mon-Thur 9.30am-10pm; Fri 9.30am-11pm; Sat 10.30am-11pm;
Sun & Bank Holidays 1pm-9pm
Closed: 25, 26 Dec & 1 Jan

Coffee shop/café on the stretch of Rupert Street south of Shaftesbury Avenue. You will discover a source of good tea, herbal infusions and coffee and the means of making them. Also stocked are the now fashionable coffee syrups in a variety of flavours, ranging from apple to marshmallow.

Tube: Piccadilly Circus/Leicester Square　　　Buses: 14, 19, 22, 38, 94

228 JEFFERIES

42 Coombe Road, Norbiton, Surrey KT2 7AF
Tel: 0181-546 0453

Open: Mon 7.30am-12.30pm; Tue 7.30am-4pm; Weds 7.30am-1pm;
Thur 7.30am-5pm; Fri 6am-5pm; Sat 6am-4pm
Closed: Sun & Bank Holidays

Popular butcher offering top quality Aberdeen Angus beef, additive-free
lamb and pork, free-range chickens and Bronze turkeys at Christmas.

Rail: Norbiton   Buses: K6

229 JEFFERSON'S SEA FOODS

17 Clifton Road, W9 1SY
Tel: 0171-266 0811

Open: Mon-Sat 9am-6pm
Closed: Sun & Bank Holidays

Expect to find a wide selection at this good fishmonger, with varieties
such as lobster, brill and turbot catering for the top-end of the market.

Tube: Warwick Avenue (5 minutes)   Buses: 6, 16, 16a, 98

230 JEKKA'S HERB FARM

Rose Cottage, Shellards Lane, Bristol, Avon, BS12 2SY
Tel: 01454 418878

Excellent supplier of fresh herbs, both usual and unusual. A book is now
available showing you how to propagate your own.

Mail Order Only

231 JEROBOAMS ★

24 Bute Street, SW7 3EX
Tel: 0171-225 2232
Branches @ 51 Elizabeth Street SW1
& 96 Holland Park Avenue W11

Open: Mon-Sat 9am-6pm
Closed: Sun & Bank Holidays (see below)

Three of London's best cheese shops. Their quick turnover (they supply
some of the areas top restaurants) means they can have hundreds of
cheeses all in peak condition. The range can be bewildering, but friendly
and knowledgeable help is always at hand. The cheeses are backed up by
a good selection of charcuterie, olive oil, chutney, mustard and char-
grilled vegetables plus unusual unpasteurised crème fraiche. The branch
at Holland Park Avenue keeps longer hours and is open between 10am-
4pm on Sunday.

Tube: South Kensington Buses: C1, 14, 49, 70, 70, 74

232 JOHN & SONS

103 Uxbridge Road, W12 8NL
Tel: 0181-743 9224

Open: Mon-Fri 8am-7pm; Sat 8am-6pm; Bank Holidays 10am-4pm
Closed: Sun, 25 & 26 Dec

A treasure trove of a delicatessen specialising in Eastern Europe, and more particularly in the area of old Yugoslavia. An excellent range of the charcuterie of the region, splendid assortment of top quality bread - ranging from those of Sally Clark (q.v) to sour-doughs from the first rate Kolos Bakery in Bradford. Other treats include various goat's cheeses, Feta from Bulgaria, flavoured olives, plus a good selection of olive oils. Many items are specially imported included preserved vegetables, Croatian mustards and Slovenian fruit juices.

Tube: Shepherds Bush   Buses: 94, 207, 260, 283, 607

233 F.C. JONES

764 Fulham Road, SW6 5CJ
Tel: 0171-736 1643

Open: Mon 9am-1pm; Tue-Fri 9am-5.30pm; Sat 8am-4pm
Closed: Sun & Bank Holidays

Useful traditional greengrocer badly needed in the area. A few more unusual seasonal items are always stocked - chicory and fresh lychee on a typical visit.

Tube: Parsons Green/Putney Bridge (10 minutes)   Buses:14, C4

234 JONES DELICATESSEN

8 Leopold Road, Wimbledon, SW19 7BD
Tel: 0181-944 7007

Open: Mon-Fri 10am-7pm; Sun 9am-6pm
Closed: Bank Holidays

Smart little deli selling all the expected basics plus a small range of Japanese products.

Rail/Tube: Wimbledon Park (10 minutes)   Buses: 156

235 HAMISH JOHNSTON ★

48 Northcote Road, SW11 1PA
Tel: 0171-738 0741

Open: Mon-Fri 9am-7pm; Sat 9am-6pm
Closed: Sun, Bank Holidays, except Good Friday

Delicatessen, with a British and French slant, run with impressive enthusiasm by William Johnston. Good general choice, plus excellent bacon and sausages from Denhay Farm; jams, chutneys and mustards from Highfield Preserves; about twenty olive oils (including some on draught you can buy if you bring a bottle) and enough varieties of cheese to make an ardent enthusiast dribble, all in peak condition. Chocolates from Montgomery Moore are hard to resist, plus excellent toffee from Penrith.

Rail: Clapham Junction   Buses: 319, G1

236 JUST FRESH
30-32 Atlantic Road, Brixton, SW9 8JW
Tel: 0171-733 5556

Open: Mon-Sat 7am-6pm
Closed: Sun & Bank Holidays

The best, and most interesting Halal butcher in the area. As well as more familiar items the needs of the West Indian community are catered for with items such as cow's feet, turkey tails, mutton, goat, goat's tripe and abadi (cow's intestine).

Rail/Tube: Brixton   Buses: 2, 3, 35, 45, 109, 118, 133, 159, 196, 250

237 KELSEY QUALITY BUTCHER
27 The Mall, Stratford Centre, E15 1XD
Tel: 0181-534 2230

Open: Mon-Sat 8am-6pm
Closed: Sun & Bank Holidays

Long established traditional butcher stocking a good selection of free-range meat and poultry.

DLR; Rail & Tube: Stratford

Buses: 25, 69, 86, 104, 108, 158, 238, 241, 257, 262, 473, D8, S2

238 KENNEDY'S
86 Peckham Road, SE15 5LQ
Tel: 0171-703 4526
Numerous branches in south-east London

Open: Mon-Fri 8.30am-5pm; Sat 8am-4pm
Closed: Sun & Bank Holidays

Sausage shops specialising in good old-fashioned bangers.

Rail: Peckham Rye   Buses: 12, 36, 171, 345, P3

239 KENT & SONS
59 St. John's Wood High Street, NW8 7NL
Tel: 0171-722 2258

Open: Mon-Sat 8am-5.30pm
Closed: Sun & Bank Holidays

This traditional butcher butcher has been supplying the needs of the local community since 1919. Expect to find plenty of free-range meat and poultry, including exceptional beef.

Tube: St. John's Wood   Buses: 13, 82, 113

240 KILBURN MARKET

Kilburn High Road, (alongside Brondesbury Road), NW6

Open: Thurs-Sat 9am-5pm

Closed: Sun-Weds & Bank Holidays

Useful market in the area, the price of basic items, rather than variety, being the main incentive. The excellent B & J Fisheries (qv) is nearby.

Tube: Kilburn Park   Buses: 16, 16a, 28, 31, 32, 98, 206

241 ELIZABETH & A.A. KING (Grocer & Butcher)

30-34 New King's Road, SW6 4ST

Tel: 0171-736 2826 & 0171-736 4004

Open: Mon-Fri 7am-5.30pm; Sat 7am-4pm

(The grocery section keeps slightly longer hours)

Closed: Sun & Bank Holidays

Useful grocer/baker also selling basic green grocery items. Traditional butcher is part of the "complex".

Tube: Parsons Green   Bus: 22

242 JAMES KNIGHT OF MAYFAIR

8 Shepherd Market, W1Y 7HT

Tel: 0171-499 2664

Open: Mon-Fri 8.30am-4pm; Sat 8.30am-10.30am

Closed: Sun & Bank Holidays

Excellent fish shop in rather a barren area of London. Weather permitting, the fish includes sea bass, brill, halibut and turbot. Undyed kippers, Arbroath smokies, fresh crabs, and oysters are normal stock items; as are a range of exotics and tuna and swordfish steaks. Cecil & Co in Islington (q.v) is under the same ownership.

Tube: Green Park   Buses: 8, 9, 14, 19, 22, 38

243 KONDITOR & COOK ★

22 Cornwall Road, SE1 8TW

Tel: 0171-261 0456

Open: Mon-Fri 7.30am-6.30pm; Sat 8.30am-2pm

Closed: Sun & Bank Holidays

Hidden away between The Cut and the river, Gerhard Jenne's baker/patisserie is run with flair and enthusiasm. Excellent in-house bread is supplemented by the best imports London can offer. Home-made biscuits, strudels, croissants made with L'Escure butter, delicious pastries and a range of chutneys, pickles, relishes and jams from Wendy Brandon are just some of the delights on offer. Martin Pitt eggs are used for baking, and available in retail packs. At lunchtime a range of tempting sandwiches and lunch boxes are offered. A licensed café operates nearby at the Young Vic. Perfect puff pastry can be supplied if a few days notice is given.

Tube & Rail: Waterloo/Waterloo East
Buses: 1, 4, 26, 68, 149, 168, 171, 171a, 176, 188, 501, 505, 521, X68

244 KORONA DELICATESSEN

30 Streatham High Road, SW16 1DB
Tel: 0181-769 6647

Open: Mon-Fri 9am-7pm; Sat 9am-6pm; Sun 9am-1pm
Closed: Bank Holidays

Mrs Wicinska has built up a loyal following at her popular delicatessen which specialises in products from Poland and Eastern Europe. The selection is wide, with plenty of French and Italian products including pasta and cheese. Wild mushrooms are a speciality, often fresh in the autumn, dried for the rest of the year.

Rail: Streatham Hill   Buses: 57, 109, 133, 137, 159, 201, 250

245 LAKELAND LIMITED

Alexandra Buildings, Windermere, Cumbria, LA23 1BR
Tel: 015394 88100

Formerly Lakeland Plastic, but as the business has developed over the last few years much more than plastic is now on offer here. A comprehensive catalogue includes items as diverse as old-fashioned mincers to knifes and high-tech microwave accessories.

Mail Order Only

246 BRIAN LAY-JONES

36 Heath Street, NW3 6TE
Tel: 0171-435 5084

Open: Mon-Sat 8am-6pm
Closed: Sun & Bank Holidays

Traditional greengrocer, enthusiastically run by the eponymous Mr Jones. The attractively laid out stock includes many exotic and out of season items (such as strawberries in January). Determination is sometimes needed to buy exactly what you went in for.

Tube: Hampstead   Buses: 46, 268

Tip

Top class free-range chickens produce more fat than battery birds. This is mainly because in their freer environment they take longer to put on weight so are not killed at such a tender age. Save this fat (a clear jug is best). It will keep well in the fridge, being excellent for sauté potatoes and your other frying needs. A little beautiful jelly will collect at the bottom and is excellent for enriching meat sauces (just add it to the gravy of your Sunday roast). If you collect this fat over a period of time, separate this jelly and use it for glazing home-made patés and terrines.

247 LEONIDAS

20 The Arcade, Liverpool Street, EC2M 7PN
Tel: 0171-626 7545
Branches @ 110 Fleet Street, EC4 (0171-353 3590);
132 St. John's Wood High Street, NW8 (0171-722 1191);
4 Colonnade Walk, Victoria, SW1 (0171-828 0848);
Selfridges Oxford Street W1 (0171-629 1234);
Unit 9, The Trocadero, W1 (0171-287 0859)

Open: Mon-Fri 7.45am-6.30pm
Closed: Sat, Sun & Bank Holidays
World-wide chain of shops selling good Belgian chocolates.
Tube: Liverpool Street Buses: 11, 5, 8, 22a, 22b, 23, 26, 35, 42, 43, 47, 48, 78, 100, 133, 141, 149, 172, 214, 243a, 271

248 LESSITER'S

167a Finchley Road, NW3 6LB
Tel: 0171-624 5925
Branch @ 75 Davies Street, W1 (0171-499 3691)

Open: Mon-Sat 9am-6pm Closed: Sun & Bank Holidays
Family run shops selling good Swiss-style chocolates mostly made in their own factory in Hatfield.
Rail: Finchley Road/Swiss Cottage   Buses: 13, 82, 113, 268, C12

249 LEWISHAM MARKET

Lewisham High Street, SE13

Open: Mon- Sat 9am-5pm
Closed: Sun & Bank Holidays
Bustling market, wedged on the wide pavement between Lewisham High Street and the modern shopping centre. Prices are keen, the main attractions being traditional fruit and vegetables and a fish stall at the southern end.
Rail: Lewisham
Buses: 47, 54, 75, 89, 108, 122, 136, 180, 181, 185, 199, 208, 261, 278, 284, 380, 484, P4

250 C. LIDGATE ★

110 Holland Park Avenue, W11 4UA
Tel: 0171-727 8243

Open: Mon-Fri 7am-6pm; Sat 7am-5pm
Closed: Sun & Bank Holidays
First rate family butcher that has built up excellent supply lines over a history of more than 130 years. All their meat is free range and some organic, and includes Glenbervie pure Aberdeen Angus beef (very expensive, but delicious) plus beef and lamb from The Prince of Wales'

farm at Highgrove; free-range chickens from Peter Onions, a splendid selection of game and Bronze turkeys from Kelly's at Christmas time. These need ordering, but even then expect long queues when collecting, as the shop is deservedly popular. Martin Pitt eggs, good bacon to accompany them, an excellent range of cheese, Cottage Delight chutneys and a selection of flavoured oils and vinegars are also on offer. Their home-made pies including steak and kidney, coq au vin and game in season have won national awards.

Tube: Holland Park   Buses: 49, 94, 295

251 LIMONCELLO ★

402 St John Street, EC1V 4NJ
Tel: 0171-713 1678

Open: Mon-Fri 8.30am-7pm; Sat 9.30am-5pm
Closed: Sun & Bank Holidays

Suzanne Heyd and Elizabeth Mitchell started this excellent delicatessen/restaurant/traiteur in 1994. Everything in the shop has been chosen with great care - delicious bread from country-wide specialists, Quickes (of Cheddar fame) butter, biscuits from The Village Bakery, Rosebud jam and marmalade, excellent chutney, pickles and mustard; cheese from Neal's Yard (q.v.). Their bacon from Richard Woodall is some of the best available, and can be accompanied by eggs from Martin Pitt. Their traiteur section includes delicious char-grilled vegetables, salads, and dishes to reheat all prepared by expert in-house chefs; plus their own patés and terrines.

Tube: Angel   Buses: 19, 38, 153, 171a

252 LINA'S ITALIAN DELICATESSEN

601 High Road, North Finchley, N12 0DY
Tel: 0181-446 6011

Open: Mon-Thur & Sat 8.30am-6pm; Fri 8.30am-7pm; Sun 10am-1pm
Closed: Bank Holidays

Useful Italian larder in the same parade of shops as Atari-Ya (q.v.). An enormous range of dried pasta plus a little fresh is backed up by a modest selection of charcuterie and a few cheeses. Good coffee.

Tube: West Finchley (10 minutes)   Buses: 263

253 LINA STORES

18 Brewer Street, W1R 3FS
Tel: 0171-437 6482

Open: Mon-Fri 7am-5.45pm; Sat 7am-5pm
Closed: Sun & Bank Holidays

Delightful little Italian grocer, very popular with the local ethnic community. All the essentials are here, including a good range of dried pasta and pulses; Parma ham and charcuterie. Italian and French bread. The shop is crammed so full that manoeuvring without knocking things over can be difficult.

Tube: Leicester Square/Piccadilly Circus   Buses: 14, 19, 22, 38, 94

254 H.S. LINWOOD & SONS ★
6 & 7 Leadenhall Market, EC3V 1LR
Tel: 0171-929 0554

Open: Mon-Fri 6am-3.30pm
Closed: Sun & Bank Holidays

Set in the splendid Leadenhall Arcade, along with a clutch of excellent fishmongers and butchers, this top notch shop offers a wide range of seafood extending from clams and lobster to sea bass, tuna and octopus.

Tube: Bank/Monument   Buses: 8, 22a, 22b, 25, 26, 35, 47, 48, 149

255 LISBOA DELICATESSEN
54 Golborne Road, W10 5NR
Tel: 0181-969 1052

Open: Mon-Sat 9.30am-7.30pm; Sun & Bank Holidays 10am-1pm
Closed: 25, 26 Dec & 1 Jan

Portuguese delicatessen offering everything from Pao bread to bacalhau (salt cod) and Iberian oils and spices.

Tube: Ladbroke Grove/Westbourne Park   Buses: 23, 52, 70, 295, 302

256 LISBOA PATISSERIE
57 Golborne Road, W10 5NR
Tel: 0181-968 5242

Open: Mon-Sat 8am-8pm
Closed: Sun, 25, 26 Dec & 1 Jan

Popular café/patisserie with the local Portuguese community, and under the same family ownership as Lisboa Delicatessen across the road. Always busy, but the wait is worthwhile.

Tube: Ladbroke Grove/Westbourne Park   Buses: 23, 52, 70, 295, 302

257 LIVEBAIT; THE FISH SHOP ★
45 The Cut, SE1 8LF
Tel: 0171-928 5570

Open: Fri noon-6.30pm; Sat 11am-5.30pm
Closed: Mon-Thur & Sun

Fishmonger attached to the excellent restaurant of the same name, and under the same ownership (Chez Gerard). Fish comes up overnight from Poole and St Mawes, so is beautifully fresh. This is mainly of the restaurant-type, so the strengths tend to be of the brill, crab, lobster, sea bass, turbot and halibut variety - the weaknesses the more mundane items. Beautiful fish stock, produced in their kitchens, is for sale by the pint; as

are Craster kippers and Martin Pitt eggs. Special orders, outside the limited opening times, can be arranged with the restaurant next door.
Tube/Rail: Waterloo
Buses: 1, 4, 21, 26, 68, 149, 168, 171, 188, 211, 501, 521

258 LOCH FYNE OYSTERS

Clachan Farm, Ardkinglas, Cairndow, Argyll PA26 8BH
Tel: 01499-600264   Fax 01499-600 234

Delivering much more than it's name implies, this excellent company supplies everything from fresh langoustines to local undyed kippers. Great efforts are made to use sustainable stocks and use only products farmed in a chemical-free environment and farmed at low densities. Their smoked salmon, which comes in three strengths, is sent around the world. They produce four types of marinated herrings, their sweet tomato variety being our particular favourite. Delivery £5-95, or free for orders over £100. 24 hours notice needed prior to despatch; delivery is then overnight.
Mail Order Only

259 LOON FUNG SUPERMARKET

42/44 Gerrard Street, W1V 7LP
Tel: 0171-437 7332
Branch Loon Fung Hong Cash & Carry @ 111 Brantwood
Road, Tottenham, N17 (0181-   365 1132)

Open: Mon-Sun 10am-8pm Closed: 25 & 26 Dec

Busy Chinese grocer/greengrocer with a splendid pavement display of fresh fruit and vegetables. All your possible needs are catered for here, including lines of deep-freezes full of everything from squid, prawns, chicken's feet, duck's tongues and ready-made dim sum. A kitchen equipment department has woks and steamers in all sizes at very reasonable prices (large woks for under £5).
Tube: Leicester Square   Buses: 14, 19, 24, 29, 38, 176

260 LOU'S BAKERY

8 Ferdinand Street, NW1 8ER
Tel: 0171-284 4644

Open: Mon-Fri 9.30am-5pm; Sat 9.30am-4pm
Closed; Sun & Bank Holidays

Excellent small bakers, just off Chalk Farm Road, run with enthusiasm by Lou Landin. Healthy-type bread is the attraction - e.g "four seed", "sesame and sunflower" - to name but two. Try the delicious pecan nut brownies and her organic marmalade. Stocks can become depleted as the day progresses.
Tube: Chalk Farm   Buses: 24, 27, 31, 46, 168

261 LOUIS PATISSERIE

32 Heath Street, NW3 6TE
Tel: 0171-435 9908

Open: Sun-Sat 8.30am-7pm Closed: 25 Dec

Popular patisserie/tea room. The large selection of cakes and pastries are let down by powdery meringues, Anglicised baguettes and heavy croissants. We will watch for improvements, and keep you informed.

Tube: Hampstead   Buses: 46, 268

262 LUIGI'S

349 Fulham Road, SW10 9TW
Tel: 0171-351 9551

Open: Mon-Fri 9am-10pm; Sat 9am-7pm
Closed: Sun & Bank Holidays

Little Italy on the Fulham Road. Practically, if not everything, is Italian including the excellent butter, jams and honey. An assortment of good fresh pasta. Five different types of Panforte alone, plus a selection of Panetone, nearly fifty olive oils, specialist flour for pasta and pizzas and a good range of charcuterie. All this makes this a haven for Italianites. Their traiteur section offers a daily soup, a pasta dish plus other specialities, including home-made tiramisu.

Tube: South Kensington (15 minutes walk)
Buses; 11, 14, 49, 211 (East-bound), 319, 345 (West-bound)

263 LYONS FISHERIES

14 Northcote Rd. SW11 1NX
Tel: 0171-978 4428

Open: Tue-Sat 7am-6pm
Closed: Sun, Mon & Bank Holidays

Popular fishmonger - the shop is surrounded by the excellent Northcote Road Market (q.v.). Even in the middle of the week they have a good selection of fish, including exotics from the Indian Ocean and Caribbean.

Rail: Clapham Junction   Buses: 319, G1

264 MACKEN BROTHERS ★

44 Turnham Green Terrace, W4 1QP
Tel: 0181-994 2646

Open: Mon-Fri 7am-6pm; 7am-5.30pm
Closed: Sun & Bank Holidays

Excellent family butcher that has largely been unaffected by our endless meat scares by only selling meat whose history is known; so the beef is grass-fed Aberdeen Angus, lamb is Wales' best, and the pork and veal free-range (something of a rarity). Everything in the shop is chosen with equal care; a good selection of game in season, about twenty varieties of their own sausages, excellent mince from grass-fed animals, and Bronze turkeys at Christmas.

Tube: Turnham Green   Buses: E3, H91, 237, 267

265 MACKEN & COLLINS

35 Turnham Green Terrace, Chiswick, W4 1RG
Tel: 0181-995 0140

Open: Mon-Thur 7am-6pm; Fri & Sat 6am-5.30pm
Closed: Sun & Bank Holidays

Deservedly popular greengrocer run by Andrew Georhiou. A wide range of fruit & vegetables is offered, the display spilling on the the pavement.

Tube: Turnham Green   Buses: E3, H91, 27, 237, 267

266 LA MADELEINE

5 Vigo Street, W1X 1AH
Tel: 0171-734 8353

Open: Mon-Fri 8am-10pm; Saturday 8am-7pm; Sunday 11am-6pm
Closed: Bank Holidays

Popular French café/patisserie just off Regent Street. Under the same ownership as Filéric (q.v.). Delicious looking fruit tarts.

Tube: Piccadilly Circus
Buses: 3, 6, 11, 12, 13, 14, 15, 19, 22, 23, 38, 53, 88, 94, 139

267 MAISON BERTAUX

28 Greek Street, W1V 5LL
Tel: 0171-437 6007

Open: Mon-Sat 9am-7.30am;
Sun & Bank Holidays 9am-1pm & 3am-7.30pm
Closed: 25 & 26 Dec

Away from the bustle of Old Compton Street this excellent patisserie is more cottagey and less glitzy than its immediate competitors (Patisserie Valerie and Amato - see entries), but standards are equally high. First class cakes and croissant. Excellent mince pies at Christmas.

Tube: Leicester Square   Buses: 14, 19, 38

268 MAISON BLANC ★

102 Holland Park Avenue, W11 4UA Tel: 0171-221 2494
Branches @ 11 Elystan Street, SW3 (0171-584 6913);
62 Hampstead High Street, NW3 (0171-431 8338)
& The Quadrant, Richmond, Surrey, TW9 (0181-332 7041)

Open: Mon-Sat 8.30am-5.30pm; Sun & Bank Holidays 8.30am-3.30pm
Closed: 25 & 26 Dec

High class fresh pastries are sold in these modern patisseries, and can also be consumed on the premises - all be it standing at a high table. A recent addition is offering bread sculptures called pain surprise for children's and adults parties; these are hollow, so can be filled with sandwiches. They come in a variety of shapes including cat, cow, elephant and lobster. Prices start at £24-50.

Tube: Holland Park   Buses: 49, 94, 295

269 MAISON BOUQUILLON

43/45 Moscow Road, W2 4AH
Tel: 0171-229 2107

Open: Mon-Sat 8.30am-9pm; Sun & Bank Holidays 8.30am-8.30pm
Closed: 25 & 26 Dec

Patisserie making splendid strawberry tarts. Other recommended items are their croissants, coming in a variety of flavours, churros (thin fried pastries that are wonderful dipped in hot chocolate) and bunuelos (deep-fried balls, resembling doughnuts, made of pasta dough filled with crème patissière - delicious!

Tube: Bayswater   Bus: 70

270 M & S FRUITS

160a Clapham High Street, SW4 7UG
Tel: 0171-498 6723

Open: Mon-Sat 7am-5pm Closed: Sun & Bank Holidays

Cheap fresh produce spills on to the pavement at this greengrocers; 5 large peaches or 3 punnets of raspberries for £1 were typical offerings on one inspection visit. Take lunch next door at Eco (q.v) to celebrate your savings. As we went to press a partial switch over from vegetables to bargain flowers was underway, the owners are major fruit and vegetable suppliers to local restaurants; so we are assured they will be continued. If planning ahead even more savings can be achieved by buying these in quantity.

Tube: Clapham Common   Buses: 60, 88, 137a, 155, 345, 355

271 MANILA SUPERMARKET

11 Hogarth Place (off Hogarth Road), SW5 0QT
Tel: 0171-373 8305

Open: Mon-Sun 9am-9pm
Closed: Bank Holidays

This self-service Filipino shop, stocks all you need to prepare a South-East Asian meal; from lime leaves and lemon grass to prepared sauces and hard to find items such as sugar-cane and palm vinegars. One room contains freezers of exotic fish and perishable items, all clearly labelled.

Tube: Earl's Court   Buses: 31, 74, C1, C3

The Gray's Guide is completely independent, and has received no payment from any of the establishments listed.

272 MANOR FARM BAKERY
108 Green Lanes, N16 9EH
Tel: 0171-254 7907

Open: Mon-Sun 7am-8pm
Closed: Bank Holidays

This Turkish bakery is deservedly popular, offering beautifully prepared bread as well as sweet and savoury pastries.

Tube: Manor House (10 mins); Rail Canonbury (5 mins)
Buses: 141, 171a

273 LA MAREE
76 Sloane Avenue, SW3 3DZ
Tel: 0171-589 8067

Open: Mon-Sat 8am-6pm
Closed: Sun & Bank Holidays

This small, but high quality, fish shop attached to La Poissonerie de L'Avenue has been run by the Rosignoli's for over twenty years. Attractive displays of rock oysters (plus natives in season), crab and lobster, scallops and fresh tuna and swordfish are all beautifully fresh. Platters of fruit de mer, plus whole poached salmon, sea bass and turbot can be prepared to order. Game in season.

Tube: South Kensington   Buses: 14, 49, 345

274 MARINE ICES
8 Haverstock Hill, NW3 2BL
Tel: 0171-485 3132

Open: Mon-Sat 10.30am-10.45pm; Sun & Bank Holidays 11am-10pm
Closed: 25, 26 Dec & 1 Jan

The Manzi family have serving good ice cream here, in their café/take-away just opposite Chalk Farm tube station, since 1931. It's all made in-house, and has become so popular they supply other shops under the name Casa Manzi.

Tube: Chalk Farm   Buses: 24, 27, 31, 168

275 MARKS & SPENCER
458 Oxford Street, W1N 0AP
Tel: 0171-935 7954
Too many branches to mention here, but some that stand out are 85 King's Road, SW3 (0171-376 5634) and 99 Kensington High Street, W8 (0171-938 3711); all are listed near the back of this book

Open: Mon, Tue, Wed & Sat 9am-7pm; Thur & Fri 9am-8pm; Sun & Bank Holidays noon-6pm
Closed: 25 & 26 Dec

The flagship M & S food department, with easily the largest range of goods. High supermarket standards are maintained, and great effort goes into producing consistent products. Good salad leaves, pre-packed vegetables and trimmed meat. Their excellent selection of traiteur dishes include those from the Italy, the Far-East and India; unfortunately they are designed to be inoffensive so tend to hold the middle-ground in the flavour stakes. The basic range has recently been joined by one called Connoisseur, developed in conjunction with Albert Roux; this includes the likes of crab cakes with chili sauce (£3·99) and monkfish with sweet pepper (£7·99) - tasty, good value and convenient. They still produce the best chicken Kiev's available; but be careful not to buy the cheaper "reformed meat" version. Excellent party nibbles.

Tube: Marble Arch/Bond Street   Buses: 2, 6, 7, 10, 12, 13, 15, 16A, 23, 30, 73, 74, 82, 94, 98, 113, 135, 137, 137A, 139, 159, 274

276 MARK'S IN KENSINGTON

17 Kensington Court Place, W8 8BJ
Tel: 0171-937 0630

Open: Mon-Fri 8.30am-5.30pm; Sat 8.30am-12.30pm
Closed: Sun & Bank Holidays

Find this good little butcher tucked away south off High Street Kensington. As well as well-sourced meat they stock a limited selection of wet fish plus British farmhouse cheese.

Tube: High Street Kensington (5 minutes)
Buses: 9, 9a, 10, 49, 52, 70 (5 minutes)

277 MARKUS COFFEE COMPANY

13 Connaught Street, W2 2AY
Tel: 0171-723 4020

Open: Mon-Fri 8.30am-5.30pm; Sat 8.30am-1.30pm
Closed: Sun & Bank Holidays

Popular little coffee shop, roasting beans on the premises.

Tube: Marble Arch   Buses: 6, 7, 15, 16, 16a, 23, 36, 98

278 MARLENE'S BAKERY & DELICATESSEN

6 Hendon Lane, N3 1TR
Tel: 0181-349 16742

Open: Mon-Thur 6am-5pm; Fri & Sun 6am-1pm
Closed: Sat & Jewish Holidays

Excellent Jewish bakery well-known for its egg cholla (produced every Thursday and Friday).

Tube: Finchley Central   Buses: 125, 143, 326

279 L & W MARSHALL

13 Tranquil Vale, SE3 0BU
Tel: 0181-852 1060

Open: Tue, Weds & Sat 8am-4.30pm; Thur-Fri 8am-6.30pm; Sun 10am-3.30pm
Closed: Bank Holidays

Traditional fishmonger offering a modest selection of beautifully fresh fish.
Rail: Blackheath   Buses: 13, 40, 44, 54, 89, 108, 202

280 W. MARTYN ★

135 Muswell Hill Broadway, N10 3RS
Tel: 0181-883 5642

Open: Mon, Wed & Fri 9.30am-5.30pm; Thur 9.30am-1pm; Sat 9am-5.30pm
Closed: Sun & Bank Holidays

Splendid tea and coffee specialist that's been run by the same family for
over 100 years. Coffee is freshly roasted and comes in about 15 blends
plus a few single bean varieties; tea includes all the familiar types, plus
some unusual flavours incorporating dried fruits. Grocery items are also
stocked, the high-point of these is a good range of jam , chutney and a
selection of excellent chocolate (including some from Ackerman's).
Tube: Highgate (15 minutes)   Buses: 43, 102, 134, 144, 234, 299, W7

281 L.S. MASH & SONS

11 Atlantic Road, SW9 8HX
Tel: 0171-274 6423

Open: Mon-Sat 7am-6.30pm
Closed: Sun & Bank Holidays

Excellent fishmonger stocking exotics, for the local West Indian and
Portuguese communities, as well as the more usual fare. The fish is all
gleamingly fresh.
Rail/Tube: Brixton   Buses: 2, 3, 35, 45, 109, 118, 133, 159, 196, 250

282 MAURO'S

229 Muswell Hill Broadway, N10 1DE
Tel: 0181-883 2848

Open: Tue-Sat 10am-4pm; Sun 11am-4pm
Closed: Mon & Bank Holidays

In the northern section of The Broadway, this shop specialises in pasta
and it's accompaniments. Dried varieties include interesting flavours like
fennel, chili, beetroot and sun-dried tomato; fresh, unusual ravioli
(perhaps gorgonzola and fig). Over 8 home-made sauces plus meat balls,
cut down cooking to a minimum. Small charcuterie section.
Tube: East Finchley/Highgate (both 15 minutes)
Buses: 43, 102, 134, 234, 299, X43

283 MAYSUN MARKET

869 Finchley Road, NW11 8RR
Tel: 0181-455 4773

Open: Mon-Sat 9am-7.30pm; Sun 10.30am-4.30pm
Closed: Bank Holidays

Excellent self-service shop supplying the groceries from seven oriental countries. Close to Golders Green tube and bus stations.

Tube: Golders Green   Buses: 28, 82, 83

284 MEAT CITY

507 Central Markets, Farringdon Road, Smithfield, EC1 9NL
Tel: 0171-253 9606

Open: Mon-Fri 9am-6pm
Closed: Sat, Sun & Bank Holidays

Bargain butchers run by Nigel Armstrong. Quality is high too, with beef from known herds in Scotland, lamb from the West Country and free-range pork from Sussex.

Tube: Farringdon   Buses: 45, 46, 63, 259

285 MEADOW VIEW QUAIL

Meadow View Farm, Church Lane, Whixall, Nr. Whitchurch,
Shropshire, SY13 2NA
Tel: 01948 880300

Suppliers of smoked salt, and herb flavoured varieties, made from specially imported Spanish sea-salt, cold-smoked over oak chips; these give a delicious lift to cruditée and to pickled or smoked quails eggs, which they also supply.

Mail Order Only

286 MEHTA FRUIT & VEG.

111/113 Upper Tooting Road, SW17 7TS
Tel: 0181-767 8214

Open: Mon-Sun 8.30am-7.30pm
Closed: Bank Holidays

Popular and large Asian grocer/greengrocer stocking every conceivable need of the local community.

Tube: Tooting Broadway   Buses: 155, 315, 355

Tip:

When buying citrus fruit always choose fruit that feels heavy, this ensures that it is full of juice. If you are using it for fruit juice, a few seconds in a microwave oven (until the fruit is just warm to the touch) will produce much more liquid than squeezing from cold.

287 MENACHEM'S

15 Russell Parade, (on Golders Green Road) NW11 9NN
Tel: 0181-201 8629

Open: Mon 8am-5.30pm; Tue & Weds 8am-6pm; Thur 8am-8pm;
Fri & Sun 8am-2pm
Closed: Sat & Bank Holidays

Kosher butcher, selling some delicatessen items such as smoked herrings and salmon, plus pre-packed charcuterie; home-made traiteur dishes such as chicken casserole, meatballs and ravioli - are all in good sauces.

Tube: Brent Cross (5 minutes)   Buses: 83, 183, 210, 240

288 MICHANICOU BROTHERS

2 Clarendon Road, W11 3AA
Tel: 0171-727 5191

Open: Mon-Fri 9am-6.30pm; Sat 9am-5.30pm
Closed: Sun & Bank Holidays

Small but excellent greengrocer, round the corner from the tube station, selling plenty of exotics as well as more mundane items.

Tube: Holland Park   Buses: 49, 94, 295

289 ANDREAS MICHLI & SONS S

33 Salisbury Road, N4 IJY
Tel: 0181-802 0188

Open: Mon-Thur & Sat 9.30am-7.30pm; Fri 7.30am-8.30pm;
Sun 11am-3.30pm
Closed: Bank Holidays

Excellent Greek family grocer/greengrocer run on old-fashioned lines. As well as the expected national staples, you will find delights such as wild spinach, hollyhock leaves and live snails. Many of the vegetables are organically grown on Mr Michli's own farm. You will find more character here than in any of the more modern shops on nearby Green Lanes.

Rail: Harringay Green Lanes (5 minutes)   Buses:29, 141, 171a

290 MIDHURST BUTCHERS

2 Midhurst Parade (off Fortis Green), N10
Tel: 0181-883 5303

Open: Mon-Fri 8am-6pm; Sat 8am-5pm
Closed: Sun & Bank Holidays

Excellent butcher and game dealer, stocking free-range and some organic meat, plus the excellent (but pricey) Peter Onions chickens. More than ten varieties of sausages are made in-house; and hens, ducks and sometimes goose eggs are supplied by Pure Suffolk Foods (real food specialists). Norfolk Bronze and Black turkeys at Christmas.

Tube: East Finchley (10 minutes)   Bus: 102

291 W.J. MILLER S

14 Stratford Road, W8 6QD
Tel: 0171-937 1777

Open: Mon & Sat 8am-1pm; Tue-Fri 8am-6pm
Closed: Sun & Bank Holidays

Hidden away amongst a clutch of shops at the Marloes Road end of
Stratford Road, this well-run little butcher unusually sells Halal meat
reared to the standards of The Organic Farmers and Growers Association.
Tube: Earl's Court/High Street Kensington (both 10 minutes)
Buses: 31, C1

292 MISE-EN-PLACE ★

21 Battersea Rise, SW11 1HG
Tel: 0171-228 4392

Open: Mon-Fri 9am-9pm; Sat, Sun & Bank Holidays 8.30am-7pm
Closed: 25, 26 Dec & 1 Jan

Under the same ownership as the popular La Bouffe restaurant nearby,
this excellent delicatessen has been tempting the local community since
1994. With the help of their restaurant experience they have conjured up
food from some of the countries best suppliers. Preserves from Bay Tree,
bacon from Sandridge of Wiltshire, flour from Doves Farm, ice cream from
Rocombe Farm and cheese from a spread of the best small producers -
from home and abroad. Good range of charcuterie is backed up by
terrines from their own kitchen, whose outside catering unit also prepare
whole dinner parties.
Rail: Clapham Junction   Buses: 35, 37

293 MR. CHRISTIAN'S

11 Elgin Crescent, W11 2JA
Tel: 0171-229 0501

Open: Mon-Fri 6am-7pm; Sat 5.30am-6pm; Sun 7am-4pm
Closed: Bank Holidays

Good delicatessen run by Glynn Christian of cookery writing and
television fame. As one would expect from a knowledgeable enthusiast,
products have been carefully chosen, and advice is at hand. Their early
morning bread is very popular.
Tube: Ladbroke Grove (5 minutes)   Buses: 7, 23, 52, 70, 302

294 MIURA FOODS

40 Coombe Road, Norbiton, Surrey KT2 7AF
Tel: 0181-549 8076

Open: Mon & Sun 10am-6pm; Tue-Sat 9am-6pm
Closed: Bank Holidays

Comprehensive Japanese grocer, with a good selection of fish prepared for making sushi.

Rail: Norbiton   Buses: K6

295 M. MOEN & SONS ★

19 The Pavement, SW4 0HY
Tel: 0171-622 1624
Branch @ 171 Kennington Lane, SE11 (0171-735 1742)

Open: Mon-Fri 8am-6.30pm; Sat 8am-5pm
Closed: Sun & Bank Holidays

This old fashioned (in the nicest sense) butcher has been run by the Moen family here since the early '70s. Most of their meat and poultry comes from The Real Meat Company or Pure Suffolk Foods, so is both free-range and organic. Their own sausages, coming in ten varieties, are deservedly popular, as are black and white puddings from Clonakilty in Ireland (these might be too on barley for some tastes). Autumn and winter bring an impressive selection of game, often including snipe and woodcock. Even more unusual items might include ostrich, emu and alligator and even locusts can be ordered. Fresh wild mushrooms in season and Bronze turkeys at Christmas. Beautifully presented meat, and excellent service.

Tube: Clapham Common
Buses: 35, 37, 60, 88, 137, 137a, 155, 345, 355

296 MONMOUTH COFFEE COMPANY ★

27 Monmouth Street, WC2H 9DD
Tel: 0171-836 5272

Open: Mon-Sat 9am-6.30pm; Sun & Bank Holidays 11am-5pm
Closed: 25, 26 December & 1 January

Shop selling coffee of the highest standard (and suppliers to some of London's better restaurants), all roasted on the premises. To keep everything fresh they restrict themselves to about a dozen varieties, which include water processed decaffeinated and an organic coffee from Papua New Guinea. These can all be bought unroast (to finish off at home), or as either dark or medium roast, according to taste - or indeed a mixture of the two. doubles up as a tasting room to help you make your choice. The coffee is backed up by delicious handmade chocolates from Weiss in Lyons, these include little novelty packets of coffee beans covered in chocolate. A flourishing mail-order business operates, and there is a local delivery service by arrangement. Enthusiastic and helpful service.

Tube: Covent Garden/Tottenham Court Road
Buses: 14, 19, 24, 29, 38, 176

Please use the forms at the back of this book
to recommend your own favourite shops

297 MONTE'S

23 Canonbury Lane, N1 2AS
Tel: 0171-354 4335

Open: Mon-Fri 9.30am-7pm; Sat 9.30am-6pm; Sun 10.30am-2pm
Closed: Bank Holidays
Popular Italian delicatessen stocking a wide range of cheese, salami and luxury items.
Tube & Rail: Highbury & Islington   Buses: 4, 19, 30, 43, X43

298 MOORE PARK DELICATESSEN

85 Moore Park Road, SW6 2DA
Tel: 0171-736 2087

Open: Mon-Fri 10am-7pm; Sat 10am-2pm Closed: Sun & Bank Holidays
Victoria Knyvett-Hoff has been running her delicatessen/traiteur, just south of Fulham Broadway station, since 1991; providing the locals with those little hard to get luxuries. Offerings include excellent biscuits, British cheese (including Quickes cheddar), some of Carluccio's products, chocolates, fudge, ice cream and Martin Pitt eggs. Filled baguettes are popular at lunchtime, and freezer-to-oven home-made meals in the evening.
Tube: Fulham Broadway   Buses: 11, 14, 22, 211

299 MOREL BROS., COBBETT & SON LTD.

Unit 7, 129 Coldharbour Lane, London SE5 9NY
Tel: 0171-346 0046

A revival of a famous name from the last century (Morels had premises at 210 Piccadilly, and held a Royal Warrant for supplying continental delicacies). They now specialise in products that you can't easily obtain elsewhere. These include caviar, keta (salmon roe), unusual oils and vinegars, pickles and mustard, confit and cassoulet plus excellent chocolates from Weiss of St. Etienne. All packaged to make excellent presents.
Mail Order (unless you're a local, when they might be persuaded to let you collect).

300 MORTIMER & BENNETT ★

33 Turnham Green Terrace, W4 1RG
Tel: 0181-995 4145

Open: Mon-Fri 8.30am-7pm; Sat 8.30-5.30pm
Closed: Sun & Bank Holidays
Delicatessen of the highest rank, run with great enthusiasm by Dan Mortimer and Diane Bennett. Lack of space must be a problem but great effort has gone into finding the best of everything; bacon from Denhay, eggs from Martin Pitt, butter from Keen's, salad leaves from Appledore, relishes from The Bay Tree Food Company and bread from Sally Clarke,

De Gustibus and Poilane - the list goes on and on. Excellent cheese, charcuterie, chocolate, olive oil and vinegar plus fresh wild mushrooms in season (sometimes gathered by the proprietors). First class fish from The Woodcock Smokery of County Cork is a recent addition.

Tube: Turnham Green   Buses: E3, H91, 27, 237, 267

301 MRS. BASSA'S INDIAN KITCHEN

Wandsworth Workshops, Unit 133, 86-96 Garret Lane, SW18 4DJ
Tel: 0181-871 4460

Excellent range of chutneys, sauces and curry pastes. Free sampling and sales every Sunday at Merton Abbey Mills. Also stocked at the The Bluebird Gastrodrome (q.v).

(Tube: South Wimbledon, opposite the Savacentre).

Shops, Mail Order and stall

302 MRS. TEE'S WILD MUSHROOMS

Gorse Meadow, Sway Road, Lymington, Hampshire SO41 8LR
Tel: 01590 673354

Well organised mail order business and popular supplier to some of London's smarter restaurants. New Forest mushrooms are generally available from the first of September to the middle of January. For the remainder of the year supplies are flown in from as far afield as California and Alaska. *Mail Order Only*

303 MRS. O'KEEFFE'S SAUSAGE SHOP

217 Kensington Church Street, W8 7LX
Tel: 0171-229 6652

Open: Mon-Sat 8.30am-7pm Closed: Sun & Bank Holidays
Useful butcher specialising in sausages in interesting flavours such as kangaroo and spicy Spanish, all made on the premises.

Tube: Notting Hill Gate   Buses: 27, 28, 31, 52, 70

304 MYDDELTONS DELICATESSEN

25a Lloyd Baker Street, WC1X GAT
Tel: 0171-278 9192

Open: Mon-Fri 7am-7pm; Sat 7am-6pm; Sun 8am-2pm
Closed: Bank Holidays
Popular delicatessen with useful opening hours. Excellent bread from Sally Clarke (q.v) plus a selection from Gail Force, an enormous range of cheese, cakes from Michael Nadell, a charcuterie selection including proper Cornish pasties, eggs from Martin Pitt to accompany their bacon with no added water and an interesting selection of sausages, are just some of the temptations on offer. Excellent sandwiches available.

Tube: Angel/King's Cross   Buses: 19, 30, 38, 63, 73

305 NADELL PATISSERIE

Units 4 & 5 White Lion Street, Islington, N1 9HJ
Tel: 0171-833 2461

Open: Mon-Fri 9am-5pm
Closed: Sat, Sun & Bank Holidays

Patisserie to the wholesale trade owned by Michael Nadell, of television fame. They are willing to supply the general public, but requirements (Wedding Cakes etc) need discussion in advance. Proper puff pastry, made with butter, is available; but only in 10 lb boxes, and even then only if ordered in advance!

Tube: Angel   Buses: 4, 19, 30, 38, 43, 73, 153

306 NATURAL HEALTH

339 Ballards Lane, North Finchley, N12 8LT
Tel: 0181-445 4397
Branch at Alternative Health Store, 1369 High Road,
Whetstone, N20 9LN

Open: Mon-Sat 9am-5.30pm
Closed: Sun & Bank Holidays

Good health-food shop stocking everything from chocolate for diabetics and Whole Earth jams to Martin Pitt eggs and the best wholemeal flour. A good range of vitamin supplements and aromatherapy oils are also available.

Rail: Woodside Park (10 mins)   Buses: 263

307 NATURE FRESH

126-128 Upper Tooting Road, SW17 7EN
Tel: 0181-682 4988

Open: Mon-Sun 8am-7pm
Closures: None

An eye-catching pavement display makes this self-service greengrocer a colourful landmark. An enormous variety of fruit and vegetables are offered catering for the local English, Asian and Caribbean communities.

Tube: Tooting Broadway   Buses: 155, 219, 355

308 NEAL'S YARD BAKERY CO-OP

6 Neal's Yard, WC2H 9DP
Tel: 0171-836 5199

Open: Mon-Sat 10.30am-5pm
Closed: Sun & Bank Holidays

Bakery producing excellent wholemeal bread from organic flour from Shipton Mill. Popular snacks at lunchtime.

Tube: Covent Garden   Buses: 14, 19, 24, 29, 38, 176

309 NEAL'S YARD DAIRY ★

17 Shorts Gardens, WC2H 9AT
Tel: 0171-379 7646

Open: Mon-Sat 9am-7pm; Sun & Bank Holidays 10am-5pm
Closed: 25 & 26 Dec

Branch & mail order dept. @ 6 Park Street, SE1
Tel: 0171-403 9544

Open: Mon-Fri 10am-6pm

Since it's conception in 1979, Randolph Hodgson has made this Britain's, as well as London's, premier cheese shop for anything worthwhile produced in the British Isles. Most of their cheeses are unpasteurised, and this is no coincidence, as uncooked milk has more character. Tasting before buying is positively encouraged, and informed advice is always on hand. As a bonus, they offer Winters Dairy ice cream throughout the year, their own Irish wild smoked salmon at Christmas and excellent apples and pears, from traditional rather than commercial strains, in season. The service is unsurpassed. An efficient mail order system operates.

Tube: Covent Garden   Buses: 14, 19, 24, 29, 38, 176

310 NEAL'S YARD WHOLE FOOD WAREHOUSE

21/23 Shorts Gardens, WC2H 9AS
Tel: 0171-836 5151

Open: Mon-Fri 9am-7pm (Thur till 7.30pm); Sat 9am-6.30pm; Sun 11am-5.30pm
Closed: Bank Holidays

Good health-food shop, now under the ownership of Holland & Barrett.

Tube: Covent Garden   Buses: 14, 19, 24, 29, 38, 176

311 NEW COVENT GARDEN MARKET

Nine Elms Lane, SW8

Open: Mon-Fri 3.30am-10.30am
Closed: Sat, Sun & Bank Holidays

Very much geared for bulk-buying, but excellent value if you have to arrange a large party or wedding.

Tube: Vauxhall   Buses: 44, 77, 77a, 322, 344

312 NEW LOON MOON SUPERMARKET

9 Gerrard Street, W1V 7LJ
Tel: 0171-734 3887

Open: Mon-Sun 10am-8pm
Closed: 25 & 26 Dec

Due to lack of space, this shop is not able to compete for Chinese varieties with the enormous Loon Fung Supermarket opposite, although their selection is still fairly comprehensive. But a separate department to the rear has an good stock of food from Indonesia, Japan, Korea, Malaysia, Phillipines and Singapore.

Tube: Leicester Square   Buses: 14, 19, 24, 29, 38, 176

313 NEWPORT SUPERMARKET
28/29 Newport Court, WC2H 7PQ
Tel: 0171-437 2386

Open: Mon-Sun 10.30am-8pm Closed: 25 & 26 Dec

Near the eastern entrance of Chinatown this shop has an excellent selection of fruit and vegetables displayed outside (from fresh lemon grass to exotic tubers). Inside, you'll find a good variety of Chinese groceries including good-value spices (e.g. 8oz Cinnamon Bark for 85p on a recent visit). There's a good selection of frozen fish - including squid, octopus and prawns, plus air-dried ducks and Chinese sausages. Under the same ownership Newport Kitchen Supplies (0171-437 2386), nearby at number 32, has plenty of woks and steamers at bargain prices so your can cook your purchases.

Tube: Leicester Square   Buses: 14, 19, 24, 29, 38, 176

314 JOHN NICHOLSON
46 Devonshire Road, W4 2HD
Tel: 0181-994 0809

Open: Tue-Fri 8am-5.30pm; Sat 8am-5pm
Closed: Sun, Mon & Bank Holidays

Good fishmonger, also selling a few delicatessen and traiteur items.

Tube: Turnham Green   Buses: 27, 237, 267, 391, E3, H91

315 NICKY'S FRUIT & VEG
98 South Ealing Road, W5 4QJ
Tel: 0181-567 2659

Open: Mon-Sat 6am-6pm Closed: Sun & Bank Holidays

The produce here always looks beautifully fresh, and the display spills out on to the street. There are generally a few unusual items as Nicky supplies local restaurants and the general public reap the benefit.

Tube: South Ealing   Buses: 65

316 NORTHCOTE ROAD MARKET
Northcote Road, SW11

Open: Mon-Sat 9am-5pm; Weds 9am-1pm
Closed: Sun & Bank Holidays

Very good market in this foodie road. Everything from exotic fruit and vegetables to excellent fish. Hamish Johnson and Dove's (q.v's) mean you can do all your shopping here at a reasonable price.

Rail: Clapham Junction   Buses: 319, G1

317 NORTH END ROAD MARKET

North End Road (south end), SW6

Open: Mon-Wed, Fri & Sat 9am-5pm; Thur 9am-2pm
Closed: Sun & Bank Holidays

This popular street market offers good-value fruit and vegetables and a fish stall with a wider than average selection. As with all street markets particular bargains are to be had near closing time.

Tube: Fulham Broadway   Buses: 14, 74, 211, 295

318 NOSH

77 Castellain Road, W9 1EU
Tel: 0171-286 2304

Open: Mon-Fri 7am-7pm; Sat 7am-7.30pm;Sun 7am-2pm;
Bank Holidays 9am-noon. Closed: 25 & 26 Dec

Unpretentious grocer/newsagent selling Martin Pitt eggs.

Tube: Warwick Avenue (5 minutes)   Buses: 6, 46 (5 minutes)

319 OFF LICENCE

100 Chalton Street, NW1 1HN
Tel: 0171-387 3937

Open: Mon-Sat 10am-10.30pm; Sun 11am-3pm & 7pm-10pm
Closed: 25 & 26 Dec

Corner shop in barricaded Somers Town, useful grocery basics and Martin Pitt eggs.

Tube & Rail: Euston (5 minutes)   Buses: 10, 30, 73, 91 (5 minutes)

320 THE OIL MERCHANT ★

47 Ashchurch Grove, W12 9BU
Tel: 0181-740 1335

First class supplier of estate bottled olive oils, nut oils and top-class vinegars; run by Charles and Sika Carey. A selection of tapenade type pastes and Italian "farmhouse made" prepared sauces are also stocked. Gift boxes and specialist books for the enthusiast make excellent presents. Prices are reasonable for the quality on offer. No mailing charge on orders over £25.

Mail Order; collection by special arrangement

321 OLGA STORES

30 Penton Street, N1 9PS   Tel: 0171-837 5467

Open: Mon-Fri 9am-8pm; Sat 9am-7pm; Sun 10am-2pm
Closed: Bank Holidays

Popular Italian delicatessen/traiteur selling pasta, good home-made sauces, plus a wide selection of cheese and charcuterie.

Tube: Angel   Buses: 30, 73, 214

322 OLIVE TREE

84 Willesden Lane, NW6 7TA
Tel: 0171-328 9078

Open: Mon, Tue, Thur, Fri & Sat 10am-6.30pm; Weds 1pm-6.30pm
Closed: Weds AM; Sun & Bank Holidays

Popular health food shop selling a good selection of organic bread and vegetables plus Martin Pitt eggs.

Rail: Brondesbury Park   Buses: 98

323 O'HAGAN'S SAUSAGE SHOP

192 Trafalgar Road, SE10 9TZ
Tel: 0181-858 2833

Open: Mon-Fri 9am-5.30pm; Sat 8.30am-5.30pm
Closed: Sun & Bank Holidays

London's first specialist sausage shop (1988), and still one of the best. Over 40 varieties include all the latest trends - ostrich, kangaroo and Thai chicken for example). Young's Real Ale flavour is a personal favourite.

Rail: Maze Hill   Buses: 108, 177, 180, 286, 386

324 THE ORIGINAL FISHERMAN

23 Electric Avenue, Brixton Market, SW9 8JP
Tel: 0171-733 3430

Open: Mon-Sat 7am-6.30pm
Closed: Sun & Bank Holidays

Very popular fishmonger, specialising in exotics for the local West Indian and Portuguese communities.

Tube & Rail: Brixton   Buses:2, 3, 35, 45, 109, 118, 133, 159, 196, 250

325 OZ FISH GALLERY AND PRAWN BAR ★

95 Ballards Lane, Finchley, N3 1XY
Tel: 0181-346 825

Open: 9am-7pm
Closed: 25 & 26 Dec

Fish shop specialising in exotics mainly sourced from Western Australia. They claim their fish is on display 24 hours after being landed, and it certainly looks very fresh. They will try to source any Australian food you might require - already stocking emu meat, kangaroo and crocodile!

Tube: Finchley Central   Buses: 82, 125, 260

326 PANADAM DELICATESSEN

2 Marius Road, SW17 7QQ
Tel: 0181-673 4062

Open: Tue-Sat 9.30am-5.45pm; Sun 10am-2pm
Closed: Mon & Bank Holidays

Zbigniew Brzeski has been running this popular Polish delicatessen since 1981. You'll find excellent home-made cheesecakes, bread from The Kolos Bakery plus a good selection of preserved herrings, meats and vegetables.
Tube/Rail: Balham. Tube: Tooting Bec   Buses: 155, 249, 355

327 PANZER DELICATESSEN
13-19 Circus Road, NW8 6PB
Tel: 0171-722 8596

Open: Mon-Fri 8am-7pm; Sat 8am-6pm; Sun 8am-2pm
Closed: Bank Holidays

Panzer's has been serving the needs of St John's Wood for over 40 years. Made up of three departments, delicatessen, green grocery and off licence, it is possible to do most of your shopping under one roof. Over fifty types of bread, including some from Sally Clarke (q.v), biscuits from around the world, excellent charcuterie, plus luxury items such as caviar and a variety of "London cure" (traditionally mild) smoked salmon.
Tube: St John's Wood   Buses: 13, 46, 82, 113

328 PAPILLON PATISSERIE
241 Muswell Hill Broadway, N10 1DE
Tel: 0181-372 7156

Open: Tue-Sat 7am-5.30pm
Closed: Sun, Mon & Bank Holidays

Popular baker/patisserie downstairs, with a tea room above. Everything is made on the premises.
Tube: East Finchley/Highgate (15 minutes)
Buses: 43, 102, 134, 234, 299, X43

329 PARIS & RIOS
93 Columbia Road, E2 7RG
Tel: 0171-729 1147

Open: Tue, Weds & Fri 9.30am-3pm; Mon & Thur 9.30am-2pm; Sat 9.30am-5pm; Sun 9am-2pm
Closed: Bank Holidays

A scattering of many delicious Spanish items inhabit Isabelle Rios' little shop. A small selection of Spanish cheeses and charcuterie includes salami and sausages. Traiteur items are all home-made - try the delicious filleted sardines in seasoned bread crumbs. This pretty street plays host to a flower and gardening market on Sunday mornings (8am-12.30pm). So the two visits could be combined.
Tube: Bethnal Green Rail: Cambridge Heath (both 10 minutes)
Buses: 26, 48, 55

330 LE PARC FRANGLAIS

94 Wickham Road, Beckenham, Kent, BR3 2QH
Tel: 0181-650 0355

Open: Mon-Fri 8am-6pm; Sat 8am-7pm; Sun & Bank Holidays 10am-2pm
Closed: 25 & 26 Dec

A useful delicatessen, with a selection of charcuterie, cheese, and cheesecakes, also bread from Delice de France. A café also operates.
Rail: Beckenham Junction/Eden Park (15 mins)   Buses: 162

331 PARTRIDGES OF SLOANE STREET

132-134 Sloane St. SW1X 9AT
Tel: 0171 730 0651

Open: Mon-Sun 8am-10pm
Closed: Bank Holidays

Grocer and delicatessen. Expensive for standard products, a modest range of charcuterie and cheeses (but little obvious attempt to search out the very best). You'll find a good range of olive oils and vinegars, their own-label dressings, preserves and sauces plus excellent free range Suffolk-cure bacon from F.E. Neave. Mail order service.
Tube: Sloane Square   Buses: 11, 19, 22, 137, 137a, 211, 319, C1

332 THE PASTA PLACE

42 Heath Street, NW3 6TE
Tel: 0171-431 0018

Open: Mon-Fri 10am-8pm; Sat 10am-6.30pm; Sun 11.30am-6.30pm
Closed: Bank Holidays

Italian delicatessen/traiteur offering a good selection of fresh pasta dishes, as depicted in the name, plus meat balls, mixed antipasti, quiches, pizza slices and individual cheesecakes. The deli section stocks good olive oil and a full range of Italian groceries.
Tube: Hampstead   Buses: 46, 268

333 PATEL BROTHERS

187/189 Upper Tooting Road, SW17 7TG
Tel: 0181-672 2792
Open: Mon-Sun 9am-6.30pm
Closed: 25 & 26 Dec

Good family-run Indian self-service grocer, selling a vast choice of everything from pistachio nuts to spices and curry paste. Many items come in enormous bags, but are no more expensive than much smaller offerings from national supermarkets.
Tube: Tooting Broadway   Buses: 155, 219, 355

334 PATISSERIE VALERIE

44 Old Compton Street, W1V 5PB Tel: 0171-437 3466
Branches @ 105 Marylebone High Street, W1
(0171-935 6240);
215 Brompton Road, SW3 (0171-823 9971);
8 Russell Street, WC2 (0171-240 0064)
& 66 Portland Place, W1

Open: Mon-Fri 8am-8pm; Sat 8am-7pm; Sun 10am-6pm
Closed: 3 days Christmas

Good patisserie producing delicious-looking fruit tarts, chocolate éclairs, and gateaux. Their French-style wedding cakes are particularly impressive, if rather expensive.

Tube: Leicester Square/Piccadilly   Buses: 11, 14, 19, 38

335 PAUL'S

62 Camberwell Church Street, SE5 8QZ
Tel: 0171-703 0156

Open: Mon-Sat 10am-7pm
Closed: Sun & Bank Holidays

Old-fashioned Greek grocer selling loose olives, fresh vegetables and ethnic staples.

Rail: Denmark Hill   Buses: 12, 36, 171, 345

336 PAXTON & WHITFIELD*

93 Jermyn Street, SW1Y GJE
Tel: 0171-930 0259

Open: Mon-Sat 9am-5.30pm
Closed: Sun & Bank Holidays

A tremendous sense of history at this excellent cheese shop, which opened it's doors for the first time just down the road at number 18 in 1797. While there are no more Paxton's or Whitfield's at the helm, the tradition of selling the best cheese, and offering advice on how it should best be kept, remains. A range of their own chutney, biscuits for cheese, traditional hams, smoked salmon and caviar is also available. A mail order service operates.

Tube: Piccadilly
Buses: 3, 6, 9, 12, 13, 14, 15, 19, 22, 23, 38, 53, 88, 94, 139

Please use the forms at the back of this book
to recommend your own favourite shops

337 PIERRE PECHON

127 Queensway, W2 4SJ
Tel: 0171-229 0746
Branch @ 27 Kensington Church Street,
W8 (0171-937 9574)

Open: Mon-Weds 7.30am-6pm; Thur-Sat 7.30am-8pm; Sun 7.30am-7pm
Closed: Bank Holidays

French baker/patisserie with a good, rather than inspiring, range of bread and cakes; strangely their baguettes are not of the highest order nor are their powdery meringues - neither would pass muster in France.

Tube: Bayswater/Queensway   Buses: 70

338 PEPPERCORN'S

2 Heath Street, NW3 6TE
Tel: 0171-431 1251

Open: Mon-Sat 10am-6.30pm; Sun 10.30-5pm
Closed: Bank Holidays

Good self-service health shop, on the corner with Perrins Lane, with stock embracing everything from dried fruit to pulses and porridge oats - many organic items. Comprehensive range of vitamin supplements.

Tube: Hampstead   Buses: 46, 243, 268

339 PEPPERCORN'S

193/195 West End Lane, NW6 2LJ
Tel: 0171-328 6874

Open: Mon-Fri 10.15am-7pm; Sat 10am-6pm
Closed: Sun & Bank Holidays

No longer connected with the above operation, although it once was; this little health shop opposite West Hampstead tube station has a good selection of pulses and tisines plus Martin Pitt eggs.

Tube & Rail: West Hampstead   Buses: 28, 139, C11

340 PIACENZA DELICATESSEN

2 Brixton Road, SW9 6BU
Tel: 0171-735 2121

Open: Mon-Sat 9am-6.30pm; Sun 10am-1.30pm
Closed: Bank Holidays

Run by the Coda family, this small shop at the northern end of Brixton Road stocks all the necessities, including several varieties of fresh ravioli. Very popular with the local Italian community, possibly because of the excellent personal service.

Tube & Rail: Oval   Buses: 3, 36, 109, 159

341 LA PICENA

5 Walton Street, SW3 2JD
Tel: 0171-584 6573

Open: Mon-Fri 9am-7.30pm; Sat 9am-5.30pm
Closed: Sun & Bank Holidays

Useful little Italian delicatessen, also selling a few emergency meat items - such as sirloin steak, veal escalopes and chicken breasts.

Tube: South Kensington (5 minutes)   Buses: 14, 49, 345

342 PLANET ORGANIC ★

42 Westbourne Grove, W2 5SH
Tel: 0171-221 7171

Open: Mon-Sat 9am-8pm; Sun 11am-5pm
Closed: Bank Holidays

This health-food supermarket is of the first rank, marvellous for health food freaks, but comprehensive enough to enable you to do all your shopping here. Nothing stocked contains any artificial additives, and as much as possible is organic, including fruit and veg, pasta and ready-made meals. The counters of cheese, fresh fish and meat are truly impressive.

Tube: Bayswater   Buses: 7, 23, 27, 70

343 PLATTERS DELICATESSEN

10 Hallswelle Parade, Finchley Road, NW11 0DL
Tel; 0181-455 7345
Branch at 83-85 Allitsen Road, St John's Wood, NW8 7AS

Open: Mon-Thur 8.30am-5pm; Fri 7.30am-5pm; Sat 7.30-4pm; Sun 7.30am-2pm; Bank Holidays 8.30am-2pm
Closed: 25 Dec

Run by the Platter family for over twenty years this Jewish delicatessen and grocery produces excellent bread, cheesecake, selilte (fish balls), latkes (potato cakes), marinated herrings and an extensive range of char-grilled vegetables and salads. Excellent smoked salmon, plus undyed kippers, buckling and red herrings. Their traiteur selection, most of which needs ordering, extends from trays of canapés and vol-au-vents to boned and decorated poached salmon, lasagne and beef Wellington.

Tube: Golders Green (10 minutes)   Buses: 82, 102, 260

344 PORTERFORD ★

6 Bow Lane, EC4M 9EB
Tel: 0171-248 1396

Open: Mon-Thur 6.30am-6.30pm; Fri 6am-7.30pm
Closed: Sat, Sun & Bank Holidays

Excellent butcher and game dealer. Carefully chosen bacon, chicken and lamb from Wales; best quality Scottish beef; Bronze turkeys; eggs from

Martin Pitt and a range of over 20 sausages, most made in-house.
Tube: Mansion House   Buses: 8, 11, 15, 17, 22b, 149, 501

345 PORTOBELLO ROAD MARKET
Portobello Road & Golborne Road, W11

Open: Mon-Sat 9am-5pm; (Thurs 1pm closing)
Closed: Sun & Bank Holidays

Excellent fruit and vegetables here at reasonable and even bargain prices,
as well as very cheap meat at of unknown quality. For good fish see J.H.
Smith (qv), and for eggs of all varieties Applewold Farm Shop (qv).
London's best foodie book shop Books for Cooks is round the corner in
Blenheim Crescent. Every Thursday from around 11am-7pm, organic
food stalls operate under the Market Tent on Portobello Green, at the
top end of Portobello Road.
Tube: Westbourne Park   Buses: 7, 23, 52, 70, 302

346 PORTOBELLO WHOLE FOODS
266 Portobello Road, W10 5TY
Tel: 0181-960 1840

Open: Mon-Sat 9.30am-6pm
Closed: Sun , 25 & 26 Dec

A branch of Neal's Yard Bakery (q.v) is situated under the Westway flyover.
Excellent bread plus vegetarian cheese, a range of specialist flour, coffee
from The Monmouth Coffee Company and a few good organic vegetables.
Tube: Ladbroke Grove   Buses: 7, 23, 52, 70, 302

347 PORTWINE & SON ★
24 Earlham Street, WC2H 9LN
Tel: 0171-836 2353

Open: Mon & Sat 7.30am-2pm; Tue-Thur 7.30am-5pm; Fri 7.30am-5.30pm
Closed: Sun & Bank Holidays

Excellent butcher specialising in free-range and additive-free meats,
including some from rare breeds. Bacon to suit all tastes (including a
strong cure from Maynard's Farm) , chickens and bronze turkeys from
Munson's (Aylesbury-type ducks to order), enormous selection of game
in season; proper mutton, boudin blanc, haggis and black pudding from
one of the countries best producers. A range of up to twenty types of
sausages make this a tempting shop to visit.
Tube: Covent Garden/Leicester Square   Buses: 8, 11, 12, 14, 19, 38

348 POSTONS
222 Hoe Street, Walthamstow, E17 3AY
Tel: 0181-520 3300

Open: Mon-Fri 8am-7pm; Sat 8am-6pm
Closed: Sun & Bank Holidays

Over 30 varieties of home-made sausages at one of London's eastern outposts; try the pork and Stilton, duck and orange or their excellent Italian varieties. While here, don't miss the chance of visiting the interesting street market round the corner.

Tube & Rail: Waltamstow Central.

Buses: 2, 20, 48, 69, 97, 97a, 230, 257, 551, W15

349 PAMELA PRICE

26 The Pavement, SW4 QJA
Tel: 0171-622 4051

Open: 8am-10pm seven days a week; Christmas Day 11am-2pm
Closed: Boxing Day

Pamela Price has been running her delicatessen since 1971, apart from her expertise in choosing the best products, the generous opening hours mean that she can provide a feast outside normal shop hours. Bread from some of the countries best bakers, carefully chosen cheese, eggs from Martin Pitt, and a selection of the best bacon and ham. A few traiteur dishes (mainly vegetarian) are available frozen, at very reasonable prices. Smoked salmon, from an excellent small producer, is available to order.

Tube: Clapham Common

Buses: 35, 37, 60, 88, 137, 137a, 155, 345, 355

350 PRIMA DELICATESSEN

192 North End Road, W14 9NX
Tel: 0171-385 2070

Open: Mon, Tue, Weds, Thur & Sat 9.30am-6pm; Fri 9.30am-7pm
Closed: Sun & Bank Holidays

Find this little Polish grocery shop on the corner with Fane Street. A good selection of preserved East-European fruit and vegetables, Polish charcuterie and Kolos bread, is accompanied by friendly service.

Tube: West Kensington   Buses: 28, 74, 190, 391

351 PRODUCTS FROM SPAIN

89 Charlotte Street, W1P 1LB
Tel: 0171-580 2905

Open: Mon-Fri 10am-5.30pm; Sat 10am-1pm
Closed: Sun & Bank Holidays

Modern grocer/delicatessen - as the name implies it specialises in all things Spanish.

Tube: Goodge Street   Buses: 10, 24, 29, 73, 134 (northbound); ten minutes walk plus 135 & C2 southbound

352 LA PROVENCAL

167 Haverstock Hill, NW3 4QT
Tel: 0171-586 2574

Open: Mon-Fri 9.30am-8pm; Sat 9.30am-7pm; Sun 9.30am-6pm
Closed: Bank Holidays

Popular delicatessen conveniently situated opposite the tube station. The wide range of goods stocked includes an excellent selection of cheese, some from Neal's Yard Dairy (q.v.).

Tube: Belsize Park   Buses: 168, C11, C12

353 WALTER PURKIS & SONS ★

52 Muswell Hill Broadway, N10 3RT
Tel: 0181-883 4355
Branch @ 17 The Broadway, Crouch End, N8 (0181-340 6281)

Open: Tue-Sat 8am-5.30pm
Closed: Sun, Mon & Bank Holidays

First class fishmonger and poulterer, with a enormous selection of fish beautifully displayed on marble slabs. Samphire is also generally available during the summer months

Tube: Highgate (15 minutes)   Buses: 43, 102, 134, 144, 234, 299, W7

354 PUTNEY HEALTH FOODS

28 Upper Richmond Road, SW15 2RX
Tel: 0181-877 0041

Open: Mon-Fri 10am-7pm; Sat 10am-6pm; Sun 10.30am-2.30pm
Closed: Bank Holidays

Useful health-shop selling Martin Pitt eggs (although they have been known to run out, so a phone call is worthwhile).

Tube: East Putney   Buses: 37, 337

355 QUEEN OF TARTS

173 Priory Road, N8 8NB
Tel: 0181-340 1854

Open: Mon-Sat 8am-5.30pm; Sun & Bank Holidays 8am-2.30pm
Closed: 25, 26 Dec, 1 & 2 Jan

Find this patisserie at the western end of Priory Road, under the shadow of Alexandra Park. An excellent selection of individual pastries is on offer, plus cakes and good bread.

Tube: Highgate (15 minutes)   Buses: 144, W2, W3

356 J. QUINN

102 Northfield Avenue, W13 9RT
Tel: 0181-567 0339

Open: Tue-Sat 8am-5pm

Closed: Sun, Mon & Bank Holidays
Good-value butcher surrounded by stiff competition; Martin Pitt eggs are a extra bonus.
Tube: Northfields (5 minutes)   Buses: E2, E3

357 RAE-RA-EL BAKERY
64 Northcote Road, SW11 6QL
Tel: 0171-228 4537

Open: Mon-Fri 8.30am-5pm; Sat 7.30am-5pm
Closed: Sun & Bank Holidays
Popular local baker that completes the picture in this foodie street. 80% of the bread is made on the premises, including good rye, West Indian types and ciabatta.
Rail: Clapham Junction (10 minutes)   Buses: 319, G1

358 RAINBOW
201 Upper Tooting Road, SW17 7TG
Tel: 0181-672 7771

Open: Mon-Fri 9am-7pm; Sat 8.30am-6pm; Sun 9am-6pm
Closed: Bank Holidays
Top-class halal butcher on the corner of Letchworth Street. Exotic fish such as Boal, Hilsha and Rohu are stocked in the deep-freeze.
Tube: Tooting Broadway   Buses: 155, 219, 355

359 RAJ SUPER STORE
7 Russell Parade, Golders Green Road, NW11 9NN
Tel: 0181-455 0134

Open: Mon-Weds & Sun 8am-9pm; Thur 8am-10pm; Fri 8am-8pm
Closed: Sat & Bank Holidays
Cash and carry in style, this shop is unusual in that it supplies a wide range of products for both the Jewish and Indian communities, the selection of flour types is impressive in it's own right. A wide range of cooking utensils is also stocked, at reasonable prices.
Tube: Brent Cross (5 minutes)   Buses: 83, 183, 210, 240

360 RANA BROTHERS
145 The Broadway, Southall, Middx. UV1 1HT
Tel: 0181-574 4481

Open: Mon-Sun 9am-9pm
Closed: Closed 25 & 26 Dec
The best of many local greengrocers selling a comprehensive range of Asian vegetables.
Rail: Southall   Buses: 95, 105, 120, 195, 207, 607, E5, H32

361 RANDALLS ★

113 Wandsworth Bridge Road, SW6 2TE
Tel: 0171-736 3426

Open: Mon-Fri 7am-5.45pm; Sat 7am-3pm
Closed: Sun & Bank Holidays

Excellent traditional butcher stocking organically-reared lamb and beef from Highgrove, free-range chickens from Munson's, a good selection of game in season, and Martin Pitt eggs. A few oven-ready dishes are offered, such as stuffed saddle of lamb with wild mushrooms, and beef Wellington. Kelly Bronze turkeys at Christmas.

Tube: Parsons Green (10 minutes)   Buses: 28, 295, C4

362 THE REAL CHEESE SHOP ★

62 Barnes High Street, SW13 9LF
Tel: 0181-878 6676
Branch @ 96a High Street, Wimbledon, SW19 (0181-947 0564)

Open: Tue-Thur 9.30am-5pm (closed 1pm-2pm); Fri & Sat 9am-5pm
Closed: Sun, Mon & Bank Holidays

First-class cheese shop, run with enthusiasm by the Handyside's. Over 150 carefully-sourced varieties are stocked at any one time, including some rarely found Swedish varieties. Interesting books on the subject. Expect to queue near the weekend, but expert advice will be on hand when your turn comes.

Rail: Barnes Bridge (5 minutes)   Buses: 209

363 THE REALFOOD STORE*

14 Clifton Road, Little Venice, W9 1SS
Tel: 0171-266 1162

Open: Mon-Fri 8.30am-7pm; 8.30am-6pm
Closed: Sun & Bank Holidays

Aptly named, this shop is enthusiastically run by Kevin Gould, who has gathered some of the best products available into one place. Excellent bread from top bakers - including Sally Clarke and De Gustibus (see entries); at least twenty varieties at any one time. Splendid British cheese from Neal's Yard Diary (q.v) plus a selection of top Italians. A range of top quality jam and honey, many from small producers with their own unique characters; ice cream from Winters Dairy. You'll find organic fresh vegetables plus a good selection of char-grilled vegetables in the delicatessen section. No meat products are stocked and no food contains any artificial additive or ingredient. A few traiteur dishes change on a daily basis.

Tube: Warwick Avenue   Buses: 6, 46, 96

364 REZA PATISSERIE, MEATS AND GROCERY

347 Kensington High St W8 6NW
Tel: 0171603 0924

Open: Mon-Sun 9am-9pm Closed: 25 & 26 Dec

Two shops side by side with a splendid street display of middle-eastern fruits, vegetables and fresh herbs; including fresh almonds in the spring. Inside there are first-rate baklavas, raisin biscuits and other ethnic pastries - made on the premises. Top quality Iranian caviar is generally available. The butchers department sells halal meat.

Tube/Rail: Kensington Olympia   Buses: 9, 10, 27, 28, 49

365 RICHARDS

21 Brewer Street W1R 3FL
Tel: 0171-437 1358

Open: Tue-Thur 8am-5pm; Fri 8am-5.30pm; Sat 8am-3pm
Closed: Sun, Mon, Bank Holidays and Tue after Bank Holidays

This popular fishmonger has been supplying the needs of Soho for nearly 40 years. As well as a good selection of standards (all beautifully fresh), they offer undyed kippers and haddock; sea-bass, brill and halibut when available as well as fresh swordfish and tuna steaks. Also lobster, crab, squid, wild salmon in season, plus excellent smoked salmon. Pike, carp and live eels are available by special order.

Tube: Piccadilly   Buses: 12, 14, 19, 22, 38,

366 RICHARDSON

88 Northfield Avenue, W13 9RR
Tel: 0181-567 1064
Branch @ 110 South Ealing Road, W5 (0181-567 4405)

Open: Mon-Thur 8am-5.30pm; Fri 8am-6pm; Sat 8am-4.30pm
Closed: Sun & Bank Holidays

Popular butcher selling Scottish beef and Sussex free-range pork. Meats prepared for the barbecue and their own smoked chickens are a summer bonus.

Tube: Northfields   Buses: E2, E3

367 RIDLEY ROAD MARKET

Ridley Road, E8

Open: Tue-Sat 9am-5pm
Closed: Sun, Mon & Bank Holidays

Versatile market for cheap and unusual food, including staples for the local Caribbean, Turkish and Asian communities; plus various surrounding halal meat shops. The popular Ridley Bagel Bakery offers filled bagels 24 hours a day.

Rail: Dalston Kingsway   Buses:30, 38, 56, 67, 76, 149, 243, 243a, 277

368 RIPPON CHEESE STORES ★
26 Upper Tachbrook Street, SW1V 1SW
Tel: 0171-931 0628

Open: Mon-Sat 8am-6.30pm
Closed: Sun & Bank Holidays
Excellent cheese shop run by Philip and Karen Rippon. Varieties stocked run into the hundreds (some rarely found in this country), but skilful storing keeps them in peak condition.
Tube: Victoria   Buses: 2, 36, 185

369 ROCOCO ★
321 King's Road, SW3 5EP
Tel: 0171-352 5857

Open: Mon-Sat 10am-6.30pm; Sun: noon-5pm
Closed: Bank Holidays
Chantal Coady has been running her superb chocolate shop, close to the junction of Beaufort Street, since 1983. The chocolates here are purely for grown ups (and it pays to be into your cocoa solids). Some of the packages make excellent presents. Expect to wait at busy periods, but when your turn comes you will have excellent service with a smile.
Tube: Sloane Square (15 minutes)   Buses: 11, 19, 22, 49, 211, 319, 345,

370 ROGG'S
137 Cannon Street Road, E1 2LX
Tel: 0171-488 3368

Open: Mon-Fri 9am-5.30pm; Sun 7am-2.30pm
Closed: Sat & Bank Holidays
Popular little Jewish delicatessen. Various types of marinated herrings are a speciality, plus jars of sauerkraut and pickled cucumbers.
DLR: Shadwell   Buses: 5, 15, 15b, 40, 100

371 ROOTS
76 High Street, Wimbledon Village, SW19 5EG
Tel: 0181-944 5105

Open: Mon-Sat 7am-7pm; Sun 9am-6pm
Closed: 25 & 26 Dec
Good self-service greengrocer, on the corner with Church Road, stocking as many organic varieties as are available at the time. Also miscellaneous items such as Parma ham, dried pasta, olive oil and Martin Pitt eggs.
Tube & Rail: Wimbledon   Buses: 93, 200
      Tip:
If you're ever stuck with a block of solid sugar, rather than throw it away, put it in a bowl without it's bag, cover with a damp cloth and leave for a few hours - it will have revived!

372 ROSSLYN DELICATESSEN ★

56 Rosslyn Hill, NW3
Tel: 0171-794 9210

Open: Mon-Sat 8.30am-8.30pm; Sun 8.30am-8pm
Closed: 25, 26 Dec & 1 Jan

Run by Helen Sherman since 1990 this is a treasure trove of a delicatessen; there are so many temptations it's difficult to leave without buying more than intended. A comprehensive charcuterie and cheese section, good bread, Hampstead's best croissant and a selection of traiteur-style dishes that need the minimum of finishing.

Tube: Hampstead   Buses: 46, 268

373 ROSTICCERIA ROMA

152 Streatham Hill, SW2 4RU
Tel: 0181-674 1901

Open: Mon-Fri 10am-7pm; Sat 10am-6pm; Sun 10.30am-1pm
Closed: Bank Holidays

Good Italian delicatessen/traiteur selling all the basic groceries plus excellent home-made dishes including a selection of pasta dishes, a Mediterranean version of chicken Kiev and the every popular tirimisu.

Rail: Streatham Hill
Buses: 57, 109, 118, 133, 137a, 159, 201, 250

374 ROTISSERIE JULES

338 King's Road, SW3 5UR
Tel: 0171-351 0041
Branch @ 6/8 Bute Street, SW7 3EX (0171-584 0600)

Open: Every day 11am-11pm
Closed: 25 Dec

Good value restaurant and traiteur operating a free delivery service. The meat choice is restricted to lamb and various cuts of free-range chicken, spit-roast as the name implies. These are backed up with a few vegetables, including ratatouille, and excellent dauphinoise potatoes. They can be persuaded to cook your own joint on their rotisserie.

Tube: Sloane Square (15 minutes)   Buses: 11, 19, 22, 49, 211, 319, 345

375 ROY'S GREENGROCER

Formosa Street, W9 1EE
Tel: 0171-286 2408

Open: Mon-Sat 8.30am-6pm; Sun 9.30am-1pm
Closed: Bank Holidays

Good greengrocer selling some exotic fruit and a few flowers.

Tube: Formosa Street   Buses: 6, 46

376 RUMBOLD

45 South End Road, NW3 2PY
Tel: 0171-794 2344

Open: Mon-Sat 8am-5pm
Closed: Sun & Bank Holidays

Excellent corner shop bakery opposite the railway station. Popular lines include American muffins, apple strudels, croissants, rye bread and an excellent multi-grain bread called "Combicorn". As with most bakers, it pays to shop early for the best selection.

Rail: Hampstead Heath; Tube: Belsize Park (10 minutes) Buses: 46, 268

377 SAFEWAY SUPERMARKETS

Head Office: Beddow Way, Aylesford, Maidstone, Kent, ME20 7AT. Tel: 0181-848 8744
Too many branches to mention here, see our listings near the back of this book

Open: 7 days a week; times vary
Closed: 25, 26 Dec & some Bank Holidays

From being a front runner only a few years ago, Safeway seem to have opted for safety, cramming their shops with mediocrity - their vegetables in particular often looking tired. A few of their products are worth a mention; their "Heritage" dry-cure bacon is the best supermarket bacon we found, and as a bonus, it's produced from animals raised outdoors. Similarly their "Heritage" range of fresh meat is to be commended. Excellent Girasolio extra-virgin sunflower oil, good Indian-style ready meals, but their Chinese counterparts do not measure up.

378 SAINSBURY SUPERMARKETS

Head Office: Stamford House, Stamford Street, SE1.
Tel: 0171-921 6000
Too many branches to mention here, see our listings near the back of this book

Open: 7 days a week, variations on Mon-Sat 8.30am-9pm, Sun 10am-5pm. Some branches are open all night on Friday and for a few days before Christmas
Closed: 25, 26 Dec & some Bank Holidays

Still with Tesco the market leader amongst supermarkets, and both have certainly raised general standards of the middle ground. However, they still rarely sell the very best of anything - the powers that be would probably blame continuity of supply as their excuse; and fish is often still thawing from the freezer. Peter Onions excellent, but expensive, organic chickens are an exception (now stocked by larger branches, deliveries seem to be on Friday) and so are their expanding range stocked in their "Specialist" section (consisting of good quality oil and luxury items).

379 ST JAMES' DELICATESSEN

56 Fortis Green Road, N10 3HN
Tel: 0181-883 0117

Open: Mon-Sat 8.30am-6pm; Sun 8.30-5pm
Closed: Bank Holidays

Attached to the restaurant of the same name this delicatessen is useful in the area, particularly because of it's Sunday opening. Be wary of artificial looking products in the chilled section, bought-in because of their competitive price rather than quality - the fluorescent looking taramasalata for example.

Tube: Highgate (15 minutes)   Buses: 43, 102, 144, 234, 299, W7

380 ST MARCUS FINE FOODS

1 Rockingham Close, Priory Lane, SW15 5RW
Tel: 0181-878 1898

Open: Mon-Sun 9am-6pm
Closed: Christmas Day

A corner of South Africa is to be found in this terrace of modern shops near Rosslyn Park Rugby Club. A comprehensive selection of biltong stretches from beef, through lamb to ostrich. The butchery counter often has kangaroo, crocodile and ostrich steaks plus venison and wild boar; and they are proud of their range of over fifty types of home-made sausages, which include English standards and recipes from around the world. Other imports include biscuits, jam and chutney. A range of traiteur dishes includes a few vacuum-packed South African specialities.

Rail: Barnes   Bus: 337

381 LA SALUMERIA

184 Trafalgar Street, SE10 9ZZ
Tel: 0181-305 2433

Open: Mon-Sat 8.30am-6pm; Sun 10am-2pm
Closed: Bank Holidays

Useful Italian delicatessen, much needed in the area, stocking all the good quality basics needed for authentic meals.

Rail: Maze Hill   Buses: 108, 177, 180, 286, 386

382 SALUMERIA ESTENSE

837 Fulham Road, SW6 5HQ
Tel: 0171-731 7643

Open: Mon-Fri 10am-7.30pm; Sat 10am-5pm
Closed: Sun & Bank Holidays

Good Italian delicatessen with a lovely atmosphere, stocking all the essentials. Helpful service and some tasty home-made dishes to reheat at home.

Tube: Parsons Green   Buses: 14

383 SALUMERIA NAPOLI

69 Northcote Rd. SW11 1NP
Tel: 0171-228 2445

Open: Mon-Sat 9am-6pm. Closed: Sun & Bank Holidays

This delicatessen contributes to the gourmet nature of this road, which is a food lovers paradise. Particularly good range of dried and fresh pasta, Italian cheese, olives, olive oils plus pancetta and Italian cold meats. Not worth a visit on its own, but is when combined with the rest of the road.

Rail: Clapham Junction (10 minutes)   Buses: 319, G1

384 SALVINO

47 Brecknock Road, N7 0BT
Tel: 0171-267 5305

Open: Mon-Sat 9am-6.30pm; Sun 10am-1pm. Closed: Bank Holidays

Brothers Steven and Tony run this popular Italian delicatessen, at the south end of Brecknock Road. Stock is carefully chosen and includes delicious rarities (a family-made goats cheese for example). Good pasta and home-made sauces.

Tube: Tufnell Park (10 minutes)   Buses: 10, C12

385 SANDRINE

233 Upper Richmond Road West, SW14 8QS
Tel: 0181-878 8168
Branch @ 38a Church Street, Twickenham, TW1 3NR
(0181-744 9197)

Open: Mon-Sat 10am-5.30pm. Closed: Sun & Bank Holidays

Belgium chocolates are the speciality at Jean Bradley's excellent chocolate shop. They make splendid presents as she takes as much trouble choosing beautiful packaging as in the chocolates themselves.

Rail: Mortlake (10 mins)   Buses: 33.337

386 SAVERA BAKERY

129 Drummond Street, NW1 2HL
Tel: 0171-380 0290
Branch @ 129 Cannon St. Road, NW1 (0171-480 7333)

Open: Tue-Sun 10am-8pm
Closed: Mon; Bank Holidays & 1pm-2pm on Fridays

Traditional Indian baker producing bread and simple pastries on the premises at bargain prices.

Tube: Euston Square   Buses: 10, 18, 30, 68, 73, 77, 77a, 168, 188

**Please use the forms at the back of this book
to recommend your own favourite shops**

387 SAPONARA

23 Prebend Street, N1 88F
Tel: 0171-226 2771

Open: Mon-Sat 9am-10pm; Sun 11am-2pm. Closed: Bank Holidays
Local Italian delicatessen with lots of delicious temptations as well as
normal groceries.

Tube: Angel (15 minutes) Rail: Essex Road (5 minutes)   Buses: 271

388 A. SCOTT ★

94 High Road, East Finchley, N2 9EB
Tel: 0181-444 7606

Open: Tue-Thur 8.30am-5.30pm; Fri 8.30am-6pm; Sat 8.30am-5pm
Closed: Sun & Bank Holidays
First class little fishmonger, cramming as much variety as possible into
their limited space. Marlin, monkfish, sea bass, sea trout and wild salmon
were all on offer on one inspection visit; plus beautifully fresh plaice,
buckling, dressed crabs and a whole lot more. Shops like this deserve
support!

Tube: East Finchley   Buses: 102, 143, 263

389 SEAFOOD AUSTRALIA

230 Essex Road, N1 3AP
Tel: 0171-354 4242

Open: Mon-Fri 9am-6pm; Sat 9am-5pm. Closed: Sun & Bank Holidays
A modern parade of shops hides this excellent source of Australian fish.
Varieties might include Moses Perch, Red Spot Emperor and Banded
Bream all gleamingly fresh. Yabbies often available, but phone before
leaving home.

Rail: Essex Road   Buses: 38, 56, 73, 171a

390 SEA HARVEST FISHERIES

14 Warwick Way, SW1V 1RX
Tel: 0171-821 5192

Open: Tue-Sat 10am-5.30pm. Closed: Sun, Mon & Bank Holidays
Popular fishmonger at the eastern end of Warwick Way. The fast turnover
ensures freshness, and interesting fish such as monk, sea bass and squid
are backed up by temptations such as dressed crab.

Tube: Pimlico/Victoria   Buses: 2, 36, 185

391 J. SEAL

7 High Street, Barnes, SW13 9LW
Tel: 0181-876 5118

Open: Mon-Fri 6.30am-5.30pm; Weds 6.30am-1.30pm; Sat 6.30am-4pm
Closed: Sun & Bank Holidays

Good traditional butcher specialising in grass-reared meat including excellent Scottish beef. Bronze turkeys at Christmas.

Rail: Barnes Bridge   (5 minutes) Buses: 209b

392 SEE WOO HONG SUPERMARKET

18/20 Lisle St. WC2H 7BA
Tel: 0171-439 8325
Branch @ Furlong House, Horn Lane, Greenwich, SE10
(0181-293 9393)

Open: Mon-Sun 10am-8pm. Closed: 25 Dec

Good selection of Chinese supplies including excellent vegetables. Large deep freeze section with everything from frozen lime leaves and spring roll wrappers to fish and air-dried duck. Friendly service.

Tube: Leicester Square   Buses: 14, 19, 24, 29, 38, 176

393 SELFRIDGES FOOD HALL ★

400 Oxford Street, W1A 1AB
Tel: 0171-629 1234

Open: Mon, Tue & Weds 10am-7pm; Thur & Fri 10am-8pm; Sat 9am-7pm; Sun noon-6pm; Bank Holidays 10am-7pm

Closed: 25 Dec, enquire about 26 Dec

Excellent food hall offering one of the most comprehensive ranges in London; unlike some, most basic necessities are available as well as luxury products. Indeed one can be spoilt for choice e.g. nearly 100 types of honey from 40 different blossoms. The charcuterie department stocks 45 types of salami alone. Splendid fresh pasta counter and another for fish, meat and baked products. Excellent bacon from Richard Woodall and smoked salmon from H. Forman.

Tube: Bond Street/Marble Arch

Buses: 2, 6, 7, 10, 12, 13, 15, 16A, 23, 30, 73, 74, 82, 94, 98, 113, 135, 137, 137A, 139, 159, 274

394 SESAME HEALTH FOODS

128 Regent's Park Road, NW1 8XL
Tel: 0171-586 3779

Open: Mon-Fri 9am-6.30pm; Sat 10am-6pm;
Sun & Bank Holidays noon-5pm Closed: 25, 26 Dec & 1 Jan

This excellent health food/vegetarian delicatessen has been pandering to the needs of Primrose Hill since the early '70s. E numbers are very thin on the ground, and many products are organic, including a selection of cheese and vegetables. Vegetarian traiteur dishes are offered every day except Sunday. Helpful service.

Tube: Chalk Farm (5 minutes)   Buses: 274

395 SEVEN SISTERS GREENGROCERS

10 Seven Sisters Road, N7 6AH
Tel: 0171-607 9070

Open: Mon-Sun 7am-8pm
Closed: Bank Holidays

Good greengrocer specialising in produce from the Caribbean.

Tube: Holloway Road (10 minutes)   Buses: 253, 259, 279

396 SHEPHERD'S BUSH MARKET

Railway Approaches, between Uxbridge/Goldhawk Roads, W12

Open: Mon, Tue, Wed, Fri & Sat 9.30am-5pm; Thur 9.30am-1pm;
Sun limited hours
Closed: 25, 26 Dec, 1 Jan & Bank Holidays

Cramped and busy market on both sides of the railway viaduct selling
good fruit and veg, including unusual varieties from the Caribbean. Best
food stalls are at the north end of the market, a good fishmonger W.H. Roe
and an interesting West-Indian grocer Moon Foods also operate from this
end of the market.

Tube: Goldhawk Road/Shepherd's Bush
Buses: 49, 94, 95, 207, 237, 260, 295, 607

397 SIMPLY SAUSAGES ★

Harts Corner, 341 Central Markets,
Farringdon Street, EC1A 9NB
Tel: 0171-329 3227
Branches @ 93 Berwick Street, W1 (0171-287 3482)
& 34 Strutton Ground, SW1 (0171-976 7430)

Open: Mon-Fri 8am-6pm; Sat 9am-2pm (9am-6pm @ Berwick St)
Closed: Sun & Bank Holidays

In our opinion London's best sausages. Generally about 35 meat
varieties to chose from ranging from the traditional to Thai, Italian and
the truly excellent duck, prune and Cognac. Meat contents are high, no
scraps or unpleasant cuts used, no artificial additives and of course
natural skins. There is an additional vegetarian selection with
temptations such as chestnut and orange, Scarborough Fair sausage (full
of fresh herbs) and Glamorgan (Caerphilly and leek). Good black
pudding from Stafford's of Derbyshire.

Tube & Rail: Farringdon   Buses: 63, 243, 259

398 SIRA CASH & CARRY

128 The Broadway, Southall, Middx. UB1 1QF
Tel: 0181-574 2280

Open: Mon-Sun 8am-9pm. Closed: No closing days

Asian grocer/greengrocer stocking everything imaginable; many of the dry products at bargain prices in enormous bags. Hasn't closed for a single day since opening in 1952!

Rail: Southall   Buses: 95, 105, 120, 195, 207, 607, E5, H32

399 J. H. SMITH

208 Portobello Road, W11 1LA
Tel: 0171-727 6223

Open: Tue, Weds & Fri 8am-5.30pm; Thur 8am-2.30pm; Sat 8am-5pm
Closed: Sun, Mon & Bank Holidays

Good fishmonger in this bustling and good value market. They always have fresh and interesting stock.

Tube: Ladbroke Grove   Buses: 7, 23, 52, 70, 302

400 SMITHFIELD MARKET

Charterhouse Street & Smithfield Long Lane, EC1

Open: Mon-Fri 5am-10.30am. Closed: Sat, Sun & Bank Holidays

You'll need a very large deep-freeze to benefit from the prices here (about half normal retail costs) and some butchery knowledge is also a benefit. But that said, you can find some smaller quantities on offer in the poultry section, plus some bargain butchers in the surrounding streets.

Tube: Farringdon

Buses: 4, 8, 22b, 25, 45, 46, 55, 63, 243, 259, 501, 505, 521

401 SONNY'S FOOD SHOP

92 Church Road, SW13 0DQ
Tel: 0181-741 8451

Open: Mon-Fri 10am-6pm; Sat 9.30am-5.30pm
Closed: Sun & Bank Holidays

Tiny delicatessen attached to Sonny's Restaurant (see "Cheap Eats"). Offerings are limited by space, but include good oils and vinegars, some of Carluccio's preserved products, Duskins apple juice and a few good traiteur dishes from the restaurant kitchen.

Rail: Barnes Bridge (10 minutes)   Buses: 209

Tip:

Never salt meat before cooking, as this will draw out the valuable juices. For a casserole this might give you a slightly better sauce but leave the meat tasteless. So when frying or cooking meat always add the salt in the last few minutes of cooking.

Likewise, when soaking dried pulses never add salt to the water, as it will make the pulses skins tough; as with meat adjust the seasoning to suit your personal tastes near the end of the cooking time.

However, when cooking fish, always sprinkle on a little salt before cooking - it improves the flavour enormously without drawing out the vital flavour in the same way as with meat!

402 SOUTHBANK FRESH FISH

Unit 26, Kent Park Industrial Estate, Ruby Street, SE15 1LR
Tel: 0171-639 6000

Open: Mon-Fri 3am-noon
Closed: Sun, Mon & Bank Holidays

Find this excellent wholesale unit in a small industrial unit behind a Kentucky Chicken Drive-In on the Old Kent Road. Although nothing is on display, a phone call will have any order of reasonable size ready for your collection - with no parking problems!

Rail: Queen's Road Peckham (10 minutes)   Buses: 21, 53, 172

403 SOUTHFIELD FRUITERERS

234b Wimbledon Park Road, SW18 5TU
Tel: 0181-870 3076

Open: Mon-Fri 6am-5.30pm; Sat 6am-5pm
Closed: Sun & Bank Holidays

Jean Grior has run this good local greengrocer since 1981, it's a refreshing shop to visit, as old-fashioned service is now a rarity, but is on offer here.

Tube: Southfields   Buses: 39

404 G.G. SPARKES

24 Old Dover Road, SE3 7BT
Tel: 0181-858 7672

Open: Mon-Sat 8.30am-5.30pm
Closed: Sun & Bank Holidays

Set in a modern parade of shops in north Blackheath, this good traditional butcher specialising in organic meat. Peter Onions chickens and a few housewife-friendly cuts are also offered - maybe rolled noisettes of lamb, delicious Italian-style liver burgers in caul fat and in summer kebabs ready for the barbecue. Cottage Delight chutney and a few well-kept farmhouse cheeses. Cheap fruit and vegetables at Apple n' Orange (q.v) almost next door.

Rail: Westcombe Park (10 minutes)   Buses: 53, 54, 108, 286

405 SPECK DELICATESSEN

2 Holland Park Terrace, Portland Road, W11 4ND
Tel: 0171-229 7005

Open: Mon-Sat 9am-9pm Closed: Sun & Bank Holidays; 2 weeks in August

You'll find this excellent Italian delicatessen and traiteur just round the corner from Holland Park Avenue. Specialities include fresh egg pasta, olive oil, Italian cheeses and salami. Ready made dishes might include king prawns with garlic and wine, osso buco with gremolata and their own pasta sauces.

Tube: Holland Park   Buses: 49, 94, 295

406 THE SPICE SHOP

115-117 Drummond Street, NW1 2HL
Tel: 0171-916 1831

Open: Mon-Sun 10am-10pm
Closed: 25 & 26 Dec

Asian grocer devoting much of it's area to whole and ground spices. As is usual in shops of this type, some of the bagged units are enormous; but offer excellent value if you have space to keep them.

Tube & Rail: Euston   Buses: 10, 18, 30, 73

407 THE SPICE SHOP ★

1 Blenheim Crescent, W11 2EE
Tel: 0171-221 4448

Open: Mon-Sat 9.30am-6pm Closed: Sun & Bank Holidays

Birgit Erath runs London's best spice shop. Their stock couldn't be more comprehensive. It encompasses spices and herbs from China, Japan and the Indian sub-continent. There are 12 types of paprika alone. None of their spices or mixes contain artificial colourings or free-flow agents. Impressive list of essential oils; excellent home-made chutneys and a good selection of pulses. Birgit has a market stall in North End Road, Fulham on Friday and Saturday, and operates a mail order system.

Tube: Ladbroke Grove   Buses: 7, 23, 52, 70, 302

408 SPITALFIELDS ORGANIC MARKET

Brushfield Street, E1
Open: Sun 10am-4pm only

Closed: remainder of week

Market selling organic fruit and vegetables plus eggs, chutney and jam on Sunday only.

Tube & Rail: Liverpool Street
Buses: 5, 8, 22a, 22b, 26, 35, 43, 47, 48, 78, 149, 243a

409 SRI THAI

56 Shepherd's Bush Road, W6 7PH
Tel: 0171-602 0621

Open: Mon-Sun 9am-8.30pm Closed: 25 Dec & some Bank Holidays

The Thepprasits have run this enterprising self-service grocers since 1986. Now familiar Thai products are backed up by an excellent green grocery section, which is replenished with the more unusual items every Tuesday by produce specially flown-in from Thailand.

Tube: Goldhawk Road/Shepherd's Bush   Buses: 72, 220, 283, 295

410 J.A. STEELE

8 Flask Walk, NW3
Tel: 0171-435 3587

Open: Mon-Sat 7.30am-5.30pm. Closed: Sun & Bank Holidays

Little butcher hidden away from the bustle of Hampstead High Street down this charming alley. Much of the meat comes from The Real Meat Company, so is organic. The affluence of their Hampstead customers gives them extra scope to have interesting items such as barbery ducks, quail and a good supply of game in season.

Tube: Hampstead   Buses: 46, 268

411 STELLA'S BAKERY

43 The Broadway, Crouch End, N8 8DT
Tel: 0181-341 7789

Open: Mon-Sat 7.30am-7pm; Sun & Bank Holidays 8am-5pm
Closed: 25, 26 Dec & 1 Jan

Good little baker under the shadow of The Broadway clock tower. Everything is baked on the premises and, apart from the rather heavyweight croissant, is excellent, particularly the apple strudels and year-round supply of hot cross buns.

Rail: Crouch End/Highgate (15 minutes)   Buses: 41, 91, W2, W7

412 STENTON ★

55 Aldensley Road, W6 9PL
Tel: 0181-748 6121

Open: Tue, Weds & Fri 7.30am-6.30pm; Thur 7.30am-1pm; Sat 7.30am-5.30pm. Closed: Sun, Mon & Bank Holidays

John Stenton has been running his excellent little butcher's shop, with the help of his family, since 1983. Meat is all free-range and quite a lot organic. Martin Pitt eggs.

Tube: Ravenscourt Park
Buses: 27, 190, 266, 267, 391, H91 (10 minutes)

413 STEPPING STONES FARM

Stepney Way, E1 3DG
Tel: 0171-790 8204

Open: Tue-Sun 9.30-6pm (dusk in winter);
incl. Christmas Day & Bank Holidays. Closed: Monday.

A visit here is great fun for kids, just like a trip to the country; with free-range chickens, sheep, goats and huge pigs all on view. They sell their own chutney, pickles, mustard and jam; plus excellent honey from Hampstead Honey farm. Martin Pitt eggs plus their own when available. Their goat's milk is also offered (depending on the time of year).

Tube: Stepney Green & Limehouse DLR   Buses: 5, 15, 15b, 40,

414 SAM STOLLER & SON
28 Temple Fortune Parade, Finchley Road, NW11
Tel: 0181-458 1429

Open: Mon 8am-2pm; Tue-Thur 7am-5pm; Fri 7am-4pm; Sun 8am-1pm
Closed: Sat & Bank Holidays
Popular fishmonger opposite M&S with large turnover and modest prices.
Tube: Golders Green (10 minutes)   Buses: 82, 102, 260

415 STROUD GREEN ROAD, N4
The drag of shops on the west-side of this road, just north of Finsbury
Park station, has an assortment of shops selling everything from halal
meat to Asian and West Indian-style vegetables, all at competitive prices.
Tube: & Rail: Finsbury Park   Buses: 210, W2, W3, W7

416 STRUTTON GROUND MARKET, SW1
Strutton Ground (between Victoria Street and Horseferry Road)

Open: Mon-Fri 11.30am-3pm Closed: Sat, Sun & Bank Holidays
Useful little market selling interesting fruit and vegetables. Stiles bakery
is worth a visit, and there is a branch of Simply Sausages (q.v's).
Tube: St. James's Park   Buses: 11, 24, 211, 507

417 SUPER BAHAR
349a Kensington High Street, W8 6NW
Tel: 0171-603 5083

Open: Sun-Sat 9am-9pm Closed: Bank Holidays
Next door to the Reza Patisserie Meats & Greengrocer, this excellent
Iranian grocer/greengrocer has an equally colourful display of fruit and
vegetables; indeed most of it's products duplicate those of it's rival.
Tube: Kensington Olympia   Buses: 9, 10, 27, 28, 49

418 SUPER HOMA & PATISSERIE
473 Finchley Road, NW3 6HS
Tel: 0171-435 2370

Open: Sun-Mon 8am-10pm. Closed: Bank Holidays
Middle-Eastern grocer specialising in sweetmeats and pastries. A small
selection of fruit, often including piles of delicious looking melons, is
also stocked.
Tube: Hampstead (15 minutes); Rail: Finchley Road & Frognal (10 minutes)
Buses: 13, 82, 113

419 SUTHERLAND'S FINE FOOD & WINE
140 Shepherd's Bush Road, W6 7PB
Tel: 0171-603 5717

Open: Mon-Fri 8.30am-7.30pm; Sat 8.30am-5pm; Sun 8.30am-3pm
Closed: Bank Holidays

Traditional delicatessen, mid-way between Hammersmith and Shepherd's Bush, selling a little of everything - all carefully chosen. Good loose olive oil, so bring a bottle.

Tube: Hammersmith   Buses: 72, 220, 283, 295

420 SWEETLAND & HOWARD

12 The Parade, Sandhurst Road, SE6 1DJ
Tel: 0181-698 3816

Open: Mon 7.30am-4.30pm;Tue, Wed & Fri 7.30am-6pm; Thur 7.30am-1pm; Sat 6.30am-1pm. Closed: Sun & Bank Holidays

Excellent family butcher on the corner of Muirkirk Road, run by the Howard's since 1957. Home-cooked ham, meat pies, salt beef and dry-cured bacon. All meat is carefully sourced, mainly from Scotland. Saturday brings the bonus of Mrs Howard's scones, plus croissant and Danish Pastries. Good crusty bread is another sideline.

Rail: Catford Bridge/Catford   Buses: 124, 181, 284

421 TACHBROOK STREET MARKET

Tachbrook Street, SW1

Open: Mon-Sat 9am-5pm. Closed: Sun & Bank Holidays

Small market with several interesting greengrocers stalls, plus an excellent fishmonger Wright & Sons, which puts many fish shops to shame.

Tube: Victoria   Buses: 2, 36, 185

422 TALAD THAI

320 Upper Richmond Road, SW15 6TL
Tel: 0181-789 8084

Open: Mon-Sat 9am-10.30pm; Sun 10am-8pm
Closed: 25, 26 Dec & Bank Holidays

Find this shop half a mile east of Putney High Street. A good selection of Thai necessities (frozen, bottled and tinned) are hidden away in the basement, under a ground floor café. Fresh produce, specially flown in, is available at the end of the week - but disappears quickly!

Rail: Putney; Tube: Putney East (10 minutes)   Buses: 74, 337

423 ENZO TARTARELLI

1 Sidmouth Parade, Sidmouth Road, NW2 5HG
Tel: 0181-459 1952

Open: Mon-Sat 8.30am-6.30pm. Closed: Sun & Bank Holidays

Although strictly a butcher/macelleria specialising in organic meat and poultry, this is combined with a few Italian delicatessen and greengrocer items plus tasty home-made Italian-style sausages. Little shops like this desperately need your support if they're to survive, the world would be a sadder place without them!

Tube: Willesdon Green (5 minutes)   Buses: 6, 52, 206, 302

424 TASTE OF THE WILD ★

31 London Stone Estate, Broughton Street, SW8 3AJ
Tel: 0171-498 5654

Open: Mon-Fri 9am-5pm. Closed: Sat, Sun and Bank Holidays
Possibly London's best source of wild mushrooms and truffles, also the supplier to over 200 of the countries top restaurants. Following the seasons, everything is stocked from fresh cepe and girolles to white Alba and black Perigord truffles, plus the rarely found huitacoche from Mexico. Good selection of dried mushrooms plus frozen summer truffles and excellent saffron. Their main business is carried out by mail-order, but customers are welcome to visit personally. Elderflowers in season and sometimes seakale grown by Sandy Pattullo on Tayside.
Rail: Queenstown Road   Buses: 137, 137a

425 THE TEA HOUSE ★

15 Neal Street, WC2H 9PU
Tel: 0171-240 7539

Open: Mon-Sat 10am-7pm; Sun noon-6pm. Closed: 25 & 26 Dec
Interesting shop selling nearly 100 types of first-class tea and tisines plus what they call "teaphernalia" - this includes pots, strainers, cosies, cups and saucers. An efficient mail order system operates.
Tube: Covent Garden   Buses: 14, 19, 24, 29, 38, 176

426 THE TEDDINGTON CHEESE ★

42 Station Road, Teddington, Middlesex TW11 9AA
Tel: 0181-977 2318

Open: Mon-Wed 9.30am-6pm; Thur & Fri 9.30am-7.30pm; Sat 9.30am-6pm
Closed: Sun & Bank Holidays
Fantastic little cheese shop, close to the railway station, run by Doug Thring and Tony Parks. Although all the household names are stocked, always from their best sources, the real strength of this shop is in seasonal cheeses from small farms. Each cheese is sold with it's own little card, containing background history etc. As many as 120 types are held at any one time. A popular mail order system operates.
Rail: Teddington   Buses: 33, 281, 285, 592, R62, R68 (5 minutes)

427 THE TEESDALE TRENCHERMAN

Startforth Hall, Barnard Castle, Co. Durham, DL12 9RA
Tel: 01833 638370

Mail order company with an interesting catalogue. Unusual items such as smoked Herdwick Macon (dry-cured sheep's ham from Cumbria), smoked pheasant and geranium jelly as well as carefully sourced standard products. Postage puts their prices up, but orders over £80 are delivered free. Í*Mail order only*

428 TEMPLE HEALTH FOODS

17 Temple Fortune Parade, NW11 0QS
Tel: 0181-458 6087

Open: Mon-Sat 9am-6pm; Sun 10am-2pm
Closed: Bank Holidays
Good health shop also selling Martin Pitt eggs.
Tube: Golders Green (15 minutes)   Buses: 82, 102, 260

429 L. TERRONI & SONS   S

138/140 Clerkenwell Road, EC1R 5LD
Tel: 0171-837 1712

Open: Mon-Fri 9am-5.45pm; Thur 9am-2pm; Sat 9am-3pm;
Sun 10.30pm-2pm Closed: Bank Holidays
Good Italian grocer/delicatessen, run by the Annessa family, supplying the
needs of the thriving local Italian community. Good range of charcuterie
and Italian cheese, vast selection of pasta, plus olives. In fact a complete
larder. Friendly, helpful service.
Tube: Farringdon/Chancery Lane (5 minutes)
Buses: 19, 38, 55, 171a, 505

430 TESCO SUPERMARKETS

Head Office: Tesco House, Delamare Rd, Cheshunt.
Tel: 01992-632222
Too many branches to list here, see our listings at the back
of this book

Open: 7 days a week; times vary. Closed: some Bank Holidays
Tesco has taken great strides in the last few years, and is without doubt
one of our best supermarkets. Their Les Landes free-range chickens won
our taste test (see introductory article on chickens and their eggs). Like
most supermarkets they balance mediocrity with convenience but stock
the occasional interesting product. Prospective food suppliers with flare
cannot be entertained unless able to supply continuity to their vast
supermarket network; and this eliminates many of the best products at
the first hurdle. An improving traiteur section includes their new "Finest"
range; this is almost as good as Marks & Spencer's and helpful to those
short of time.

431   PAUL THOROGOOD

113 Northfield Avenue, Ealing, W13 9QR
Tel: 0181-567 0339

Open: Mon-Sat 7am-5pm. Closed: Sun & Bank Holidays
Go ahead butcher specialising in organic and additive-free meat. Martin
Pitt eggs. Deliveries.
Tube: Northfields   Buses: E2, E3

432 TODAYS LIVING HEALTH FOODS

92 Clapham High Street, SW4 7UL
Tel: 0171-622 1722

Open: Mon-Sat 9am-6.30pm Closed: Sun & Bank Holidays
Health shop stocking Martin Pitt eggs.
Tube: Clapham North; Rail: Clapham High Street
Buses: 88, 155, 345, 355

433 TOM'S

226 Westbourne Grove, W11 2RH
Tel: 0171-221 8818

Open: Mon-Fri 8am-7pm; Sat 8am-6pm; Sun 10am-4pm
Closed: Bank Holidays & Sun of Notting Hill Carnival
Deservedly popular café/delicatessen. Lack of space is limiting, but all the
stock is carefully chosen and of the top quality. Excellent ice cream from
Winters Dairy is one of the many temptations.
Tube: Bayswater   Buses: 23

434 TOOTING MARKET

Upper Tooting Road, SW17

Open: Mon-Sat 9.30am-5pm; Weds 9am-1pm
Closed: Sat, Sun & Bank Holidays
Indoor market with good fruit, vegetables, far-eastern groceries, meat
and fish stalls, the standard of which is generally higher than that of
Broadway Market, almost next door. Cut-Price Fishmongers (0181-682
3044) have an excellent selection of exotic fish, and are worth a visit .
Tube: Tooting Broadway   Buses: 155, 219, 355

435 TURKISH FOOD CENTRE

227-229 Lewisham High Street, SE13 6LY
Tel: 0181-318 0436
Branches @ 89 Ridley Road, E8 (0171-254 6754)
& 332 Walworth Road, SE17 (0171-703 9765)

Open: Mon-Sat 8am-9pm. Closed: Sun & Bank Holidays
The smell of freshly baked bread will entice you to enter this shop which
sells a comprehensive selection of Turkish groceries, fresh vegetables,
sticky pastries and halal meat.
Rail: Lewisham   Buses: 47, 54, 75, 89, 108, 122, 136, 180, 181,
185, 199, 206, 261, 278, 284, 380, 484, P4

436 R. TWINING & CO.

216 Strand, WC2R 1AP
Tel: 0171-353 3511

Open: Mon-Fri 9.30am-4.30pm. Closed: Sat, Sun & Bank Holidays

Easily found opposite The Royal Courts of Justice, this narrow shop and museum covers some of the ground occupied by the coffee shop started by Thomas Twining in 1706. Many years ago, the emphasis switched to tea, all of which are available here (including a few normally for export only). Coffee has not been forgotten however, as over ten varieties are still stocked, plus a variety of tea pots and presentation packs. A mail order system operates.
Tube: Aldwych   Buses: 4, 11, 15, 23, 26, 76, 171a

437 TWO PEAS IN A POD

85 Church Road, Barnes, SW13 9HH
Tel: 0181-748 0232

Open: Mon-Sat 8am-5.30pm; Sun 10am-1pm
Closed: Bank Holidays

Don't be put off by the size of this little greengrocer, everything bought has been carefully chosen by the owner Malcolm Louis and includes plenty of organic produce. His stock follows the seasons, so don't expect tasteless produce just to fill up the display; on the other hand you will probably find delicious raspberries from Kent in early November.
Rail: Barnes Bridge (10 minutes)   Buses: 209

438 VALENTINA S

210 Upper Richmond Road West, East Sheen, SW14 8AH
Tel: 0181-392 9127

Open: Mon-Fri 9am-8pm; Sat 8.30am-6pm;
Sun & Bank Holidays 9.30am-3pm. Closed: 25 & 26 Dec

The Borfecchia's have run this excellent little Italian delicatessen since 1991, and it is deservedly popular as it's brimming with temptations; including the best Parma ham, dried and fresh pasta and traiteur dishes at affordable prices. The marinated semi-dried tomatoes are a must!
Rail: Mortlake   Buses: 33, 337

439 VB & SONS

218 Ealing Road, Wembley, HA0 4QG
Tel: 0181-795 0387
Branch @ 736 Kenton Road, Kingsbury Circle, Kenton,
Harrow, NW9 (0181-206 1770)

Open: Mon-Fri 9.30am-6.45pm; Sat 9am-6.45pm; Sun 11am-5pm
Closed: 25 Dec

A beautiful smell of ground spices greets you at this Indian self-service supermarket. Like many Asian suppliers, rice, nuts, pulses and spices come in enormous bags - but the prices will take you back years.
Tube: Alperton   Buses: 79, 83, 224, 297

440 VICTORIA HEALTH FOODS

99 Muswell Hill Road, Muswell Hill, N10 3RS
Tel: 0181-444 2355
Branch @ 12b Ealing Broadway Centre, W5 (0181-840 6949)

Open: Mon-Sat 9am-6pm. Closed: Sun & Bank Holidays
Good selection of vitamins and food supplements, plus oats and pulses;
friendly staff to give advice. Martin Pitt eggs.
Tube: Highgate (15 minutes)   Buses: 43, 102, 134, 144, 234, 299, W7

441 VILLAGE BAKERY

44 Tranquil Vale, SE3 0BD
Tel: 0181-318 1916

Open: Mon-Sat 8.30am-5.30pm. Closed: Sun & Bank Holidays
Peter Squire has been running this little bakery since 1978. His excellent
bread tends to run out by lunchtime, so an early visit brings the best
choice. A few excellent "home-style" biscuits and cakes and patisserie
items are also offered.
Rail: Blackheath   Buses: 13, 40, 44, 89, 202

442 THE VILLAGE PANTRY

133 Pitshanger Lane, Ealing, W5 1RH
Tel: 0181-997 4776

Open: Mon-Fri 9am-7pm; Sat 9am-6pm; Sun & Bank Holidays 10am-2pm
Closed: 25 & 26 Dec
Popular and well stocked delicatessen rather like Aladin's cave - offering
everything from caviar and rye bread to farmhouse cheeses and
charcuterie. Try the excellent Polish doughnuts. Proper old-fashioned
service with a smile.
Tube: Ealing Broadway (15 minutes)   Buses: E2, E9

443 VILLAGERS SAUSAGES

91 High Street, Beckenham, Kent BR3
Tel: 0181-325 5475

Open: Mon-Sat 8.30-6pm. Closed: Sun & Bank Holidays
Good sausages are made on the premises here, with flavours such as
Caemarvon Leek, Scrumpy Jack, Duck à l'Orange and Pork and Blue Stilton.
Rail: Beckenham Junction   Buses: 54, 351, 361, 367

444 VILLANDRY FOODSTORE RESTAURANT ★

170 Great Portland Street, W1N 5TB
Tel: 0171-631 3131

Open: Mon-Sat 8.30am-8pm. Closed: Sun & Bank Holidays
Now firmly established in smart new premises this excellent shop/
restaurant is skilfully run by Jean-Charles Carrarini. This is without doubt

one of London's best delicatessen's. Marvellous bread from their own bakery, plus some from The Bread Factory and Max Poilane (Paris). Home-made cakes, excellent charcuterie, cheese from Phillip Olivier and Neal's Yard, the very best jam and marmalade, an impressive fruit and vegetable spread often includes salad leaves from Appledore - the list goes on and on. A buzzy restaurant (q.v) to the rear of the shop offers a menu that begins with breakfast and then moves on to a French bistro-style. The kitchen here prepares terrines and many of the other temptations for sale in the shop. Martin Pitt eggs.

Tube: Great Portland Street/Warren Street
Buses: 2, 13, 30, 74, 82, 113, 135, 139, 159, 274

445 VIVIAN'S ★

2 Worple Way, Richmond, Surrey, TW10 6DF
Tel: 0181-940 3600

Open: Mon-Fri 9am-7pm; Sat 8.30-6pm; Sun 8.30am-noon
Closed: Bank Holidays & Sun if Mon is Bank Holiday

Delicatessen, run by Vivian Martin and Deborah Watson, setting the highest standards. A glance through the index gives some indication but little justice, as it gives no clue to the dedication shown in seeking out the very best products. Charcuterie includes items from Denhay and Richard Woodall, and might also include terrines or black pudding from the kitchen of Stephen Bull (of restaurant fame). Cheeses number about 100, again from the very best sources - nothing less has shelf space here - and their olive oils number over 30, about 14 of which are sold loose if you bring your own bottle. A few excellent traiteur items are a new addition, and often include London's best pecan tart.

Tube & Rail: Richmond (10 mins)   Buses: 33, 337, 371, R69

446 WAINWRIGHT & NEILL

284 Battersea Park Road, SW11 3BT
Tel: 0171-350 2035

Open: Mon-Fri 9.30am-7.30pm; Sat 9am-6pm; Sun 10am-7pm
Closed: Bank Holidays

Useful delicatessen in the area, also selling Martin Pitt eggs.

Rail: Battersea Park (10 minutes)   Buses: 44, 49, 319, 344, 345

447 WAITROSE

Head Office: Doncastle Rd, Southern Industrial Estate,
Bracknell. Tel: 01344-424680
Too many branches to mention here, see our listings at the
back of this book

Open: times vary. Closed: some Bank Holidays
Good example of how supermarkets have improved in the last few years.

A comprehensive fruit and vegetable department has interesting exotics, fresh herbs and a few organic vegetables. The pre-packed meat section includes items such as organic beef from Eastbrook Farm, and good free-range "Farmhouse" ducks. Like all supermarkets the fish counter relies too heavily on pre frozen products. Cheese again has too many types of the plastic-wrapped variety, but unpasteurised Montgomery Cheddar is available. Similarly the charcuterie looks impressive but relies on fast moving items, rather than better specialist products, but Denhay ham is a bonus. Good baguettes and sometimes excellent sour-doughs from The Village Bakery. If seeking dried cepes, chose their own brand in the vegetable department - they are half the price of the branded variety (which are displayed on a shelf elsewhere). You may be surprised to find organic ice cream (excellent), eggs, milk and cheddar.

448 WALTHAMSTOW MARKET

Walthamstow High Street, E17

Open: Mon-Sat 8am-6pm. Closed: Sun & Bank Holidays

Bustling market stretching from Pretoria Avenue in the west to Hoe street in the east, and said to be Britain's longest. It's certainly great fun and full of food bargains from the stalls and the shops on either side. If you like sausages Postons (q.v) round the corner is a bonus. Avoid Saturdays if you hate crowds!

Tube & Rail: Walthamstow Central

Buses: 2, 20, 34, 48, 58, 69, 212, 215, 251, 257, 275, 505, 551, W11, W15

449 WANG THAI MARKET

103 Kew Road, Richmond, TW9 2PN
Tel: 0181-332 2959

Open: Mon-Sun 10am-8pm; Bank Holidays 11am-2pm
Closed: 25, 26 Dec & Easter Day

Useful supplier of Thai and Far-Eastern groceries. Products are mainly dried, tinned or frozen, but all the basics are available. Fresh vegetables are sold from a chilled cabinet (which is just as well, as the shop can be very hot) - the best of these are to be had towards the end of the week.

Rail/Tube: Richmond (10 mins)

Buses: 65, 90, 190, 290, 371, 391, 415, H22, R61, R68, R70

450 WEMBLEY EXOTICS ★

133/135 Ealing Road, Wembley, HAO 4BP
Tel: 0181-900 2607

Open: Mon-Sun 24 hours. Closures: None

Rather smarter in appearance than many surrounding shops, this Asian greengrocer is the place to buy emergency items night and day. Their selection is impressive by any standards and includes all European staples as well as exotics from the Indian sub-continent such as addo, turia and long beans. Prices are modest.

Tube: Alperton   Buses: 79, 83, 224, 297

451 WHITTARD

Head Office: Union Court, Union Rd, SW4.
Tel: 0171-627 8885
Too many branches to mention here, see our listings towards the end of this book

Open: Times vary, but Mon-Sat 10am-6pm; Sun 11am-5pm is typical
Closed: Bank Holidays (City branches closed on Sun)

Whittard's have been supplying coffee and tea to London since the 1880's. Over 50 types of tea are on offer, this is of a high quality and includes varieties from single estates. We have not found the coffee of equal quality, it is not roasted in individual branches, and perhaps distribution and freshness is a problem? Good range of tisines.

Also mail order from 73 Northcote Rd, SW11 (0171-924 1888)

452 WHOLE FOOD

24 Paddington Street, W1M 4DR
Tel: 0171-935 3924

Open: Mon-Thur 8.45am-6pm; Fri 8.45am-6.30pm; Sat 8.45am-1pm
Closed: Sun & Bank Holidays

Organic fruit and vegetables as well as health-food items cram this shop which was ahead of it's time when it opened in 1960. If you're in need of an organic orange or banana, this is your place - salads, in particular, always look beautifully fresh.

Tube: Baker Street (5 minutes)
Buses: 2, 13, 30, 74, 82, 113, 139, 159, 274

453 WHOLE FOOD BUTCHERS

31 Paddington Street, W1M 3RG
Tel: 0171-486 1390

Open: Mon-Thur 8am-6pm; Fri 8.30am-6.30pm; Sat 8am-1pm
Closed: Sun & Bank Holidays

Only additive-free and organically-reared meat is sold at this excellent butchers, just off Baker Street. So all is free of hormones and the indiscriminate use of antibiotics. This peace of mind comes at a premium, as animals naturally take longer to mature when reared by this method - the flavour, and the knowledge that they've had a happy life, makes this worthwhile.

Tube: Baker Street (5 minutes)
Buses: 2, 13, 30, 74, 82, 113, 139, 159, 274

454 WILD OATS WHOLE FOODS ★
210 Westbourne Grove, W11 2RH
Tel: 0171-229 1063

Open: Mon, Wed, Thur, Fri 9am-7pm; Tue 10am-7pm; Sat 9am-6pm; Sun & Bank Holidays 10am-5pm. Closed: 25, 26 Dec & 1 Jan

Self-service health food shop of the first rank. Their enormous range of products, mostly housed in an expansive basement, includes everything imaginable (see index), all free of artificial additives and many organic. Comprehensive selection of gluten free products and organic fresh herbs and vegetables.

Tube: Bayswater/Notting Hill Gate (10 minutes)   Buses: 23

455 WING YIP ★
550 Purley Way (A23), Croydon, Surrey, CRO 4RF
Tel: 0181-688 4880
Branch @ 395 Edgware Road, (near Staples Corner)
Cricklewood, NW2 6LN

Open: Mon-Sat 9.30am-7pm; Sun 11.30am-5.30pm
Closed: Bank Holidays

Chinese cash and carry type operation catering for both the restaurant trade and the general public. Every conceivable item is stocked from frozen dim sum to Peking duck. A large selection of frozen fish, such as barracuda, grouper, sea-bass, shark and tuna steaks is backed up by a fresh fish department selling live carp and lobsters. There is a useful kitchen section selling woks etc. at bargain prices. The Croydon branch has an excellent café/restaurant.

Rail: Waddon (10 minutes)   Buses: 119, 289

456 WOOLWICH MARKET
Beresford Square, SE18

Open: Tue-Sat 8.30am-5pm; Thur 8.30am-1pm
Closed: Sun, Mon & Bank Holidays

Good market for fruit, vegetables, meat and fish.

Rail: Woolwich Arsenal
Buses: 51, 96, 99, 122, 177, 178, 180, 244, 272, 380, 422, 469, X53

457 YASAR HALIM
493/495 Green Lanes, N4 1AL
Tel: 0181-340 8090
Branch @ 182 Uxbridge Road, W12 (0181-740 9477)

Open: 7 days a week 9am-10pm. Closed: Bank Holidays

Turkish supermarket with a halal meat department and popular bakery producing sticky temptations.

Rail: Harringay Green Lanes   Buses: 29, 141,

458 YOAHAN SUPERMARKET & FOOD COURT

Yoahan Plaza, 399 Edgware Road, NW9 0JJ
Tel: 0181-200 0009

Open: Mon-Sat 10am-8pm; Sun & Bank Holidays noon-6pm
Closed: 25, 26 Dec & 1 Jan

The Yoahan Plaza complex describes itself as "All Japan under one roof", and this is probably close to the truth, with shops of all descriptions selling Japanese products - including one where everything is £1 (selling useful plastic food containers). The supermarket section offers enough standard "western" items for you to do your complete shop here. There is also a good Chinese section. Beware - there's a Segadome amusement arcade, which draws in children of all ages!

Tube: Colindale (5 minutes)   Buses: 32, 142, 204, 292, 303

Tip:

Bought spring rolls will never match what can be achieved at home, and they are easy and fun to make (if you lack the enthusiasm for this, Sainsbury produce the best shop version we found). If making your own, try to buy Banh Trang Vietnamese rice wrappers (see index, under rice wrappers, for suppliers) as they will give you far lighter rolls than the more usual Chinese wrappers which are made with wheat flour - these are thicker and give rather clumsy results. Rice wrappers have the added advantage of needing no refrigeration, whereas the more traditional Chinese version will need to be kept in the deep-freeze or will keep for only a few days in the fridge.

CHEAP EATS

Excellent food at reasonable prices:

Adams Café
77 Askew Road, Shepherds Bush, W12
Tel: 0181-743 0572

Excellent day time café, changing to a Mediterranean/North African operation in the early evening. Prices are modest and service comes with a smile.

Open: Mon-Sat 6.30am-11pm
Closed: Sun & Bank Holidays

Andrew Edmunds
46 Lexington Street, Soho, W1. Tel: 0171-437 5708

Possibly London's best bistro. Not cheap in the true sense, but excellent value for money - and just having one course here is a treat! The style is set by dishes such as braised lamb shank in a red wine sauce or bruschetta of grilled vegetables with mozzarella and tapenade. Main courses are priced at about £7. Booking essential.

Open: Mon-Sun noon-3pm (Sat & Sun from 1pm) & 6pm-10.45pm
(Sun till 10.30pm)
Closed: 1 week Christmas & 4 days Easter.

Big Easy
332 King's Road, SW3. Tel: 0171-352 4071

American-style restaurant, which is fun for children and easy on their parents pocket - as one child can eat free for each paying adult; all day every day. Unlike many themed restaurants the food here is excellent and the general value good. Not suitable for those who loath loud music.

Open: noon-midnight; (Fri & Sat till 12.30am)
Closed: 25 & 26 Dec

Eco
162 Clapham High Street, SW4. Tel: 0171-720 0738
Branch @ 4 Market Row, Electric Lane, Brixton, SW9
Tel: (0171-738 3021)

Some of London's best pizzas are to be had here at this ultra-modern restaurant near next door to M&S Fruits (q.v.). The evenings can be frantic affairs, but shoppers can enjoy lunch in more peaceful surroundings at very reasonable prices (pizzas start at about £5). There is also a selection of oven-baked dishes.

Open: Mon-Fri 11.30am-3pm & 6.30am-11pm; Sat 11.30am-4.30pm &
6am-11.30pm; Sun noon-5pm & 6am-11pm

Emperor Junior

366 King's Road, SW10
Tel: 0171-823 3368

New addition to the Emperor Chinese Restaurant (next door), ideally suited to shoppers requirements. The operation is based around dim sum, all priced at £2-10, and bowls of tasty noodles, starting at around £5. A welcome addition to New Culture Revolution (q.v) opposite, which can be very busy.

Open: noon-11.30 daily
Closed: 25 & 26 Dec

Florians

4 Topsfield Parade, Middle Lane, Crouch End, N8
Tel: 0181-883 8368

Italian restaurant offering good-value lunches and early evening meals in a front wine bar section (£5-95 for two courses and coffee).

Open: noon-3pm (Sun till 3.30pm) & 7pm-11pm
Closed: 3 days Christmas

Jirocho

134 Wardour Street, Soho, W1
Tel: 0171-437 3027

Friendly little Japanese restaurant which offers rarely found "family-style" dishes (such as stewed pork with potato and chicken teriyaki bowl) as well as the more usual sushi. Lunchtime set menus are about £5.

Open: Mon-Fri noon-2.30pm & 6pm-10.30pm
Closed: L Sat; all Sun & some Bank Holidays

Madhu's Brilliant

39 South Road, Southall, Middlesex
Tel: 0181-574 1897

This excellent Indian restaurant, specialising in Punjabi food, is worth a special trip, and a must if you're in the area. It's hard to recommend individual items, because everything is so good, but the alu tikkie (potato with chick peas and coriander), korai gosht (lamb) stick in the memory and the crisp bhatura bread is not to be missed.

Open: Mon, then Weds-Fri 12.30pm-3pm; Mon-Sat 6pm-11.30pm
Closed: L Sat & Sun, all Tues; 25 Dec.

Mezzonine Restaurant

100 Wardour Street, W1
Tel: 0171-314 4000

This is the ground floor, and mid-priced section, of the Mezzo complex. Dishes have a strong Pacific-Rim bias, but include the likes of five-spice

duck spring rolls, braised vegetables with Indian spices in broth and tea -
smoked quail with miso and aubergine relish , all at very reasonable
prices. For those in a hurry Café Mezzo (with a separate entrance) offers
sandwiches and excellent pastries.

Open: Mon-Sun noon-2.50pm & 5.30pm-12.50am
Closed: 25 & 26 Dec

Mutiara

14 Walworth Road, Elephant and Castle, SE1
Tel: 0171-277 0425

Good value restaurant selling authentic Indonesian/Malaysian dishes.
Their £2-95 set lunch is a bargain by any standards.

Open: Mon-Fri noon-2.30pm; Mon-Sat 6am-11pm
Closed: L Sat, all Sun & Bank Holidays

New Culture Revolution

305 King's Road, SW3. Tel: 0171-352 9281
Branches @ 42 Duncan St, Islington, N1 (0171-833 9083)
& 43 Parkway, Camden Town, NW1 (0171-267 2700)

Good value eaterie offering a few healthy-type starters and big bowls of
steaming oriental-style noodles. Expect to queue at peak times.

Open: noon-11pm daily
Closed: 3 days Christmas

Rotisserie Jules

338 King's Road, SW3. Tel: 0171-351 0041
Branches @ 6 Bute Street, SW7 (0171-584 0600)
& 133a Notting Hill Gate, W11 (0171-221 3736)

A simple menu comprising of spit-roast free-range chicken and lamb is on
offer here at reasonable prices. A home delivery service is also available.

Open: 11am-11.30pm daily
Closed: 25, 26 Dec & 1 Jan

Royal China

13 Queensway, Bayswater, W2. Tel: 0171-221 2535

Smart Chinese restaurant of particular interest to shoppers as it offers
London's best dim sum at very reasonable prices; this coupled with
friendly service. Eating from the main menu is more expensive. Avoid
Sunday lunch unless you can arrive very early.

Open: Mon-Sun noon-5pm & 6pm-11pm
Closed: 23-25 Dec.

Sonny's

94 Church Road, Barnes, SW13. Tel: 0181-748 0393

For a civilised break while shopping in Barnes try Sonny's, a serious restaurant with a relaxing atmosphere. To entice you in throughout the day, a café menu is offered with items ranging from excellent sandwiches to more serious dishes such as pan-fried Skate wing with sorrel sauce. Prices are very reasonable ranging from about £2 to £7.

Open: Mon-Sat 12.30am-11pm; Sun 12.30pm-2.30pm

Sohail's Charcoal Kebab Centre

238a Ealing Road, Alperton, W10. Tel: 0181-903 6743

When exploring the excellent cluster of food shops in this area, this little café deserves a visit. It adds a quality rarely seen in standard-issue kebabs with pitta bread. About ten varieties are offered, included vegetarian paneer, all cooked before you on a charcoal barbecue. A selection of simple curries includes the ever-popular chicken tikka masala. Prices are modest, and service friendly. Only halal meat is used. Unlicensed, so drink lassi.

Open: Mon-Thur noon-10pm; Fri-Sun noon-10.30pm.
Closed: 25 Dec. No credit cards.

Stick & Bowl

31 Kensington High Street, W8. Tel: 0171-937 2778

Sit at a bar on high stools at this excellent-value Chinese eatery - ideal for Kensington shoppers. Main courses are about £4, and arrive quickly. Not suitable for very young children. Plenty of Chinese customers show the quality of the food.

Open: Sun-Sat 11.30am-11pm
Closed: 25 & 26 Dec. No credit cards.

Stockpot

273 King's Road, SW3. Tel: 0171-823 3175

Simple reliable food at bargain prices, but no frills, at this Chelsea restaurant. Starters, such as field mushrooms with tartare sauce are about £1-50; plenty of main course choice for under £3 and desserts for about a pound. Famous regulars show the quality of what's on offer! We have found this branch to have the edge on those listed below. Branches @ 40 Panton Street (off Haymarket), SW1 (0171-839 5142); 6 Basil Street, Knightsbridge, SW3 (0171-589 8627) & 18 Old Compton Street, Soho, W1 (0171-287 1066). No credit cards.

Open: Mon-Sun 8am-midnight (Sun from noon). Closed: 25 & 26 Dec

Toffs

38 Muswell Hill Broadway, N10. Tel: 0181-883 8656

Family run fish and chip restaurant of the first rank. Fish is either coated in batter or matzo meal (60p extra). Prices start at about £8 for cod and chips. There are also daily specials such as fish soup fisherman's pie, plus a children's menu.

Open: Tues-Sat 11.30am-10pm. Closed: Sun, Mon, & 2 weeks Aug-Sept.

Villandry

170 Great Portland Street, W1N 5TB. Tel: 0171-631 3131

Excellent brasserie-style restaurant to the rear of the shop (entrance from Bolsover Street in the evening). The daily changing menu has starters from about £4, main courses from £8; with food to suit all tastes. Booking advised. No smoking.

Open: Mon-Sat Breakfast 8.30am-11.30pm; Lunch noon-3pm; Tea 3pm-7pm; Dinner 7am-10pm. Closed: Sun & Bank Holidays

Wing Yip

550 Purley Way, Croydon, Surrey, CRO. Tel: 0181-688 3668

This cash & carry style Chinese supermarket (q.v) has an excellent café/restaurant attached; making it an ideal break from the exhausting shopping imposed by the cluster of warehouse-shops on this drag - these include Comet, Curry's, Habitat, Ikea, PC World and Tempo to name but a few.

Open: Mon-Sat 11am-11pm; Sun 11am-10pm
Closed: Bank Holidays

Woodlands

77 Marylebone Lane, W1. Tel: 0171-486 3862

Smart, but unpretentious South Indian vegetarian restaurant offering excellent Thalis and the like at bargain prices. Set lunch £4-95. Branches @ 37 Panton Street (off Haymarket), SW1 (0171-839 7258) & 402a High Road, Wembley (0181-902 9869)

Open: Mon-Sun noon-3pm & 6pm-11pm
Closed: 25 & 26 Dec

The Wren

St James' Church, Piccadilly, 35 Jermyn Street, SW1.
Tel: 0171-437 9419

This split-level restaurant, owned by the church, specialises in vegetarian dishes. Lunch might include the likes of chili bean casserole with baked potato, quiches and salads - all around the £2-50/£4 mark. Homemade cakes in the afternoon. Unlicensed and no smoking.

Open: Mon-Sun 8am-7pm (Sun 9am-5pm)
Closed: Most Bank Holidays. No credit cards.

What to do with Salt Cod

Widely available from fishmongers with a Portuguese or French following, these unattractive strips of dried fish can easily be turned into a delicious dish. The skill needed is minimal and the long preparation time (which is simply soaking to re-hydrate and remove the salt) is largely unattended.

Brandade de Morue;
(A traditional dish from South-West France):

Ingredients:
1lb (750g) salt cod
$1/2$ Pint (284ml) olive oil, slightly warmed
$1/2$ pint (284ml) milk, slightly warmed
1 large clove garlic, peeled and finely chopped
A squeeze of lemon juice
A little freshly ground pepper
A little grated nutmeg

Method:
1. Soak the fish in cold water for 48 hours, completely changing the water twice a day.
2. Drain the fish, putting it in a big pan of cold water.
3. Slowly bring to boiling point and simmer for for 15 minutes, or until the fish flakes easily. Cooking too agressively will result in a stringy texture.
4. Remove the fish from the liquid and remove any skin and small bones.
5. Heat the oil and milk separately until they are warm.
6. In a big bowl flake the cod segments with the chopped garlic until fairly smooth; then gradually add the warmed oil and milk alternately a spoonful at a time, mixing all the time, and incorporating each addition thoroughly before any more is added.
7. Add the lemon juice, pepper and nutmeg mixing until you have a fairly smooth paste. Serve in the same way as taramasalata or houmous with good French or pitta bread.

8. *The mixture can be made in a food processsor, but great care has to be taken to leave some texture.*

TIPS WHEN BUYING AND NAMES TO SEEK OUT

Apples: As with all fruit it is important to follow the seasons of the Northern and Southern Hemispheres. For example an English Cox (which has had months in cold store) will very likely be disappointing in April, whereas an example from New Zealand or Chile should be fresh and delicious. Shops might offer both varieties - so beware.

Bacalhau: see Salt Cod.

Bacon: Pigs were the most popular source of meat in mediaeval times; pork being the only meat which tastes better cured than fresh; fresh meat in winter months was a rarity. This British tradition is something we should have perfected by now; however, apart from a few passionate bacon producers, things are going from bad to worse!

Supermarkets haven't grasped the nettle in the same way they have with bread, eggs and to a certain extent fruit and vegetables.

Instead of seeking out unadulterated forms of bacon - such as those recommended in this book - the meat is often flooded with added water and sodium nitrate. All this results in making it hard to crisp, and the fact that it often oozes the now familiar white pus-like substance. One of the problems seems to be that modern cross-breds, reared to produce less fat, seem to be incapable of weaning their young in a free range habitat. The process no longer comes naturally to them and they tend to lie on their piglets. The small sacrifice therefore seems to be, that to have bacon that is (a) pus-free (b) full of flavour (c) to be easily crisped - one has to put up with a little extra fat!

The latest production benefit for the manufacturers; but certainly no advantage to the discerning consumer, is to replace the natural smoking process with a bath in a liquid smoke solution; this produces a smoke flavour more quickly and with less hassle to the producer. So far this procedure doesn't even have to be mentioned on the label, and the bacon can be labelled "smoked"!

Rather than extend the range with a natural product; varieties such as "peppered bacon" are appearing in supermarkets, to take up valuable shelf space.

Pigs used for dry cured bacon are bred to have a high proportion of fat otherwise their meat would become dry and hard when heated. It is important not to remove this fat before cooking, as it keeps the bacon moist and adds to the flavour; it can always be left at the side of your plate if you don't want to eat it, then gently rendered down to keep in the fridge; this will provide you with a delicious cooking medium for your next sauté potatoes.

It is worth remembering that bacon cures tend to gain in strength the further north in the country they are produced.

If you seek out the bacons mentioned below, you will add a delight to your breakfast not shared by the masses for many years. You never know a shift in buying habits might make the genuine product more widely available!

Names to look out for: bacon produced by: Maynards, Denhay Farms, Heal Farm, Mooreland Foods, F.E. Neave Richard Woodall. and Eastbrook Farm. See also under **Pork**.

Balsamic Vinegar: until fairly recently this was only made by the well-off families of Modena (who had their own vineyards). It took at least 12 years to make good vinegar; and for an exceptional one, many years more. In the middle-ages it was sometimes listed as part of a lady's dowry. The precious liquid being transferred at least five times from barrels made from different woods. These wood-type might include ash, juniper, apple, pear and mulberry; each one imparting it's own flavour to the precious liquid.

Vinegar is still made by this method and sold labelled aceto balsamico tradizionale; needless to say it is very expensive.

Balsamic vinegar must by law still be made around Modena; but the commonly found commercial varieties lack the extreme depth of flavour of the tradizionale. There are many price points so experiment and find the cheapest that you like; Sainsbury's own version is a good starting point.

Beef: there are three distinct types of beef on the market, plus a fourth; dairy-cow which we will talk about in a moment.
1. Grass-reared animals reared for beef, as opposed to milk production - these are usually fed on silage (fermented grass/hay) in the winter months; most, if not all herds reared in this way have been almost totally BSE free for the whole of the beef crisis.
2. Animals fed on natural cereals only throughout the year - so might have had a life indoors. Herds reared in this way have also generally been free of even a single case of BSE. Beef fed this sort of diet tends

to produces good but paler meat with less character than that from grass-reared herds.

3. Animals fed a proprietary brand of animal feed from a commercial supplier - problems start at this stage of the proceedings; but as animals reared for beef are killed at an early age, it's possible that the very early stages of the disease might not have manifested itself.

If the government is guilty of anything it is in not pointing out the complete safety in eating naturally, particularly organically-reared animals; it is surely largely the publics bewilderment that has so damaged the beef industry. It is also possible that their instructions compelling farmers to use high doses of pesticides on their fields compounded the issue.

The animal food manufacturers must take the bulk of the responsibility in adulterating their feed-stuffs with bone meal, unnaturally turning herbivores into cannibals, or at the very least, meat eaters; and farmers for taking this cheaper option by letting pound notes fill their eyes, rather than letting their animals graze naturally. A government, of any political denomination, surely can't be blamed for the actions of greedy industrialists, any more than they can examine what goes into every tin of pet food!

The most worrying cases of BSE come from worn out dairy-cows, which in our opinion should never have been sold as beef at all, but as cow (as opposed to meat from steers or heifers [young females]). These carcasses enter the food chain when animals high-yield milking days are over; their meat then being put onto the market as beef.

Because they are bred to produce milk rather than meat, they are more lightly structured, and their flesh skimpier on the bone. Their meat is commonly sold by butchers who have less pride in their product, and also commonly found in cheaper sausages, burgers, meat pies and other processed items. Unscrupulous restaurants can also be tempted to use this meat, and to pass on to the unsuspecting public as top-class beef, even using it for steaks. Meat of this type should from the start have been labelled cow; the BSE crisis would then have been much easier to isolate. All our recommended butchers have actively sought out safe beef supplies, and those with stars often offer a choice from single known herds.

Black Pudding: generally made with pigs blood in England and sheep's blood in Scotland and parts of Ireland. Irish blood pudding is generally padded out with barley, which might not suit all tastes. Occasionally

Vivian's, in Richmond, has excellent pudding from the kitchens of
Stephen Bull - another experience from commercial brands altogether!
Bloaters: similar to kippers (but more lightly salted and smoked), and
left unsplit - so resembling a fish in appearance; more difficult to find
than kippers because their shelf live is shorter.

Bottarga: a form of pressed fish roes, often made from tuna (and
coming from Sardinia), and hard to find fresh. For lovers of smoked
salmon or taramasalata it's an experience not to be missed - expensive,
but a little goes a long way, as it is eaten cold in wafer-thin slices, or
perhaps grated into olive oil as the basis of a pasta sauce.

Bread: A slow bread revolution is taking place to rival that of the return of
the free-range egg; all connected with peoples wish to eat more healthily.

Although stone-ground flour, producing a heavier style loaf, is still not
popular with many of the younger generation; it has many nutritional
benefits. These are because the grinding stones don't produce the heat
generated by the stainless-steel rollers used in mass production - this
cooler technique destroys fewer vitamins than it's more modern alternative.

Our tastes have largely become accustomed to packaged sliced bread
"aerated" by being made by the Chorley Wood method; this produces
bread which feels very light for it's size, giving a false sense of value! The
process also saves 60% of production time, as the rising period is largely
cut out, and more yeast and cheaper flour can be used.

It should be remembered that Sour-Dough bread has a much longer
shelf life than it's yeast made cousin, this has helped establish the sales
of excellent bakeries such as The Village Bakery, Melmerby and The
Kolos Bakery of Bradford miles away from their local patch.

Many of these smaller bakeries use organic flour and bake with traditional
wood-fired ovens. Traditionally-made bread might seem expensive
compared to the factory-style loaves we've become accustomed to, but
you are buying quality flour and flavour rather than air and water.

French baguettes have improved enormously in quality here, largely
because much of the dough is imported, already shaped in its frozen
state. These loaves produce pretty good bread, but cannot rival the very
best; unfortunately their convenience is also threatening the survival of
village bakeries in their home country, as they can easily be produced by
any supermarket, and are often sold by them as a loss-leader. For the

best French bread look out for Poilane, which is imported from Paris on a regular basis by some of our best delicatessen; Villandry amongst them.

Don't necessarily think that brown bread is more nutritious that white, for unless it is labelled wholemeal, it is very likely made from white flour coloured brown with caramel. In addition, white flour used in bread-making has to contain certain added vitamins, to make up for any loss in processing.

Inevitably, supermarkets are scrambling to keep up with fashion; but in their wild attempts to offer what the customer wants, they can't resist adding "improvers" such as mono and di-acetyltartaric acid and esters of mono and di-glyerides of fatty acids - all this, perhaps, in a supposedly Italian-style focaccia - items unheard of to a housewife here or to a baker in Tuscany; where even adding salt to bread is illegal! The end result is often a loaf containing a little olive oil, vaguely resembling focaccia in shape, but tasting more like plastic-wrapped sliced bread!

Brill: this excellent flat fish is a cheaper alternative to Turbot (the two can be used interchangeably). It's a thinner fish than Turbot, so not quite the same flesh to bone ratio, but a 3lb fish will provide four good helpings - plus an excellent frame for stock or soup.

Buckling: another style of preserved herring; similar to a bloater, but beheaded and gutted. They are lightly brined before smoking, so keep quite well.

Buckwheat: used to make flour, but actually no relation of wheat but a member of the rhubarb family. Makes interesting pancakes when added to plain flour in a ratio of 1:3.

Butter: Because Anchor butter had to travel from New Zealand for weeks by sea, generations have grown up in this country thinking salt is a natural addition to butter. Pure butter is made from unadulterated milk, this in turn being flavoured by the excellence of the pasture where the cows have grazed, the addition of salt will simply camouflage it's delicate character. Excellent English butters include Appleby's, Denhay, Duckett's, Keen's and Lane's (who also make Winters Dairy Ice Cream). French butters to look out for are Lescure and the rather expensive Echiré. Italian butter is of a generally excellent standard, but it is often made with German milk.

Buttermilk: traditionally the liquid that is left after cream has been churned to produce butter. Nowadays this is often cultured by adding bacteria to milk. Ideal for making soda bread.

Caviar: The hard roe of the female sturgeon. Most caviar on sale in this country has been decanted from big tins into much smaller containers. This means it has often been exposed to the air since originally being packed. So only buy caviar from a shop with a fast turnover, then keep in the coldest part of your fridge (but do not freeze).

Charcuterie: to cover language differences we have rather cheekily used this word to cover all cooked meats, thus covering everything from French paté to ham and Italian salami. The selection now on offer would have amazed our parents. Unfortunately the need to be ever more competitive has led to modern processes which might mean the beautifully presented packet of turkey breast or roast pork you see before you has been made from reformed meat - designed to resemble uniform but genuine slices. Good delicatessens, rather than supermarkets, are far more likely to stock slices cut from a joint of real meat.

Cheese: *Unpasteurized cheese, while having more flavour and character should not be given to the pregnant or very elderly.*

Storing: once cut open, all cheese is best kept in tin foil in the fridge; this is better than cling wrap, as the cheese can still breath a little (and cling wrap still lets strong flavours like melon through). There is also the hanging worry that high-fat foods should not be wrapped in cling wrap - particularly brands including PVC - per se.

Soft cheese, if uncut, ripen at room temperature until you are happy, then they should be kept in tin foil in the fridge.

Hard and blue cheese: can be kept in the fridge either in a clean damp cloth or wrapped in tin foil.

A few cheeses that stand out:

> **Brie:** seek out Brie Fermier, which is unpasteurized, never buy Brie which smells of ammonia. Best from early summer to late autumn.

> **Camembert:** Buy whole rounds rather than portions; and as for Brie try to find Camembert Fermier, which is again unpasteurized and has more flavour. Best from early summer to late autumn.

> **Cheddar:** Although cheddar-type cheeses are now made worldwide, with varying degrees of success, there are only about ten farms left in the West Country making real traditional cheese. What is important is to remember that unless Cheddar is allowed to develop naturally in

cheesecloth, it can't breathe and won't mature properly. Anything wrapped in plastic rind is a sealed unit, and will have little character; any strength will have come from the addition of salt, not from the natural evaporation of moisture. Cheeses to look out for are those by Quickes, made on six farms and producing good pasteurised and unpasteurized cheese; the truly excellent Montgomery, or Keen's which are both unpasturised; the latter being more nutty and sharper in flavour than the former. These three cheeses are still made by their respective families in the West Country. Denhay in Hampshire also make very good cheese. The best Cheddar will have matured for nine months or more, so if the age is advertised bear in mind that the most lush grass is available when it rains - perhaps September to March, and this will produce the best product.

Blue: There are far too many to list, but some really stand out and need a mention. Cashel Blue, made by Louis Grubb from cow's milk in Tipperary, is delicious with soft, creamy texture. Scotland gives us the excellent Lanark Blue, still made with raw (unpasteurized) milk. For something milder the best Gorgonzola is hard to beat, having more oomph and character than it's creamier cousin Dolcelatte.(See also: sheep's cheese, goat and Stilton).

Cheshire: Britain's oldest surviving cheese was being made before the Roman invasion. The last Cheshire made from unpasturised milk is made by The Appleby family in Shropshire; this should be available at most of our starred cheese shops, and is worth seeking out.

Goat's Cheese: for British cheese look out for Poulcoin or Ticklemore for hard cheeses, Golden Cross, Perroche or St.Tola for soft and Harbourne for blue. Spain offers good soft Monte Enebro and the French Crottin de Chavignol is excellent for grilling on croûtes for warm salads.

Lancashire: Mrs Kirkham's unpasteurized cheese stands head and shoulders above rivals, she only makes about four cheeses a day, so they're not widely available; but most of our starred cheese shops will have regular supplies.

Parmesan: no list would be complete without mentioning Parmesan, the original and best of which is Parmesan Reggiano. This must still only be made within the provinces of Parma and Reggio Emilia; processes have changed little since the 14th century and production is confined to small factory units. Cheese made by a similar method, but without the strict controls is made in the surrounding regions and sold as Grana Padano. The whey left over from cheese production is fed to the pigs reared for the production of Parma ham.

Sheep's Cheese: a good selection of excellent British cheeses in this department. For hard cheese look out for Spenwood and Wigmore; for blue, Beenleigh and for soft Emlett, Little Ryding and in certain places (including Neal's Yard [qv]) Fetta which, unlike most of it's Greek models is not now made from cow's milk. Italy produces various Pecorino the name of which is a generalisation - like Cheddar; but some of our recommended Italian delicatessen's offer as many as eight types ranging from a hard Parmesan-style (traditionally correct for pesto sauce) to fairly soft. France, of course, offers Roquefort, much of which is now made in Corsica, the AOC protection insists that all is brought to maturity in the traditional natural caves of Mont Combalou.

Stilton: Look for cheeses produced at Colston Bassett. These have unfortunately all been made of pasteurised milk since the listeria scarce of 1990. Although they might have lost a little character they are still easily the best available. The 1990 scarce did the cheese industry unjustifiable harm; food poisoning cases from cheese only run at about one a year, whereas those from chicken still run into thousands! Stilton is at it's best from November to early spring, hence it's popularity at Christmas.

Chickens: The flavour of hens reared for the table largely depends on their bred. Some of the more old-fashioned varieties take a few more weeks to mature, and so over the years have fallen out of favour with the mass-producers.

Under factory farming methods poussin might be killed at 4 weeks, and a mature bird at any time after 6 weeks. This is simply not enough time for their meat to develop any noticeable flavour (10 weeks seems to be the minimum time for this to happen).

After numerous tastings Tesco's Les Landes chickens, as advertised by Dudley Moore, had the best flavour of any widely available. The supermarket giant didn't respond to questions about their diet (the label implying they are fed corn), and whether they were automatically fed antibiotics; maybe they'll be more forthcoming by our next edition. They are doing something right, however, as their flavour was only matched by those reared organically by Peter Onions - which are considerably more expensive - these are stocked by a few specialist butchers and, towards the end of the week, by larger branches of Sainsbury.

The skin-colour of birds is largely governed by their bred, not their diet - one chicken might be constantly fed corn, yet have white skin, while another fed a mass-producers feed, yellow - your taste buds, not your eyes, must be the main judge at the end of the day!

A small price to pay for a more mature chicken is a higher proportion of fat; but this can always be saved for, like bacon or duck fat, it is excellent for sauteing potatoes and for other frying needs, for which you might normally use butter.

Chocolate: Chocolate began it's British life as a drink after the English captured Jamaica from the Spanish in 1655 cocoa-houses quickly sprang up all over London. Later, influential Quaker families, such as the Cadbury's and Rowntree's, tried to promote it as an alternative to alcohol, which was very cheap at the time.

Solid chocolate bars were not invented until about 1828 (although chocolate almonds were available as early as the 1670's), when Joseph Fry used a recently developed press and put to good use the left over solids after the much sought after cocoa butter had been extracted.

Over the years the British have developed a preference for milk chocolate, which is very convenient for manufacturers as it is generally very low in expensive cocoa solids. For real chocolate aim for chocolate with cocoa solids of over 60%; the very best contains over 70% of the real thing.

A visit to either Ackerman's or Rococo (q.v's) is a chocolate-lovers delight. Valrhona is quite widely available and top-class Tschirren Swiss chocolates are stocked by Harrods, but their price puts them in the special occasion category.

For scoffing pleasure, or for cooking at an affordable price, supermarket own-brands often outshine more familiar varieties.

Chutney, pickles and relishes: The Cottage Delight range is widely found and good; for the very best look out for Wendy Brandon's excellent range from Wales, those from Highfield Preserves (who also make mustard, jellies and herb-flavoured oils), the products of The Bay Tree Food Company and The Wiltshire Tracklement Company (see under mustard) plus Harvey Nicholls in-house selection. Mrs Brassa's (q.v) range of Indian pickles and chutneys is excellent and good value.

For pickled onions, the best we have found are made by Garners of Worcestershire; these have the added benefit of being made totally of natural ingredients. They are becoming increasingly available in London, and are regularly stocked by Sainsbury, Waitrose and The Bluebird Gastrodrome.

Coffee: Coffee beans keep very well for many years, and indeed may even improve if stored in the right conditions in their unroasted state. Roasting releases the essential oils, and these evaporate slowly from that moment. Storing roasted beans in a air-tight tin and preferably in the fridge gives them a life of about two weeks before any loss of flavour becomes apparent. None of the specialist coffee shops recommended by us holds vast quantities of roasted beans, and many are roast on the premises. Ground beans should be kept in the same way, but will have deteriorated noticeably after four to five days. So grind your own as required if at all possible; the beautiful smell makes this chore worthwhile.

Once you have found your favourite coffee, you can often make worthwhile savings in both money and travelling time by buying in larger quantities. For example, at the time of writing 1lb of Colombian Medellin Supremo at the excellent Monmouth Coffee Company is £6 while a 12lb bag (which needs to be ordered a day in advance) is £1 per lb cheaper. It's useful to know that whole beans freeze very successfully, and can be ground straight from the deep-freeze.

Confit: literally means preserve, and was a method used primarily in South-West France for keeping duck, rabbit and other meats through the winter months by first smothering them in herbs and salt, then very slowly cooking in duck or goose fat. The word has been somewhat abused by restaurants, who in seeking to be constantly different from their rivals are offering confit of everything from aubergine to bamboo shoots - with varying degrees of culinary success.

Croissant: rolled dough (generally shaped into the shape of a crescent), the very best of which should be layered with half as much butter as the weight of flour, in the manner of puff pastry. In practice this is a rarity in this country, but 100% butter rather than butter substitutes should be the basic aim. The very best we tasted are the all butter unbaked variety as supplied to restaurants and hotels by Leatham's Larder (Tel: 0171-252 7838); we have so far been unsuccessful in finding any shops they supply. If you have a big deep-freeze you could buy these wholesale! All our recommended shops sell above average examples.

Dover Sole: to many the king of fish. Needs to be at least a day old before it's possible to remove the skin without also removing too much flesh. The wise will ask their fishmonger to do this. Avoid buying them during March and April when they can be heavy with roes.

Denhay: farm near Bridport in Dorset whose initial aim was to produce first quality Farmhouse Cheddar; the left over whey from this process is now used to make butter and to fed an ever-expanding herd of pigs, from which they produce excellent dry-cured bacon and a "Parma" style ham. The meat for the hams is first cured in a blend of Dorset apple juices, local herbs and honey, before being lightly smoked over oak chippings. The process is then completed by air-dried for several months. The hams are available on the bone, but more usually in 4oz and 8oz vacuum packs.

Eggs; hens: The bleak days of the 1970's and '80's seem to be behind us, with the commercial reemergence of free-range eggs. But although everything in the garden looks rosier, there are important facts to remember.

1. A few open trap doors to the outside world and a surrounding area of open ground are often all that differentiates between free-range birds and those labelled as barn or perchery eggs. Perchery chickens can be housed at a stocking density of 25 birds per square metre plus enough perching area to give them 15cm each. Much better than caged birds, but in no way generous.

2. Chickens originated on the Indian sub-continent and naturally lived in areas which gave them plenty of tree cover and hence a certain protection from birds of prey; they are still inherently agoraphobic. So allowing them access to the outside world does not necessarily mean that the option is taken up without encouragement.

3. Grandly labelling eggs as being free-range gives no indication of the quality of their food, or indeed the amount of antibiotics they might automatically be given. Like us, chickens are what they eat; so an egg labelled as free-range is little better than a normal battery product if the hens are fed the cheapest proprietary brands of feed and not encouraged to venture outside - in other words a marketing ploy!

The only eggs recommended in this volume come from sources which we know - so they are all sourced from happy proper free-range birds, and are certainly fed a wholesome natural diet.

Free-range birds can only achieve a small proportion of their requirements by grubbing, so their diet is actually as, or more, important than their living conditions.

For the above reasons we highly recommend eggs produced by Martin Pitt in Wiltshire, and have marked shops selling these with a * in the index). They are genuine free-range eggs, from happy chickens, and luckily widely available in our area. Their taste will make your hunt worthwhile!

His hens are actively encouraged to roam outside, while their indoor accommodation is up to three-times the legal requirement. They are fed a completely natural diet of largely home-grown wheat, barley, maize and grass meal, blended on the farm with a little natural seaweed and sunflower oil. Scatterings of oyster shell give strong egg shells. No chemicals, hormones or artificial yolk colourants are added, and antibiotics are not part of the routine.

Birds are kept in small flocks, in fields often shared with cattle, sheep and horses; while their eggs are collected four times a day, and almost always delivered to outlets within 24 hours of being laid.

Knowledge on his subject means he travels the world lecturing. A visit to one of his farms is more than welcome. For further information call 01672 512035.

The view, still held by a few, that brown eggs are superior to white is nonsense - different breeds of chicken simply produce different coloured eggs!

The life of true free-range birds highlights the cruelty subjected to battery chickens, who at the time of writing have a legal space allocation of only 250cm√/kg (for birds up to 2 kg) barely giving them room to turn around; much needed new EU regulations are soon to enforce a fraction more space.

Next time you buy eggs from a battery chicken, remember they are kept in cages where they can hardly move, and stand on legs that because of their lack of exercise can hardly hold their weight. If you can live with these facts, all well and good!

If the extra cost of our recommended free-range eggs make them out of the question, we recommend "Four Grain" eggs from Stonegate; which are widely available. They are produced from perchery hens fed on a diet of wheat, barley, maize and oats; have good flavour, and seem more honest than the profusion of eggs labelled free-range, but from unknown sources and fed unknown diets.

Essence: for dishes needing an almond or vanilla hint always use a bottle saying "essence" as opposed to "flavour" - which although cheaper, will not produce the same results.

Fishmongers: The standard for entry is very high, so all are endorsed by us. Those given a star are extra special, and always willing to order unusual items, such items as pike (in season), fresh anchovies and live eel and langoustines. However, as the weather fluctuates and seasons change, always phone to check stocks before travelling. Even the best fishmonger might have brill one day, and turbot the next - but rarely both. When buying white fish, look for bright clear eyes and skin markings, plus flesh that recovers its shape quickly when pushed with your finger.

Fruit: for tasty fruit follow world-wide seasons - see apples (above).

Game Seasons:

Grouse - August 12th to December 12th
Hare - August 1st to the end of February
Partridge - September 1st to February 1st
Pheasant - October 1st to February 1st
Pigeon - all year
Rabbit - all year
Snipe - August 12th to January 31st
Venison - July 1st to end of February
Wild Duck - September 1st to January 31st
Woodcock - October 1st to January 31st

Garlic: There are three main types of garlic. White is the mildest and also has the shortest keeping time (about four months), violet bulbs are of medium pungency; while red garlic is the strongest of all; this will keep for up to a year if hung up in a cool airy place. New seasons garlic (of all types) is fairly mild, and can be spotted by it's thick moist skin which has not yet had time to dry to the papery state of it's more mature cousin.

The flavour of garlic mellows the longer it is cooked, and if used in conjunction with onions or leeks you can often cut down on the quantity used, as their flavours are complementary.

Genetically modified food: this might be the biggest issue by our next edition, as people have already died in the U.S.A from vegetables modified with genes from fish! For those who worry, soya is the main problem at the moment, as it's hard to avoid. The American firm of Monsanto is a, if not the major supplier to Europes food processing industry and at the time of writing is committed to modified beans. These emerge in such unlikely products as baby foods, chocolate, ice cream and ready meals as well as the more obvious bread and biscuits. Tomatoes are not far behind, their taste being sacrificed for a longer shelf life and increased frost resistance. Iceland (not at the moment listed in this book) are championing the cause of genetically unmodified food (their own labelled products are guaranteed to contain none); they deserve support. They recommend those worried about the situation to contact societies such as Friends of the Earth, 26-28 Underwood Street, London N1 7JQ (Tel: 0171-490 1555), sending an sae; or themselves on 0990 133373 for more information.

Monsanto are in the middle of a vast advertising campaign, and their admirers tell us nature has been adapting plants for years; maybe, but not with genes from something other than plants.

The possibilities of what might happen when seeds from a genetically modified crop are spread naturally by the wind into surrounding fields, to contaminate neighbouring plants, might make the seriousness of the beef crisis pale into insignificance. Part of the grand scheme of things is to introduce altered crops that will tolerate more insecticide; this will result in certain wild grasses disappearing, and with them the wildlife they support (we can therefore expect a few birds and rare butterflies to come under threat) - in the long run true organic farming might be difficult in certain areas.

It is a strange situation when a percentage of the population is seeking organic produce, while big business is wooing farmers to use more and more insecticide on unnatural plants!

Goose: The only remaining seasonal type of poultry. No amount of coercion has persuaded geese to bred more than twice a year, so their eggs are much sought over, and in practice they are only available in the shops between Michaelmas (29th September) and Christmas. We will keep searching for more suppliers of Easter geese. The deep-freeze is often the only answer! Look for geese reared by G.B. Geese of Lincolnshire, Homewood Partners of Abingdon or Goodman's of Worcester, and for mail order The Holly Tree Farm Shop (q.v).

Ham: by tradition, this should only be made from the rear leg of a pig, but packet items of reformed cured pork are now sold under this blanket name. Furthermore, a generation of Englishmen have been brought up to believe one of the main ingredients in ham is water. This is in no way traditional, but introduced by the injection of brine into the meat to speed up the curing process; so although the symptoms are different, ham has suffered the fate of Cheddar - that of being manufactured by the convenience of the mass producer.

All is not lost, for air-dried hams look out for Parma (from Italy) and Serrano or the extremely delicious and expensive Pata Negra (both from Spain), and excellent products from enthusiastic English producers such as Denhay of Dorset (where the pigs feed on whey from the dairy herd, and honey from their hives sweetens the brine), Richard Woodall (Cumbria) and Mooreland Foods (Cheshire).

For home-style hams, our recommended shops either cure their own, often in secret blends of beer, molasses and apple juice, or stock a product cured by an enthusiast; again look out for the names Mooreland, Richard Woodall, plus Heal Farm, Slacks and The Country Victualler. The best hams are produced as part of the natural linkage between pigs and dairy cows; e.g. the pigs for Parma Ham are fed the whey left over from the making of Parmesan Cheese (see Pork).

Ice Cream: names to look out for - Winters Dairy (produced by S.E.Lane in Kent), Loseley from Hampshire and Rocombe Farm from Devon. While not quite in the same league, Marine Ices (qv) also produce good ice cream, supplying a few other shops under the name Manzi.

Irradiation: a method of treating perishable food by radiation, so destroying micro-organisms and extending its shelf life. It prevents the sprouting of potatoes, onions and garlic, and also kills salmonella. Some food, including rice, has been treated in this way in Japan since the 1970's.

 Irradiation plants are expensive to build, and this cost must be born by the consumer. There are also worries about nutritional loss by food treated in this manner; making the products worse in every way except staying power. In our opinion the process is not as worrying as genetic engineering, as the consumer will still have a choice; and untreated food can't be affected (as by the wind-born distribution of corrupted seeds). More research needs doing into any possible carcinogenic implications.

Jam, Preserves and Marmalade: An excellent selection is available, many from small producers. After many hours of tasting Wilkin & Sons

"Tiptree" brand was a clear winner of those widely available. In our opinion it easily outshone it's main rival Bonne Mamam, which is nearly always more expensive, has a lower fruit content and often disappointed in our taste tests. As a nation we are often still guilty in believing imported goods must be better, especially when cleverly marketed. When buying an unknown make, take just a few seconds to look at the ingredients and fruit content; some famous marmalade names in particular might surprise you - a darker colour might seem to indicate quality, but is often simply caramel.

Kippers: The lightest smoking treatment for herrings, developed in Northumberland in the mid 1800's, based on method for smoking salmon, which is called kippering.

Unfortunately as a nation we are still a nation of visual shoppers, so shops are still crammed with bright yellow artificially-dyed smoked fish - we have to use the word "smoked" loosely, for as with bacon, and for the convenience of the producer (certainly not yours) immersing the fish in a smoke flavoured liquid is becoming more common - so it doesn't see any smoke at all. We can say with certainty that the best fish will never be this bright colour, but a less uniform pale gold, which is not so bright and dramatic in appearance.

The best kippers are smoked over oak chips in the Isle of Man, where dying them is illegal (these tend to be small); Craster in Northumberland, some small producers in Scotland plus a few enterprising London fishmongers - Box's of Fulham and Condon's of SW8 spring to mind.

Do you really want to fill your stomach with an unnecessary yellow chemical, however natural it is claimed to be, it's not natural to the fish!

Lardo: a delicious traditional product from Northern Italy; this is preserved fat, cut into sections from the rump of a pig. Good for sweating vegetables when starting a stew (as in Italian soffritto). Try also very-thinly sliced on toast or good bread.

Marron glacés: Chestnuts that have undergone a time consuming process of being repeatedly dipped into vanilla syrup until they have a melting consistency. This tedious procedure puts them in the luxury price bracket.

Meat: shops have only been recommended for meat if their meat comes from known sources, and has passed our inspectors taste tests.

Middle-Eastern groceries: for the purpose of simplicity, we have grouped these countries, spreading east from Turkey to Iran, together.

Mushrooms and Funghi: more varieties than ever are becoming readily available; and although wild mushrooms are seasonal (roughly from the beginning of September to the middle of January in the Northern Hemisphere), suppliers now extend this to include most of the year by importing them from further afield. If you have a choice, always buy mushrooms loose rather than pre-packed, as they lose moisture (and hence weight) quickly when sitting at room temperature.

Apart from familiar cultivated mushrooms, the most common varieties found in our shops are -

Chanterelle (Cantharellus cibarius): sometimes known as Girolle. Now available in up market supermarkets (i.e. Waitrose in the King's Road, SW3) as well as speciality shops. Try adding a few chopped and lightly fried Chanterelles and a glass of red wine next time you make Shepherds Pie for a real treat. They are also delicious in scrambled eggs. Flown in from California and Oregon when supplies are short here.

Cepe (Boletus edulis): The most delicious member of the Boletus family; these are known as Porcini in Italy. Along with Chanterelles and Morels these are the royalty of the mushroom kingdom. Delicious chopped in sauces or fried with olive oil and a little garlic. When out of season here these are often flown in from South Africa. The small packets of dried mushrooms may look expensive, but go a long way when reconstituted by soaking for a few minutes in warm water.

Field Mushrooms (Agaricus campestris): The wild mushroom that spawned the cultivated mushrooms familiar to us all. Excellent flavour, particularly when very fresh. Treat as for cultivated mushrooms: if they are big, peel the thin skin from the top - this can be used for flavour in stocks, but can be tough if left on the mushroom.

Girolle: see Chanterelle.

Horn of Plenty (Craterellus cornucopioides): also known as Trompettes-des-morts: disappointing.

Lion's Mane: attractive looking fungus, seemingly being promoted by Sainsbury, virtually tasteless - don't bother!

Morel (Morchella esculenta): usually only found dried or tinned. If you find them fresh they need very careful rinsing, as the gills can hide lots of grit. Excellent when cooked in cream sauces. They often come from Alaska when not available closer.

Oyster Mushrooms (Pleurotus ostreatus): a mild flavoured mushroom which is found wild in France, but more often than not has been cultivated when found on sale here. Becoming a supermarket standard. Use as ordinary cultivated mushrooms.

Pied-de-Mouton: excellent delicate flavour. Often sourced from Portugal and the U.S.A. Sometimes now found in posh supermarkets.

Puffball (Lycoperdon giganteum): fun for their novelty value - they are quite good thickly sliced, then fried in olive oil with a little garlic. Always use a stainless steel knife when cutting, or the flesh discolours.

Shitake (Lentinus edodes): Originally a wild species from the far-east, but those on sale here are generally cultivated in a similar way to the Oyster Mushroom - they both grow on tree trunks - although they have more flavour. Widely available in supermarkets. Use as you would ordinary mushrooms. If you buy them dried - perhaps from a Chinese outlet - remove and discard the stalk, which becomes tough, before soaking for 20 minutes in warm water.

Truffles (Tuber melanosporum): So far these have proved elusive to cultivate, although it is possible to reproduce "ideal" conditions with a certain success and oak and filbert trees have been inoculated with truffle spores with limited success; they therefore remain very expensive. The tubers grow underground, often under the above-mentioned trees and are "hunted" by trained pigs and dogs. They come in two basic types - black and white. France is the main supplier of the black variety, the very best coming from the Perigord; where they seem to be becoming even more scarce - pollution is blamed! The white are even more expensive and come to us from Italy. Tinned truffles are available, but much flavour is lost in the canning process.

Sometimes tinned truffle peelings can be found; although still pricey they are delicious added to sauté potatoes or scrambled eggs; and a little goes a long way; any leftover can be frozen for another time. Not the same as fresh truffles, but a way of enjoying them at a more affordable price.

A fresh truffle is best stored in the fridge buried in a bowl of Arborio rice (where it will flavour your next risotto), or in a bowl of eggs (again in the fridge) where it will help flavour an omelette.

Mushrooms: Storing: store in a paper bag, if possible in the warmest part of a fridge, but never in plastic, as they tend to sweat and go slimy. For truffles see above.

Mussels: Because of improved refrigeration and cleaning techniques these shellfish are now available barnicle-free throughout the year. Always check that most are alive by giving them a good shake and that most close - if this is not the case buy on another day or find an alternative supplier. Either way always rinse thoroughly in cold water and discard any mussels that refuse to close when tapped.

Mussels; Green-lipped: Widely available in half-shells, these have arrived frozen from New Zealand, so should not be refrozen. They are delicious with garlic butter, sprinkled with a few breadcrumbs, then lightly grilled. A chemical in these mussels appears to be beneficial to arthritis sufferers.

Mustard:
English Mustard: The Wiltshire Tracklement Company make a range of widely found excellent mustards including flavours such as English beer, Spiced Honey and Green Peppercorn; Highfield Preserves of Tiverton make a wide range of interesting flavours and Burnham Hot English Mustard from Tiptree (of jam fame) is also very good. Harvey Nichols in - house mustards are also impressive, and like most of their goods nicely packaged. If making your own mustard at home always allow it to stand for a few minutes after mixing to allow the flavour to develop.

French Mustard: look for Dijon (not Dijon-style) mustard. Additives are strictly controlled by law, grape juice and vinegar are about the only permitted additives.

Nougat: although proper nougat comes from Montélimar in France, many countries have their own excellent versions, and for the purposes of this book we have included the best of these.

Pasta: you wouldn't have thought such a supposedly simple product could vary so enormously. In Italy, as a general rule, pasta is made with flour and eggs in the north and flour and water in the south. In theory all areas use the very hard durum wheat, but Italian labelling is not always as accurate as it might be; a recent BBC survey showed that none of the supermarket "own branded" pastas were 100% durum wheat (although all were clearly marked as such). Anything less than pure durum tends to become sticky when cooked, so cooking it al dente is virtually impossible.

Pasta is like all things, you get what you pay for. Pasta flour is becoming more widely available here, so you can have fun making your own. So called fresh egg pasta (often coming vacuum-packed) can be very disappointing. Stuffed shapes are good from our recommended shops and are worth making at home if you have time. For the less rich, egg-less, southern types De Cecco is a widely available standard while the only recently available Mario & Simon organic pasta and their accompanying Mediterranean sauces (produced by our sponsers) are both good quality and excellent value for money. As mentioned earlier, budget-priced pasta uses poorer quality flour, and seldom excites.

Italian logic has developed basic rules for which pasta shape is suitable for which sauce. Our generally corrupted Bolognese sauce would never be served in it's home town with spaghetti, but with lasagne, or perhaps a shell-shape more able to hold the sauce.

Pasta names vary throughout Italy, for example what is called spaghetti in the middle of Italy, becomes vermicelli in the south and bigoli in Venice.

Interesting shapes, and coloured pasta made from natural ingredients can turn this basic product into a special dish. Try to find a copy of Antonio Carluccio's excellent book " A Passion for Pasta" (BBC Books).

Pesto Sauce: we failed to find any shop-bought pesto to warrant the savings of the few minutes it takes to make your own. Simply combine the following in a food processor; 2 cloves of peeled garlic, 2oz (50g) of pine nuts, 4 tablespoons of grated Pecorino sardo or Parmesan and a good bunch (about 2oz) fresh basil leaves and stems; whiz these up quickly, then with the motor running add $1/2$ pint (300ml) good olive oil. Season with salt and pepper and keep in a jar in the fridge.

Of the bought pesto tested, Harvey Nichols own brand and the new brand of our sponsors Mario & Simon were easily the best, but do cost a little more than their dreary supermarket conterparts. However, they have a long shelf life, so are a good larder standby.

Pork: The best pork is produced in association with a cheese/dairy herd, as each product naturally supports the other as depicted below:

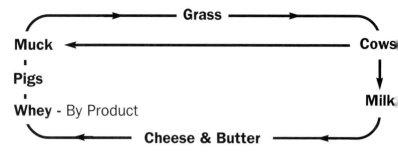

Although after making cheese the whey from about eight cows is needed to feed one pig.

Tenderloin/Fillet is a by-product in the production of bacon; in normal butchery this cut would be visible as the "eye" of a loin chop. Although lacking in flavour like it's beef counterpart, it's an excellent and economical cut for stir fries as it cooks quickly, and there is little waste. Sainsbury, as bacon producers, are a good source.

Potatoes: it makes an enormous difference to use the correct type of potato for the dish in hand. There are two distinct types of potato - floury and waxy, (3 if salad varieties are included); within these types there are more than 400 varieties, less than 50 of which are produced commercially in this country - to visit a country such as Peru is said to be a potato education.

Baking & mashing - both floury and waxy varieties produce good results, but flavour is important, so buy Desiree, Maris Peer, King Edwards, Marfona or Golden Wonder (available early in the year from Scottish sources). Supermarkets promote the adequate Cara, mainly because it suits their purposes, growing in a nice regular shape so it looks good at their point of sale; but this variety generally lacks flavour.

Old potatoes for boiling: either type can be used, as it's a matter of taste whether you prefer floury or waxy potatoes. However, very floury potatoes such as King Edwards can split and disintegrate unless carefully watched. Best floury - Maris Peer and King Edward; best waxy Bintje, Desiree or Nicola (generally from Cyprus or Egypt).

New potatoes for boiling: From the end of April Jersey Royals are available, and after the first week quickly come down in price; however they seem to lose their flavour after the end of June. Nicola's (see above) are also a kidney-shaped potato and when new are also excellent, so are Ulster Sceptre's and the small salad-type potatoes such as Charlotte and Pink Fir Apple.

Chips: Majestics are the chip shops favourite, but this is largely because they absorb less oil than other varieties - so being cheaper to produce. For crisp chips with a soft centre you need floury potatoes such as Maris Pipers or the marvellous King Edward. The most important point in producing good chips is to cook them at two temperatures - the first at about 160C (325F) to cook them; they can then be kept at this stage until needed (even overnight if necessary); to finish they need a blast at 200C (400F) to make them crisp. A few minutes soak in cold water, before frying, removes any excess starch.

Roasting: The best roast potatoes are those in which the edges have "caught" in the oven to produce loose flakes rather than hard edges, so choose floury types such as Arran Chief, Kerrs Pink, King Edward and Maris Piper.

Gratins: floury potatoes will fall to pieces, so choose waxy potatoes such as Wilja, Nicola or Charlottes.

Prawns: if North Atlantic prawns are being advertised as fresh (i.e. having never been frozen) they should have long thin whiskers; when prawns are frozen these become brittle and invariably break off near the head. If buying King Prawns, which will have come from the Pacific or Indian oceans, the best buys for flavour and value are those which have had their heads removed but their tails intact. Buy uncooked if at all possible; the smaller sizes tend to be more tender than more expensive giants; either way they are cooked when they develop their glorious colour, which will take only a couple of minutes - so when stir-frying, they are best added near the end. Do not freeze without inquiring, as they have almost certainly been frozen previously.

Pulses: the soaking time of these can vary enormously, depending on their age. It's worth buying from a shop with a quick turnover.

Red Herrings: The strongest preservation method for these little fish - so highly salted and highly smoked. Fairly rare these days, but worth trying if you find them. Soak for 6-8 hours in cold water, changing this once or twice, then cook as kippers.

Salad Leaves: Gone are the days when the most exciting salad leaves were from a Cos or Webbs Wonder lettuce. While these are still on offer, and can form a good salad basis, being slightly bitter or crisp to suit your mood.

Because of the increased interest in food over recent years, restaurants have encouraged specialist producers to grow delicious varieties and re-introduced varieties that have been popular here in the past. Rocket , which was popular in Victorian times, instantly springs to mind; strangely many regard it as a foreign newcomer - so much so that it is often "smartly" called by it's French name Roquette!

Perhaps the best of these growers is Francis Smith, who operates under the name of Appledore Salads; these are available throughout the year from Mortimer & Bennett and Villandry (q.v's) - perhaps as lettuce-types in the summer, but smaller leaves and herbs are still produced in winter months. A few a these will add flavour to any salad.

Supermarket salad bags often contain some of these interesting leaves with their unusual names, shapes and colours, but their natural flavour is generally in short supply. Of the supermarkets our favourite packaged bags are those of Sainsbury; their "Gourmet Lettuce Selection" includes red chard, red mustard, mizuna, rocket and the padding of lollo biondi; Waitrose and Marks & Spencer also offer a wide range, but other supermarkets seem to lag way lag behind, sometimes with bags of cut leaves oozing brown iron.

Salt Cod; (Bacalhau): Found in Spanish, Portuguese and West Indian shops plus a few up market fishmongers (small pieces are available in Sainsbury); these dried fillets look like a cross between cardboard and a strange type of pumice stone. They need soaking in cold water for 24 hours (or until soft), changing the water several times; the revived fish then makes an easy and delicious dish called Brandade, emanating from south-west France - see recipe page 135, plus numerous dishes from the Iberian peninsula. The fish itself is often not cod, but hake, which when dried is given the mysterious name of stockfish!

Samphire: becoming increasingly available, generally from good fishmongers, this late spring and summer vegetable grows in sea-side salt marshes. Because of this it can be excessively salty for some tastes. The trick is to wash it carefully (removing any roots at the same time) then blanch it in boiling water from 1 minute - discarding this water - before steaming or boiling until tender but still holding it's shape. Serve with melted unsalted butter; delicious!

Sauerkraut: if using tinned sauerkraut, drain before using, squeeze dry, then give it a lift by adding to a pan of a few lightly-fried onions - add a teaspoon of paprika and mix well in. This will improve the dish enormously. Left over cooked meat, poultry or game can also be added to make a delicious light meal.

Sausages: these have improved enormously in the last few years. The specialist sausage shops buy in prime cuts of meat to make these, so there is no question of unsavoury body parts being incorporated as might have been the case in the past. This of course comes at a price, but sausages can now form the basis of a smart meal; while interesting vegetarian varieties mean non-carnivores need not be excluded.

Scallops: Buy scallops straight from the shell if at all possible. If not make sure that they are not soaking in iced water, as this is a fishmongers trick to increase their weight. When scallops treated in this way are cooked they will shrink back to their natural size and exude the extra liquid you have paid good money for!

If you are lucky you may find Queen Scallops - the shells of these have a normal diameter of about 6cm. Just the right size for holding a dollop of garlic butter. Scallops need very little cooking or they become tough.

Smoked Salt: Delicious treat to be used in the same way as celery salt; so very good to liven-up hard boiled eggs and with cruditée. When mixed with a little butter and rubbed into a chicken, it produces a good smoky flavour when the bird is roasted - plus an extra crisp skin.

Smoked Salmon: there are two distinct styles of smoked salmon. A strong cure, favoured by the Scots, Irish and Canadians; and an altogether lighter (so less salty) cure favoured by London producers. This results in a more delicate flavour, that although doesn't produce the same keeping qualities, allows the true flavour of the fish to express itself to a greater degree.

In addition to styles, there is a great difference between smoked salmon made from a wild as opposed to a farmed fish. The latter is naturally a more oily in its natural state (having not burnt off extra fat in pursuing a vigorous and dangerous life like its wild cousin). This is carried forward to produce a moist style of smoked salmon, while a wild fish might seem a little gamy and dry for some modern tastes.

Seek out salmon smoked by H. Forman & Sons (q.v), this is widely available. Donal Box's shop-smoked salmon available from his shop in Wandsworth Bridge Road is also worth a special trip.

Snails: tinned snails are widely available; shells are often charged as an extortionate extra, so after using wash carefully then boil and keep for future use. Boil them again just before reusing. The only shop we have found selling live snails is Andreas Michli (q.v).

Soup: we haven't found a single "fresh" variety we can wholeheartedly recommend; natural ingredients and no preservatives unfortunately are no substitutes for lack of flavour; often, if blindfolded, you would never guess what the main ingredients were meant to be. We haven't given up and will keep searching! Supermarket own-brands (particularly Sainbury) often seem to "out-taste" their more expensive competitors.

Sourdough Bread: risen with a little retained and soured dough from previous batches, perhaps with a very little wild yeast (Conran uses a yeast culture from his own vines). Bread made by this method has a heavier style than bread risen with yeast; but much better keeping qualities.

With this in mind, when making yeast-risen bread at home try using half the recommended quantity of yeast and let it rise over many hours - this will give your own bread much better keeping qualities. An alternative is to make your own sourdough mother by leaving a flour and water dough to ferment at about 27 C (80 F) for 7-8 days; then retaining a little dough from each batch for future use.

Soy Sauce: the big bottles of Soy Sauce on offer at Chinese supermarkets offer excellent value for money, but unlike Japanese soy, they are made by a short-cut method which uses an extract and isn't naturally fermented. Because of this they don't have the same depth of flavour. So pay your money and take your choice. Personally we use the Chinese for stir-fries and Japanese as a condiment - when the difference is more noticed. Chinese mushroom soy sauce makes an interesting change.

Speck: of Austrian originality, this air-dried and smoked pork is very popular in Northern Italy as a cheaper substitute when Parma ham might be called for in a recipe. Slice thinly or cut into small dice when using.

Squab: the French Pigeonneau, which are specially reared young pigeons. Tender but expensive.

Squid: best cooked in one of two distinct methods - grilled very quickly until translucent; or slowly stewed in a sauce - anything in the middle and it will end up being tough and rubbery.

Stock cubes: nowadays indispensable. The trick seems to be to find your favourite (ours is Knorr) then dilute the cube with twice the recommended amount of water (or use half a cube).

If you have time, try sweating equal quantities of chopped onion, leek, carrot and celery (plus a little garlic) in butter before adding the diluted stock cube. Simmer until the vegetables are soft, strain, and you will have something with more character for only a little extra effort.

Taramasalata: the traditional Greek fish "paté" now known and loved by us all. This was originally made with the preserved roe of the grey mullet, but even in Greece is now made with imported smoked cod's roe. We found most of the widely available varieties very disappointing; particularly in flavour (not surprising as some only contained 10% fish and could almost be mistaken for mayonnaise), but also in their extravagant use of unnecessary pink colouring.

Of the shops recommended most made their own, of the others Waitrose's own version stood head and shoulders above the rest.

Tea: a plant in the Camellia family. The British Isles consumes about half of the worlds tea output. Tea is generally named after the area in which it is grown (i.e. Assam, Darjeeling and Ceylon etc.). Like grape vines, tea bushes are much affected by climate and soil types; as a general rule, the higher the altitude at which tea is grown, the more delicate it's flavour becomes; the best Darjeeling (whose price has been forced to astronomical levels, like a rare wine) being grown at an altitude of about 5, 000 feet. As well as it's area of production, tea comes in four main types -

1. **Black:** this is what most of use would regard as a cup of tea. The picked leaves go through a complicated process of fermentation before being dried.
2. **Oolong:** only lightly fermented before drying; tea of this type retains much of it's localised character, so much so that a lifetime could be spent in it's discovery.
3. **Green;** natural dried tea leaves - a light refreshing drink.
4. **Flavoured:** Earl Grey is an example of this style; this can be an invitation for unscrupulous manufacturers to use inferior leaves, the flavour - bergamot, in the case of Earl Grey - is simply sprayed on to black tea leaves. Lapsang Souchong can be included in this category, although it is smoked rather than spray-flavoured.

Most tea is still picked by hand, as only the top few leaves of each branch are picked at any one time. In the best quality tea, these tips can be clearly visible.

Recent research has shown that black tea acts as a anti-carcinogen (the fat in milk is meant to nullify this effect). Contrary to popular belief, tea is high in caffeine; about 80-140 mg per 6oz cup depending on strength, this is about 60% of the levels found in coffee. For a special treat, try single estate varieties from our ★ recommended shops.

Toffee: we have given stars to shops selling toffee from The Toffee Shop in Penrith, which we feel is the best that is widely available.

Traiteur: we have used this word to encompass both food completely ready for the table, and that that might need the minimum of unskilled finishing.

At the cheaper end of the market, both the Marks & Spencer and Tesco's new up market ranges stand out as being widely available and reasonable in both price and quality. At the top end The House of Albert Roux, and more modestly Hand Made Food are excellent.

Trelough Duck: reared by Barry Clark of The Hereford Duck Company (qv) from a Rouen strain, with a high ratio of meat to bone. Their feed includes no antibiotics, chemicals or animal proteins. They take about 14 weeks to mature, hence their high price.

Truffles: see Mushrooms and Funghi.

Turbot: more expensive than it's cousin the brill (q.v) but culinarily interchangeable; the fish produces thicker fillets so a 3⁄ lb fish can feed 6 people. It can be distinguished from brill by bony nobbles scattered on the dark side of it's skin.

Turkey: these were originally domesticated in Mexico and central America, but our modern birds far outclass anything the Pilgrim Fathers would have encountered; as these would have had their proportion of breast meat to body weight at less than 20% (so very skinny). The king of turkeys is the Bronze breed (so called because of the colour of it's feathers) this has good flavour and a breast ratio of approximately 32%. Their source is important however as unscrupulous farmers now breed bronze-feathered birds, which are not the true Bronze strain, most of which come from small producers who feed them a natural diet, and only have free-range birds.

A good family butcher is the answer here - see our index. Producers to look out for are Kelly's Turkey Farm, Copas Brothers, Eastbrook Farm, John Homewood and Munson's.

Vanilla Pods: seemingly rather expensive, but can be used many times. Once used for flavouring your custard or whatever, wash gently in cold water and keep in a sealed container or alternatively buried in a jar of caster sugar (to make vanilla sugar). For vanilla essence, see under essence.

Veal: this has become a taboo meat for many people over the last few years, largely because of the conditions many of the animals are subjected to; both in transportation and in their day-to-day confinement. The incessant demand of restaurants, and the expectation of the public for sheet-white meat, has led to the animals being fed on a diet which denies them any iron; they thus become anaemic.

They are more often than not kept in small crates (making movement, let alone exercise, practically impossible - in this way they they put on weight quickly, so boosting the producers profits).

Holland is the main supplier of calves reared in this way, and at the moment there is no EU legislation in the pipeline to outlaw the practice. Furthermore, when British beef is given the export all-clear, it will be illegal for Britain to unilaterally forbid the export of live veal calves, as this would be considered a restrictive practice.

All the butchers recommended by us sell free-range veal; and it's worth noting that Sainsbury have recently introduced West Country free-range veal escalopes. Do expect them to have a natural pink tinge.

Verjuice: made from the juice of unripe green grapes (or in mediaeval times crab apples if grapes were not available) verjuice used to be popular at this time in Britain, and is still a larder requirement of the housewife in south-west France. It's a marvellous tenderiser when used as a marinade; the strong acid flavour becomes beautifully sweet when cooked. Worth seeking out for the enthusiastic cook. See under Carr Taylor (q.v).

Vietnamese Rice Wrappers: when making spring rolls use these; they are much thinner than their Chinese flour-made counterparts. They have the added advantage that they keep for months in the larder, being simply revived by soaking in warm water for a few seconds.

Yoghurt: see the index for our recommended shops, and if you buy live yoghurt it is easy to make your own by holding a little back then mixing it with good quality milk and then holding at about blood heat for 8-10 hrs, stirring occasionally. This can be done easily in an airing cupboard.

Keep a little back again and repeat the process and you will never have to buy yoghurt again. Fancy machines are completely unnecessary.

York Ham: a traditional method of producing dry-cured ham, where the only additives used are salt and saltpetre. The relatively short maturing time (perhaps ten weeks) produces looser-textured meat than either Parma or Denhay (which takes up to twelve months).

TEN RECOMMENDED COOKERY BOOKS

Alan Davidson; North Atlantic Seafood: excellent book, which both gives descriptions of our native fish, and interesting recipes on how to bring the best out of them. Published by Penguin.

Elizabeth David; French Provincial Cooking: the most versatile of Ms David's many interesting books (all of which should be compulsory reading). A successful restaurant could be run purely from its pages, and it's also an excellent bed-time read. Published by Penguin.

Jane Grigson; Good Things: like Elizabeth David, it is difficult to choose just one book from such an interesting output. But Good Things is such a delight to read, and includes recipes and background information hard to find elsewhere. Published by Penguin.

Ken Hom; Chinese Cookery: our favourite (and possibly the first) from a wide selection. There's nothing too difficult for the enthusiastic novice and ingredients are clearly explained. BBC Books.

Madhur Jaffrey; Indian Cookery: perhaps the best of Ms Jaffrey's many books.

Alaistair Little; Keep it Simple: excellent book with mainly Italian, plus a few Oriental recipes clearly written by one of Britain's top chefs. Conran Octopus.

Readers Digest Cookery Year: almost encyclopaedic, encompassing everything from your Sunday roast to a Victoria sponge.

Nancie McDermott; Real Thai: all the basics of Thai cooking, simply explained.

Claudia Roden; Middle East Cookery: excellent book, good enough for bed-time reading.

Delia Smith; Summer Collection: this good cookery book, with nothing too daunting even for the complete beginner, has deservedly become a best seller. Well illustrated. Published by BBC Books.

Yan-Kit's; Classic Chinese Cookbook: readers are shown illustrated step-by-step techniques in this excellent book by Yan-Kit So. Recipes range from Singapore noodles to Peking duck, and include many for vegetarians.

Not in the same league as the above, but a useful little book none the less is **Simon Scrutton's; Foolproof Entertaining:** giving simple, sometimes unusual, bistro-type recipes designed for the working cook.

The dishes are designed to be finished off in a few minutes, after earlier mise-en-place (preparation) has taken place at a more convenient time. Published by Cheyne Publications, so we are a little biased. If you find this difficult to obtain, it's available by mail order from:
Simon Scrutton, 1 Willoughby Mews, London SW4 OQH.
Send £6.95 to include postage. Please make payment to: Simon Scrutton.

Location	ESTABLISHMENT	Ref. No	Bread	Afro Caribbean	Chinese & Far Eastern	Cheese	Coffee	Chocolate	Tea	Delicatessen	Fruit & Veg	Fish	Eastern European	Greek	Health	Indian Sub Continent	Japanese	Meat	Middle East	Pâtisserie	Sausages	Spanish & Portuguese	Traiteur	Open on Bank Holidays	Open Late	Open Sunday
BR1	Cope's of Bromley	110										●*														
BR5	Importers	220					●*		●*																	
	James's Cheese Shop	224				●																				
	Le Parc Français	330								●														●		●
	Villagers	443																			●					
CR6	Sainsbury	378			●		●		●	●	●*								●		●				●	●	●
	Wing Yip	455			●*																						●
E1	Eastern Grocers	146															●*										
	Hussey's	218																	●								
	Rogg's	370								●																	●
	Safeway	377			●	●	●		●	●	●								●						●	●	●
	Sainsbury	378			●	●	●		●	●	●*								●						●	●	●
	Spitalfields Organic Market	408	●							●	●								●								●
	Stepping Stones Farm	413								eggs																	
E2	Bethnal Green Road Market	47																									
	Friends Foods	172	●								●					●											
	Paris & Rios	329			●		●		●	●	●	●							●				●	●	●	●	●
	Tesco	450			●		●		●	●	●*								●						●	●	●
I3	Safeway	377			●		●		●	●	●								●						●	●	●
	Tesco	430	●		●		●		●	●	●*								●						●	●	●
E4	Sainsbury	378			●		●		●	●	●*								●						●	●	●
F6	Sainsbury	378			●		●		●	●	●*								●						●	●	●

Location	ESTABLISHMENT	Ref. No	Afro Caribbean	Bread	Chinese & Far Eastern	Cheese	Coffee	Chocolate	Tea	Delicatessen	Fruit & Veg	Fish	Eastern European	Greek	Health	Indian Sub Continent	Japanese	Meat	Middle East	Pâtisserie	Sausages	Spanish & Portuguese	Traiteur	Open on Bank holidays	Open late	Open Sunday
E8	Ridley Road Market	367									•					•		•	•							
E4	Sainsbury	378				•	•		•	•	• *							•						•	•	•
	Turkish Food Centre	435																	•					•	•	•
E9	H. Forman	160										•														
	Hoo Hing	216			• *																			•	•	•
	Tesco	430		•	•	•	•		•	•	• *							•						•	•	•
E10	Tesco	430		•	•	•	•		•	•	• *							•						•	•	•
E13	Tesco	430		•	•	•	•		•	•	• *							•						•	•	•
E14	Billingsgate Market	54										•														
	Chrisp Street Market	99								•	•															
	Tesco	430				•	•		•	•	• *							• *						•	•	•
E15	Kelsey Quality Butcher	237																	•								
	Sainsbury	378			•	•	•		•	•	• *							•						•	•	•
E17	Poston's	348																				•					
	Sainsbury	378		•	•	•	•		•	•	• *							•						•	•	•
	Tesco	430			•	•	•			•	•	•						•						•	•	•
	Walthamstow Market	448								•	•	• *	•				•		•	•							
E18	Sainsbury	378		•	•	•	•		•	•	• *							•						•	•	•
EC1	Bliss	56																			•						
	Freshlands Wholefoods	171		•						• (eggs)					•									•			
	G. Gazzano	182		•						•														•	•		•
	Limoncello	251				•				• *													• *			

Location	ESTABLISHMENT	Ref. No	Afro Caribbean	Bread	Chinese & Far Eastern	Cheese	Coffee	Chocolate	Tea	Delicatessen	Fruit & Veg	Fish	Eastern European	Greek	Health	Indian Sub Continent	Japanese	Meat	Middle East	Patisserie	Sausages	Spanish & Portugese	Traiteur	Open on Bank Holidays	Open Late	Open Sunday
EC1	Meat City	284																*								
	Safeway	377		●		●			●	●	●								●						●	●	●
	Simply Sausages	397																				*					
	Smithfield Market	400																	*								
	L. Terroni & Sons	429				●	●		●	*																	●
	Whittard	451					●																				●
EC2	International Cheese Centre	221				*																					
	Leonidas	247						*																			
	Tesco	430		●		●	●		●	●	*								●						●	●	●
	Whittard	451					●		*																		
EC3	R.S. Ashby	24																	*					●			
	Ashdown	25											*														
	Butcher & Edmonds	72																	*								
	Charbonnel & Walker	88						*																			
	Godiva	188						*																			
	H.S. Linwood	254					●						*														
	Whittard	451							*																		
EC4	L. Booth of St. Paul's	59									●	●															
	Leonidas	247						*																			
	Porterford	344					●												*								
	Whittard	451							*																		
HA0	Big Market Retail	53				●					●	●													●	●	●

Location	ESTABLISHMENT	Ref. No	Afro Caribbean	Bread	Chinese & Far Eastern	Cheese	Coffee	Chocolate	Tea	Delicatessen	Fruit & Veg	Fish	Eastern European	Greek	Health	Indian Sub Continent	Japanese	Meat	Middle East	Patisserie	Sausages	Spanish & Portuguese	Traiteur	Open on Bank Holidays	Open Late	Open Sunday
HA0	VB & Sons	430													●									●		●
	Wembley Exotics	450									●*							●*						●	●	●
NF2	R.A. Bevan	48																								
	Fratelli	166								●													●			
	Jarvis & Sons	226										●*														
	Jefferies	228																								
	Miura Foods	294															●*	●								
N1	Amalfi	10								●													●			
	Barstow & Barr	41				●*						●*												●	●	●
	Cecil & Co.	84										●*														
	Chapel Market	87									●															
	Dugan's Chocolates	143						●*																		
	James Elliott	151								●								●								
	Gallo Nero Delicatessen	177				●				●																
	Steve Hatt	206										●*														
	Monte's	297				●				●																●
	Nadell Patisserie	305																	●*							
	Olga Stores	321								●													●			
	Sainsbury	378			●	●	●		●	●	●*							●						●	●	●
	Sapanora	387								●														●	●	●
	Seafood Australia	389										●*														
N2	Amici Delicatessen	14								●																

Location	ESTABLISHMENT	Ref. No	Afro Caribbean	Bread	Chinese & Far Eastern	Cheese	Coffee	Chocolate	Tea	Delicatessen	Fruit & Veg	Fish	Eastern European	Greek	Health	Indian Sub Continent	Japanese	Meat	Middle East	Patisserie	Sausages	Spanish & Portuguese	Traiteur	Open on Bank holidays	Open Late	Open Sunday
	Chorak	97		●																●						
	Graham's	193																●*								●
	A. Scott	388										●*														●
N3	Marlene's Bakery & Delicatessen	278		●*																				●		●
	Oz Fish & Prawn Bar	325								●*		●*												●		●
	Tesco	430		●	●	●			●	●		●						●						●	●	●
N4	Andreas	16																		●			●	●	●	●
	Antepliler	18		●																					●	●
	France Fresh Fish	164										●*														
	Andreas Michli & Son	289								●				●*												
	Sainsbury	378			●	●	●		●	●	●*							●						●	●	●
	Stroud Green Road	415								●	●															
	Tesco	430		●	●	●	●		●	●	●*					●		●	●					●	●	●
	Yasar Halim	457		●															●	●				●	●	
N5	Da Rocco	126																					●			
	La Fromagerie	173				●*				●																●
	Frank Godfrey	187																●*								
N6	Highgate Butchers	212																●*								
N7	Bumblebee	69				●				●					●*								●			
	L'Europa	154								●																
	Fresco Fish	169										●*														
	Gibber of Holloway	185									●															

Location	ESTABLISHMENT	Ref. No.	Afro Caribbean	bread	Chinese & Far Eastern	Cheese	Coffee	Chocolate	Tea	Delicatessen	Fruit & Veg	Fish	Eastern European	Greek	Health	Indian Sub Continent	Japanese	Meat	Middle East	Patisserie	Sausages	Spanish & Portuguese	Traiteur	Open on bank holidays	Open Late	Open Sunday
N7	Safeway	377			●		●		●	●	●	●						●						●	●	●
	Salvino	384								●												●		●		●
	Seven Sisters Greengrocers	395									●														●	●
	Waitrose	447		●	●	●	●		●	●	●*							●						●	●	●
N8	Bunces	70		●						●												●				●
	Dunn's	144		●																						
	Freeman's Butchers	168																●*								
	Haelan Centre	197												●*											●	●
	Walter Purkis	353										●*														
	Queen of Tarts	355		●																●				●		●
	Stella's Bakery	411		●																●				●		●
N9	Tesco	430		●	●	●	●		●	●	●*							●						●	●	●
N10	Cheeses	92				●																				
	W. Martyn	280					●*		●*																	
	Mauro's	282																					●			●
	Midhurst Butchers	290																●*								
	Papillon Patisserie	328		●																	●					
	Walter Purkis & Sons	353										●*														
	Sainsbury	378			●	●			●	●	●*								●					●	●	●
	St. James' Delicatessen	379								●																●
	Victoria Health Foods	440								Eggs				●											●	
N12	Atari Ya	27									●					●						●				●

Location	ESTABLISHMENT	Ref. No.	Afro Caribbean	Bread	Chinese & Far Eastern	Cheese	Coffee	Chocolate	Tea	Delicatessen	Fruit & Veg	Fish	Eastern European	Greek	Health	Indian Sub / Continental / Japanese	Meat	Middle East	Patisserie	Sausages	Spanish & portuguese	Traiteur	Open on Bank Holidays	Open Late	Open Sunday
N12	Lina's Italian Delicatessen	252					●			●															●
	Natural Health	306								Eggs					●										
	Sainsbury	378		●	●	●			●	●	●*						●						●	●	●
	Tesco	430		●	●	●			●	●	●*						●						●	●	●
	Waitrose	447			●	●			●	●	●						●						●	●	●
N13	Safeway	377			●	●			●	●	●*						●						●	●	●
	Tesco	430		●	●	●			●	●	●						●						●	●	●
N15	Tesco	430		●	●	●			●	●	●*						●						●	●	●
N16	Aziz Baba Pastahanesi	31																●	●			●	●	●	●
	The Cooler	109								●															
	The Fish Centre	159										●													●
	Gallo Nero Delicatessen	177				●				●															
	Manor Farm Bakery	272		●																					
	Safeway	377			●				●	●	●						●						●	●	●
N17	Loon Fung Hong Cash & Carry	259			●*					●															
	Sainsbury	378			●	●			●	●	●*						●						●	●	●
N18	Safeway	377		●	●				●	●	●						●						●	●	●
	Tesco	430			●	●			●		●*						●						●	●	●
N20	Natural Health	306								Eggs					●										
	Waitrose	447		●	●	●				●	●*						●						●	●	●
N21	Sainsbury	378			●	●				●	●*						●						●	●	●
N21	Tesco	430		●	●	●				●	●*						●						●	●	●

Location	ESTABLISHMENT	Ref. No.	Afro Caribbean	Bread	Chinese & Far Eastern	Cheese	Coffee	Chocolate	Tea	Delicatessen	Fruit & Veg	Fish	Eastern European	Greek	Health	Indian Sub Continent	Japanese	Meat	Middle East	Patisserie	Sausages	Spanish & Portugese	Traiteur	Open on bank Holidays	Open Late	Over Sunday
N22	Safeway	377			•				•	•	•							•						•		•
	Sainsbury	378			•	•	•		•	•	*							•						•	•	•
NW1	Austrian Sausage Centre	30																			•					
	Camden Coffee Shop	76					*																			
	Inverness Street Market	222									•															
	Lou's Bakery	260		•																						
	Off Licence	319			•					eggs														•	•	•
	Safeway	377			•	•	•		•	•	•							•						•	•	•
	Sainsbury	378			•	•	•		•	•	*							•						•	•	•
	Savera Bakery	386		•						•																
	Sesame Health Foods	394								•					*									•	•	•
	The Spice Shop	406								•						•								•	•	•
NW2	Bifulco	51																		•						
	Safeway	377			•	•	•		•	•	•							•						•	•	•
	Enzo Tartarelli	423								•								•						•		
	Tesco	430		•	•	•	•		•	•	*							•						•	•	•
	Wing Yip	435			*													•								
NW3	Barretts	38																•								
	Belsize Village Delicatessen	64				•				•													•			•
	Crescent Fruiterers	118									•															•
	The Delicatessen Shop	133								•																
	Giacobazzi's Delicatessen	184								•													•			

Location	ESTABLISHMENT	Ref. No	Afro Caribbean	Bread	Chinese & Far Eastern	Cheese	Coffee	Chocolate	Tea	Delicatessen	Fruit & Veg	Fish	Eastern European	Greek	Health	Indian Sub Continent	Japanese	Meat	Middle East	Patisserie	Sausages	Spanish & Portuguese	Traiteur	Open on Bank Holidays	Open Late	Open Sunday
NW3	M & D Grodzinski	195		•														•						•	•	
	Hampstead Butchers	200																•								
	Hampstead Seafoods	201										•														
	Brian Lay-Jones	246									•															
	Lessiter's	248						•																		
	Louis Patisserie	261																		•				•	•	•
	Maison Blanc	268		*																*				•	•	•
	Marine Ices	274								Ice Cream														•	•
	The Pasta Place	352								•												•			•
	Peppercorn's	358													•										
	La Provencal	352								*•															
	Rosslyn Delicatessen	372			•					*•									•				•	•	•
	Rumbold's	376		•																						
	Sainsbury	378			•	•	•		•	•	*•							•		•					•	•
	J.A. Steele	410																•								
	Super Homa & Patisserie	418																	•	•				•		•
	Waitrose	447		•	•	•	•		•	•	*•							•						•	•	
	Whittard	451							*•																	•
NW4	Hendon Bagel Bakery	209		•																•				•	•	
	Tesco	450		•	•	•	•		•	•	•	*•						•						•	•	•
	Waitrose	447		•	•	•	•		•	•	•	*•						•						•	•	•
	Whittard	451							*•																	•

Location	ESTABLISHMENT	Ref No	Afro Caribbean	Bread	Chinese & Far Eastern	Cheese	Coffee	Chocolate	Tea	Delicatessen	Fruit & Veg	Fish	Eastern European	Greek	Health	Indian Sub continent	Japanese	Meat	Middle East	Patisserie	Sausages Spanish & Portuguese	Traiteur	Open on Bank Holidays	Open Late	Open Sunday
NW5	B & M Fisheries	37										•						•							
	Dillo's	138								Eggs													•		•
	Fish & Fowl	158										•						•							
NW6	Ackerman's	5						•*																	
	B & J Fisheries	36										•													•
	David's Foodstore	127								Eggs															
	Kilburn Market	240									•														
	Olive Tree	322								Eggs					•										
	Peppercorn's	339													•										
	Safeway	377			•	•			•	•	•							•					•	•	•
	Sainsbury	378			•	•	•		•	•	•*							•*					•	•	•
NW7	Cooksley's Butcher	107								•								•					•	•	
NW8	Ambra	13								•															
	Brown's	66										•*													
	Church Street Market	101									•														
	Le Connaisseur	106																		•			•		•
	Kent & Sons	239																•*							
NW8	Leonidas	247						•																	
	Panzer Delicatessen	327		•	•	•			•	•	•							•					•	•	•
	Tesco	450		•	•	•	•		•	•	•*							•					•	•	•
NW9	Safeway	377			•				•	•	•							•					•		•
	Sainsbury	378			•	•	•		•	•	•*							•					•		•

Location	ESTABLISHMENT	Ref No	Afro Caribbean	Bread	Chinese & Far Eastern	Cheese	Coffee	Chocolate	Tea	Delicatessen	Fruit & Veg	Fish	Eastern European	Greek	Health	Indian Sub Continent	Japanese	Meat	Middle East pâtisserie	Sausages Spanish & portugese	Traiteur	Open on Bank Holidays	Open Late	Open Sunday
NW9	VB & Sons	459										●				*						●		●
	Yoahan S/Mkt & Food Court	458			*						●	●					*	●				●	●	●
NW 10	B & J Fisheries	46										●												●
	Hoo Hing	216			*																			
	Tesco	430		●	●	●	●		●	●	*	●						●				●	●	●
NW 11	Carmelli Bakeries	79		●																		●	●	●
	J.A. Corney	114										●												●
	Daniel Bagel Bakery	125																				●	●	●
	M & D Grodinski	195		●																		●		●
	Importers	220					*		*															
	Maysun Market	283			●																		●	
	Menachem's	287									●													
	Platters Delicatessen	343		●						●											●		●
	Raj Superstore	359															*			●			●	●
	Sainsbury	378				●	●		●	●	*								●				●	●	●
	Sam Stoller	414										●												●	●
	Temple Health Foods	428									Eggs					●								
	Waitrose	447		●		●			●	●	*								●				●		●
SE1	Aberdeen Sea Products	1										*												
	Borough Market	60											●												
	Butlers Wharf Gastrodome	74		*							*		●										●	●	●
	Konditor & Cook	243		*																*			●	●	●

Location	ESTABLISHMENT	Ref. No	Afro Caribbean	Bread	Chinese & Far Eastern	Cheese	Coffee	Chocolate	Tea	Delicatessen	Fruit & Veg	Fish	Eastern European	Greek	Health	Indian Sub Continent	Japanese	Meat	Middle East	Patisserie	Sausages	Spanish & Portuguese	Traiteur	Open on bank holidays	Open Late	Open Sunday
SE1	Livebait – The Fish Shop	257										*														
	Neal's Yard Dairy	309				●*	●		●	●	*							●						●	●	●
	Tesco	430			●	●			●	●	●							●						●	●	●
SE3	Apple'n Orange	19									●															
	Hand Made Food	202								●													*			
	L & W Marshall	279										●														
	Safeway	377							●	●	●							●						●	●	●
	G.G. Sparkes	404			●													●*								
	Village Bakery	441		●																						
SE5	Paul's	335		●											●											
	Safeway	377		●	●	●	●		●	●	●							●*						●	●	●
SE6	Sweetland & Howard	420		●																	●					
	Tesco	430		●	●	●			●	●	●*							●						●	●	●
SE8	Deptford Codfather	154										●														
	Deptford High Street Market	135									●															
SE9	Sainsbury	378			●	●	●		●		●*							●	●					●	●	●
SE10	The Cheeseboard	91				●*																				
	Dring Brothers	141																●								
	O'Hagan's Sausage Shop	523																			●*					
	La Salumeria	381																									
	See Woo Hong Supermarket	592			●*																				●	●	●
SE11	Max Angle	17										*															●

Location	ESTABLISHMENT	Ref. No	Afro Caribbean	Bread	Chinese & Far Eastern	Cheese	Coffee	Chocolate	Tea	Delicatessen	Fruit & Veg	Fish	Eastern European	Greek	Health	Indian Sub Continent	Japanese	Meat	Middle East	Patisserie	Sausages	Spanish & Portuguese	Traiteur	Open on Bank Holidays	Open on Bank Holidays	Open Late	Open Sunday
SE1	M. Moen & Sons	295																*									
SE12	Sainsbury	378			●	●	●		●	●	*							●						●	●	●	●
SE13	Gennaro Delicatessen	183								●																	
	Lewisham Market	249									●	●						●									
	Sainsbury	378			●	●			●	●	*							●						●	●	●	●
	Tesco	430		●	●	●			●	●	*													●	●	●	●
	Turkish Food Centre	435																	●					●	●	●	
SE14	Sainsbury	378			●	●			●	●	*							●									●
SE15	Choumbert & Rye Lane Market	98									●	●															
	Kennedy's	238																		●							
	Safeway	377			●	●			●	●	●							●						●	●	●	●
	Southbank Fresh Fish	402										*															
SE17	East Street Market	147									●																
	Safeway	377			●	●	●		●	●	*							●						●	●	●	●
	Tesco	430		●	●	●	●		●	●	*							●						●	●	●	●
SE18	Sainsbury	378			●					●	*							●						●	●	●	●
	Woolwich Market	456									●	●						●									
SE19	La Gastronoma	180								●																	
SE22	Andreas	15												*												●	●
	The Cheese Block	90				*																					●
	Sainsbury	378			●	●	●		●	●	*							●						●	●	●	●
SE23	Sainsbury	378			●	●	●		●	●	*							●						●	●	●	●

ESTABLISHMENT	Location	Ref. No	Afro Caribbean	Bread	Chinese & Far Eastern	Cheese	Coffee	Chocolate	Tea	Delicatessen	Fruit & Veg	Fish	Eastern European	Greek	Health	Indian Sub Continent	Japanese	Meat	Middle East	Patisserie	Sausages	Spanish & Portuguese	Traiteur	Open on bank holidays	Open Late	Open Sunday
La Gastronoma	SE24	180								•																
Safeways	SE25	377			•				•	•	•							•						•	•	•
Sainsbury		378			•		•		•	•	*							•						•	•	•
Ada's	SE26	5								Ice Cream															•	•
Safeways		377			•				•	•	•							•								
Gunn's	SE27	196			•					•	•							•								
Safeways	SE28	577			•				•	•	•							•						•	•	•
Charles	SW1	89										•														
The Chocolate Society		96						*•																		
Ciaccio		102																				•				
Da Baere		128	*•																	*				•	•	•
Drone's the Grocer		142				•				• Eggs		•												•	•	•
Eaton's Continental		148								•														•	•	•
Gastronomia Italia		181				•				•																
Godiva		188			•		*•	*•		•								•								
Harrods		203				*	*	*•	*	•	•	*						*•	*•	*						
Harts (Victoria) Ltd		204								*								•								
Harvey Nichols		205				*	*	•	*	*•	•	*				•	*•	•	•						•	•
The House of Albert Roux		217								*•	•							*						•		•
International Cheese Centre		221				*•																				
Jeroboams		231				*•																				
Leonidas		247						*•																		

Location	ESTABLISHMENT	Ref No	Afro Caribbean	Bread	Chinese & Far Eastern	Cheese	Coffee	Chocolate	Tea	Delicatessen	Fruit & Veg	Fish	Eastern European	Greek	Health	Indian Sub Continent	Japanese	Meat	Middle East	Patisserie	Sausages	Spanish & Portuguese	Traiteur	Open on Bank Holidays	Open Late	Open Sunday
SW1	Partridges	331				●				●														●		●
	Paxton & Whitfield	336				●*																				
	Rippon Cheese Stores	368				●*																				
	Sainsbury	378			●	●	●	●	●	●*	●*	●						●						●	●	●
	Sea Harvest Fisheries	390										●														
	Simply Sausages	397																			●*					
	Strutton Ground Market	416	●																							
	Tachbrook Street Market	421								●	●															
	Tesco	430		●	●	●	●	●		●	●*	●						●						●	●	●
	Whittard	451					●	●	●*																	●
SW2	Roticceria Roma	373								●													●			
	Tesco	430		●	●	●	●	●	●	●	●*	●						●						●	●	●
SW3	Jane Asher	26																								
	Baker & Spice	33		●*																●*						●
	Beverley Hills Bakery	40		●																●						
	Bibendum Crustacea	50									●															
	Bluebird Gastrodrome	57		●*		●*	●*	●*	●*	●*	●*	●*						●*		●*				●	●	●
	B's	67									●															
	The Chelsea Fishery	91										●														
	Finn's of Chelsea Green	157								●													●			
	Fry's of Chelsea	174									●															
SW5	Maison Blanc	268		●*																			●*			

Location	ESTABLISHMENT	Ref. No	Afro Caribbean	Bread	Chinese & Far Eastern	Cheese	Coffee	Chocolate	Tea	Delicatessen	Fruit & Veg	Fish	Eastern European	Greek	Health	Indian Sub Continent	Japanese	Meat	Middle East	Patisserie	Sausages	Spanish & Portuguese	Traiteur	Open on bank holidays	Open Late	Open Sunday
SW3	La Marée	273						•				•														•
	Marks & Spencer	275		•		•	•			•	*								•					*		•
	Patisserie Valerie	354		•																	*				•	•
	La Picena	341								•												•				
	Rococo	369						*																*		•
	Rotisserie Jules	374																							•		•
	Safeway	377			•	•	•		•	•	•								•						•	•
	Waitrose	447			•	•	•		•	•	*								•					•	•	•
	Whittard	651			•		•		*																	•
SW4	Devonia	136								•																
	M & S Fruits	270									•															
	Moen & Sons	295																	*							
	Pamela Price	349								•	*															
	Sainsbury	378			•	•	•		•		*								•					•	•	•
	Today's Living Health Foods	632								Eggs					•										•	
SW5	Manilla Supermarket	271			*																					•
SW6	Amandine	11		•															•						•	•
	Box's of Fulham	61										*														•
	The Catch	82										•														
	Cope's Seafood Co.	111										*														
	Eaton's Delicatessen	149								•																
	F.C. Jones	233									•															

Location	ESTABLISHMENT	Ref. No	Afro Caribbean	Bread	Chinese & Far Eastern	Cheese	Coffee	Chocolate	Tea	Delicatessen	Fruit & Veg	Fish	Eastern European	Greek	Health	Indian Sub Continent	Japanese	Meat	Middle East	Patisserie	Sausages	Spanish & Portuguese	Traiteur	Open on Bank Holidays	Open Late	Open Sunday
	A.A. & E. King	261		•						•								•								
	Moore Park Delicatessen	298								•																
	North End Road Market	317									•															
	Randalls	361										•						•*								
	Safeway	377			•				•	•	•													•	•	•
	Sainsbury	378			•	•	•		•	•	•*												•	•	•
	Salumeria Estense	382								•*													•*			
SW7																										
	Bagatelle	32		•*						•*													•*			
	Bute Street Boucherie	73																•*								
	De Baere	128		•*						•										•*				•	•	•
	Fileric	156		•																•				•	•	•
	Jeroboams	231				•*				•																
	Sainsbury	378			•	•	•		•	•	•*							•						•	•	•
SW8																										
	Condon Fishmongers	105										•*													•	
	Di Lieto	157		•																						•	
	Hyams & Cockerton	219									•															•	
	New Covent Garden	311									•*															•	
	Sainsbury	378			•	•	•		•	•	•*							•						•	•	•
	Taste of the Wild	424									•*																
SW9																										
	A & C Continental	2								•																
	Brixton Market	62	•*																								
	Brixton Wholefoods	63		•											•*			•									

Location	Establishment	Ref. No	Bread	Afro Caribbean	Cheese	Chinese & Far Eastern	Coffee	Chocolate	Tea	Delicatessen	Fruit & Veg	Fish	Eastern European	Greek	Health	Indian Sub-Continent	Japanese	Meat	Middle East	Patisserie	Sausages	Spanish & Portugese	Traiteur	Open on bank holidays	Open Late	Open Sunday
	Funchal Patisserie	176	●																	●						●
	Granville Arcade	194		●*							●*										●					
	Just Fresh	236																●								
	L. S. Mash & Sons	281										●*														
	The Original Fisherman	324										●*														
	Piacenza Delicatessen	340			●					●													●			●
SW10	Chelsea Catering Company	93																					●			●
	City Meats	105																●*								
	Currick	120																●								
	The Italian Fruit Company	223										●*														
	Luigi's	262								●*													●	●	●	
SW11	Battersea Market	42										●														
	R. F. Cutting	121								Eggs								●								
	Dove & Son	140																●*								
	The Hive	214								Honey ●*																
	Hamish Johnson	235			●*			●*		●*																
	Lyons Fisheries	263											●													
	Mise-en-Place	292	●		●*					●*	●												●	●	●	●
	Northcote Road Market	316									●	●														
	Rae-Ra-El Bakery	357	●																							
	Salumeria Napoli	383								●																
	Wainwright & Neill	446								●																●

Location	ESTABLISHMENT	Ref. No	Afro Caribbean	Bread	Chinese & Far Eastern	Cheese	Coffee	Chocolate	Tea	Delicatessen	Fruit & Veg	Fish	Eastern European / Greek	Health	Indian Sub Continent / Japanese	Meat	Middle East	Patisserie	Sausages	Spanish & Portugese / Traiteur	Open on Bank Holidays	Open Late	Open Sunday
SW12	Balham Market	34	•								•												
	Balham Wholefood	35								Eggs				•									
	Bon Vivant Delicatessen	58				*				*										•			
	Hildreth Street Market	213	•								•					•							
	Safeway	377			•				•	•	•					•					•	•	•
	Sainsbury	378			•	•	•		•	•	*					•					•	•	•
SW13	Alexander & Knight	6										•											
	Arkwright's	23																	*				
	The Real Cheese Shop	362				*																	
	J. Seal	391														*			•				
	Sonny's Food Shop	401								•													
	Tesco	430		•		•			•	•	*										•	•	•
	Two Peas in a Pod	437								•	*											•	•
SW14	Ceres Wholefoods	85								Eggs				•									
	Safeway	377			•	•			•	•	•					•					•		•
	Sandrine	385						*															
	Valentina	438								•													
	Waitrose	447		•	•	•	•		•	•	*					•					•	•	•
SW15	Giuliano	186								•													
	Health & Diet Centre	208								Eggs				•									
	Putney Health Foods	354								Eggs				•								•	•
	Sainsbury	378			•	•			•	•	*					•					•		•

Location	ESTABLISHMENT	Ref No	Afro Caribbean	Bread	Chinese & Far Eastern	Cheese	Coffee	Chocolate	Tea	Delicatessen	Fruit & Veg	Fish	Eastern European	Greek	Health	Indian Sub Continent	Japanese	Meat	Middle East	Patisserie	Sausages	Spanish & Portuguese	Traiteur	Open on bank holidays	Open Late	Open Sunday
SW15	St Marcus Fine Foods	380								•								•			*			•		•
	Talad Thai	422			*																			•		•
	Waitrose	447		•	•	•	•		•	•	*							•						•	•	•
	Whittard	451					•	•	*															•		•
SW16	Chuanglee Oriental Supermarket	100			*																					•
	Korona Delicatessen	244								•			•											•		•
	Safeway	377			•					•	•	•							•					•	•	•
	Sainsbury	378			•	•	•		•	•	*							•					•	•	•
SW17	Broadway Market	64								•	•														•
	Coppin Brothers	112													*										
	Dadu's Cash & Carry	122												*	*							•		•
	Deepak Cash & Carry	130												*	*							•		•
	Everfresh	155									*											•		•
	Fox's of Wandsworth	162								•														•
	Mehta Fruit & Vegetables	286									*													•
	Nature Fresh	307									*											•		•
	Panadam Delicatessen	326		•						•														•
	Patel Brothers	333												*								•		•
	Rainbow	358															•							•
	Tooting Market	434				•				•	•	•						•						•
SW18	Brotherhoods	65																						•
	S. A. Elliott	152															Closed							

Location	ESTABLISHMENT	Ref. No	Afro Caribbean	Bread	Chinese & Far Eastern	Cheese	Coffee	Chocolate	Tea	Delicatessen	Fruit & Veg	Fish	Eastern European	Greek	Health	Indian Sub Continent	Japanese	Meat	Middle East	Patisserie	Sausages	Spanish & portugese	Traiteur	Open on Bank Holidays	Open Late	Open Sunday
SW18	Sainsbury	378			•	•	•		•	•	*							•						•	•	•
	Southfield Fruiterers	403									•													•	•	•
	Tesco	430		•	•	•	•		•	•	*							•						•	•	•
SW19	Robert Edwards	150																•								
	W. A. Gardner	179																•								
	Gitliano	186								•							•									
	Jones Delicatessen	234				•				•														•		•
	Roots	371									•													•		•
	Safeway	377			•				•		•							•								•
	Sainsbury	378			•	•			•		*													•		•
TW1	Sandrine	385					•	*																•	•	•
TW9	Maison Blanc	268		*															*					•	•	•
	Wang Thai Market	449			*																			•		•
TW10	Vivian's	445		•		*	•			*													•	•		•
TW11	The Teddington Cheese	426				*																		•		•
UV1	Best Fruit Fare	46									*													•		
	Dokal	159												*										•		•
	Rana Brothers	360									*													•		•
	Stra Cash & Carry	398												*										•	•	•
W1	Algerian Coffee Stores	7					*																	•	•	•
	Allen & Co	8																*								

Location	ESTABLISHMENT	Ref. No	Afro Caribbean	bread	Chinese & Far Eastern	Cheese	Coffee	Chocolate	Tea	Delicatessen	Fruit & Veg	fish	Eastern European	Greek	Health	Indian Sub Continent	Japanese	Meat	Middle East	Patisserie	Sausages	Spanish & Portuguese	Traiteur	Open on bank holidays	Open Late	Open Sunday
W1	Alwadi Alakhdar	9																	*						●	●
	Amato	12		●																●				●		●
	Arigato	22															●						●		●	●
	Berwick Street Market	45									*	●									*					
	Biggles	52																			*					
	Blagden Fishmongers	55										*														
	Café Mezzo	75		*																*				●	●	●
	I. Camisa	77				●				*																
	Caviar Kaspia	83										Caviar *														
	Charbonnel & Walker	88						*																●		
	De Gustibus	131		*																						
	Fortnum & Mason	161				*		●	*	*																
	Fratelli Camisa	165								*													●			
	Godiva	188						*																		
	H.R. Higgins	211					*																			
	International Cheese Centre	221				*																				
	Japan Centre	225															*							●		●
	Java Java	227					*																	●	●	
	James Knight of Mayfair	242										*														
	Leonidas	247						●																		
	Lessiter's	248						*																		
	Lina Stores	253								*																

Location	ESTABLISHMENT	Ref. No	Afro Caribbean	Bread	Chinese & Far Eastern	Cheese	Coffee	Chocolate	Tea	Delicatessen	Fruit & Veg	Fish	Eastern European	Greek	Health	Indian Sub Continent	Japanese	Meat	Middle East	Patisserie	Sausages	Spanish & Portuguese	Traiteur	Open on bank Holidays	Open Late	Open Sunday
W1	Loon Fung Supermarket	259			*																			●	●	●
	La Madeleine	266		●																●					●	●
	Maison Bertaux	267		●																*				●	●	●
	Marks & Spencer	275		●		●	●			●	*	●						●					*	●	●	●
	New Loon Supermarket	312			*																			●	●	●
	Patisserie Valerie	334		●																*				●	●	●
	Products From Spain	351																			●					
	Richard's	365										●														
	Selfridges Food Hall	393		●		*	*	*	*	*	●	●						●		*		●		●	●	●
	Simply Sausages	397																			*			*		
	Tesco	430			●	●		●	●	●	*							●				●		●	●	●
	Villandry	444		*		●	●	●	●	*	*									●					●	
	Whittard	451					●		*																	
	Wholefood	452									●															
	Wholefood Butchers	453																*								
W2	Archie	21																	●						●	●
	Athenian	28												●										●	●	●
	Maison Bouquillon	269																		●				●	●	●
	Markus Coffee Co	277					*																	●		
	Pierre Pechon	337		●																●			●			●
	Planet Organic	362		*		*					●	*			*			*				●			●	●
	Safeway	377				●			●	●	●							●						●		●

Location	ESTABLISHMENT	Ref No	Afro Caribbean	bread	Chinese &	Far Eastern	Cheese	Coffee	Chocolate	Tea	Delicatessen	Fruit & Veg	Fish	Eastern European	Greek	Health	Indian Sub	Continent	Japanese	Meat	Middle East	Patisserie	Sausages	Spanish & Portugese	Traiteur	Open on Bank Holidays	Open Bank Holidays	Open Late	Open Sunday
W3	Safeway	377			•					•	•	•								•						•	•	•	•
W4	Adamou	4									•	•			•											•		•	•
	Buckingham Butchers	68									Eggs									•									
	The Corner Shop	113									Eggs																		•
	Covent Garden Fishmongers	117										•								*									
	Macken Brothers	264									•									•									
	Macken & Collins	265																											
	John Nicholson	314											•												•				
	Sainsbury	378			•		•		•	•	•	*								•						•	•	•	•
	Whittard	451						•		*																			
W5	T. H. Carr	80											•																
	Cornucopia	116									Eggs					•													
	Importers	220						*		*																			
	Nicky's Fruit & Veg	315										•																	
	Safeway	377			•					•	•	•								•						•	•	•	•
	Victoria Health Foods	440					•				Eggs					•													
	The Village Pantry	442		•						*	Eggs *															•		•	•
	Whittard	451								*																			•
W6	Bushwacker	71														*													
	Safeway	377			•					•	•	•								•						•	•	•	•
	Sri Thai	409			*																									•
	Stenton	412																			*									

Location	ESTABLISHMENT	Ref. No.	Afro Caribbean	Bread	Chinese & Far Eastern	Cheese	Coffee	Chocolate	Tea	Delicatessen	Fruit & veg	Fish	Eastern European	Greek	Health	Indian Sub Continent / Japanese	Meat	Middle East	Patisserie	Sausages	Spanish & Portuguese / Traiteur	Open on Bank Holidays	Open Late	Open Sunday
W6	Sutherland's Food & Wine	419								*													●	
	Tesco	430		●	●	●	●	●			*						●					●	●	●
W7	G.H. Baxter	43															●						●	●
W8	Barstow & Barr	41				*																			●
	& Clarke's	104		*		*	*		●	●														
	Hamlin's of Kensington	199				●				●												*			
	Marks & Spencer	275		●			●			●	*											*	●	●	●
	Mark's in Kensington	276																							
	W. J. Miller	291																●							
	Mrs. O'Keefe's Sausage Shop	303																*			*				
	Pierre Pechon	337		●																					
	Reza	364									●							●	*	●			●	●	●
	Safeway	377			●				●	●	●							●		●			●	●	●
	Super Bahar	417									●								*				●	●	●
	Whittard	651					●		*															●	
W9	Jefferson's Sea Foods	229											●											●	
	Nosh	318									Eggs											●		●	
	The Real Food Store	363		*		*				●	●													●
	Roy's Greengrocer	375										●													
W10	L'Etoile de Sous	153		●																●					
	Fudco	175														*							●	●	●
	Golbourne Fisheries	189											*												

Location	ESTABLISHMENT	Ref. No	Afro Caribbean	Bread	Chinese & Far Eastern	Cheese	Coffee	Chocolate	Tea	Delicatessen	Fruit & Veg	Fish	Eastern European	Greek	Health	Indian Sub Continent	Japanese	Meat	Middle East	Patisserie	Sausages	Spanish & Portuguese	Traiteur	Open on Bank Holidays	Open Late	Open Sunday
	Lisboa Delicatessen	255								•												•*		•		•
	Lisboa Patisserie	256																		•				•		
	Portobello Wholefoods	346		•*		•*			•*		•				•*									•	•	•
	Sainsbury	378			•	•			•	•	•*							•						•		•
W11	Applewold	20								Closed																
	Chalmers & Gray	86										•*														
	Cullen Patisserie	119																		•				•		•
	De Baere	128		•*																•*					•	•
	R. Garcia & Sons	178																				•*				
	Jeroboams	231			•*																					•
	Lidgates	250																•*								
	Maison Blanc	268		•*																•*				•		•
	Michanicou Brothers	288								•*	•*													•		
	Mr. Christian's	293		•*																						
	Portobello Road Market	345									•	•														
W1	J.H. Smith	399										•														
	Speck	405								•*													*		•	
	The Spice Shop	407								Spice*																
	Tesco	430		•	•	•			•	•	•*						•						•	•	•
	Tom's	433		•		•			•	•	•*													•	•
	Wild Oats Wholefoods	454								•*	•				•*									•		•
W12	Damas Gate	123								•	•							•	•					•	•	•

Location	ESTABLISHMENT	Ref. No	Afro Caribbean	Bread	Chinese & Far Eastern	Cheese	Coffee	Chocolate	Tea	Delicatessen	Fruit & Veg	Fish	Eastern European	Greek	Health	Indian Sub Continent	Japanese	Meat	Middle East	Pâtisserie	Saucisses Sausages	Spanish & Portuguese	Traiteur	Open on Bank Holidays	Open Late	Open Sunday
W12	John & Sons	232								●			●	●				●						●		●
	Shepherd's Bush Market	396	●								●	●														●
	Safeway	377			●				●	●	●							●						●	●	●
	Yasar Halim	457		●														●	●	●				●	●	●
W13	Au Gourmet Grec	29								●			●	●												
	J. Quinn	356								Eggs								●								
	Richardson	366																●								
	Sainsbury	378			●	●	●		●	●	*							●						●	●	●
	Paul Thorogood	431								Eggs								*								
	Waitrose	447			●	●	●		●	●	*							*						●	●	●
W14	Buckingham Butchers	68								Eggs								●								
	Prima Delicatessen	350											●													
WC1	Myddleton's Delicatessen	391								●																
	Safeway	377			●				●	●	●							●							●	
WC2	Carluccio's	78								*	●												*		●	
	Earlham Street Market	145									●														●	
	Golden Gate Supermarket	190			*																			●	●	●
	Good Harvest	191					*					*												●	●	●
	Monmouth Coffee Company	296					*	●																	●	●
	Neal's Yard Bakery Co-op	308		*																				●	*	●
	Neal's Yard Dairy	309				*																			●	●
	Neal's Yard Wholefood Warehouse	310													*											●

193

Location	ESTABLISHMENT	Ref. No	Afro Caribbean	Bread	Chinese & Far Eastern	Cheese	Coffee	Chocolate	Tea	Delicatessen	Fruit & Veg	Fish	Eastern European	Greek	Health	Indian Sub Continent	Japanese	Meat	Middle East	Patisserie	Sausages	Spanish & Portugese	Traiteur	Open on bank holidays	Open Late	Open Sunday
	Newport Supermarket	313			*																			•		•
	Patisserie Valerie	334		•																*						
	Portwine & Son	347																								
	See Woo Hong Supermarket	392			*													*						•		•
	The Tea House	425							*															•		•
	Tesco	450		•	•	•	•		•	•	*							•						•	•	•
	R. Twining & Co.	436					•		*																	
	Whittard	451					•		*																	•

Multiples Addresses

Health & Diet Centre
31 Tranquil Vale, SE3 0181-318 0448
243 Muswell Hill Broadway, N10 0181-444 7717
5 Jerdan Place, SW6 0171-385 0015
151 Putney High Street, SW15 0181-788 0944
Centre Court Shopping Centre, Queen's Rd, SW19 0181-947 3583

Marks & Spencer
Brixton, 446 Brixton Rd, SW9 0171-274 6811
Camden Town, 143 Camden High St, NW1 0171-267 6055 Chiswick, 236
Chiswick High Rd, W4 0181-994 2236
Clapham Junction, 45 St. John's Rd, SW11 0171-228 2545
East Ham, 143 High St. North, E6 0181-472 1137
Hackney, 347 Mare St, E8 0181-986 3821
Islington, 5 Liverpool Rd, N1 0171-837 2744
Kilburn, 66 Kilburn High Rd, NW6 0171-624 7322
Mill Hill, 3 The Broadway, NW7 0181-906 8220 Moorgate, 70 Finsbury
Pavement, EC2 0171-786 9500
Muswell Hill, 126 Muswell Hill Broadway, N10 0181-365 2882
Putney, 59 Putney High Street, SW15 0181-788 2544
Walworth, 311 Walworth Rd, SE17 0171-703 6263

Safeway
Acton, King St, W3 0181-993 6566
Balham, 134 Balham HighRd, SW12 0181-675 4939
Barbican Shopping Centre, Whitecross St, EC1 0171-628 2317
Blackheath, Stratheden Parade, SE3 0181-858 2331
Bloomsbury, Brunswick Shopping Centre, WC1 0171-278 4965
Bow, 564a Roman Rd, E3 0181-980 1882
Brent Cross, Tilling Rd, NW2 0181-450 3274
Camberwell, Butterfly Walk, Daneville St, SE5 0171-708 4656
Camden, Chalk Farm Rd, NW1 0171-428 0405
Chelsea, 35 King's Rd, SW3 0171-730 9151
Ealing, Unit 10, Ealing Broadway Centre, W5 0181-840 3502
East Sheen, 284 Upper Richmond Rd, SW14 0181-876 7302
Edgware Rd, 159 Edgware Rd, W2 0171-723 1946
Edmonton, Sterling Way, N18 0181-807 6031
Fulham, North End Rd, SW6 0171-381 8738

Hammersmith, 2 King's Mall, W6 0181-748 0092

Holloway, 10 Hertslet Rd, N7 0171-700 4744

Kensington, 150 Kensington High St, W8 0171-937 0694

Kilburn, 142 Kilburn High Rd, NW6 0171-328 0191

Palmers Green, Aldemans Hill, N13 0181-886 0224

Peckham, 1 Rye Lane, SE15 0171-732 3518

Queensbury, Honeypot Lane, NW9 0181-204 6958

Shepherds Bush, 114 Shepherds Bush Green, W12 0181-743 5744

South Norwood, 18 Station Rd, SE25 0181-653 4853

Southwark, Walworth Rd, SE17 0171-701 1337

Stamford Hill, 1 Amhurst Park, N16 0181-800 2686

Stamford Hill, 49 Stamford Hill, N16 0181-809 7705

Streatham, 350 Streatham High Rd, SW16 0181-769 0691

Sydenham, 74 Sydenham Rd, SE26 0181-659 1914

Thamesmead, 2 Joyce Dawson Way, SE28 0181-311 6699

Upper Norwood, 64 Westow St, SE19 0181-653 5000

Wapping, Thomas More St, E1 0171-702 2863

Wembley, Blackbird Hill, NW9 0181-200 6424

Wimbledon, 33 The Broadway, SW19 0181-946 9981

Wood Green, N22 0181-881 4801

Sainsbury

Balham, 149 Balham High Rd, SW12 0181-675 1162

Camden Town, 17 Camden Rd, NW1 0171-482 3828

Chingford, 13 Hall Lane, E4 0181-529 1204

Chiswick, 31 Essex Place, W4 0181-994 9128

Clapham, Park Rd, SW4 0171-498 9396

Cromwell Road, 158a Cromwell Rd, SW7 0171-373 8313

Dalston Cross Shopping Centre, E8 0171-241 6942

East Dulwich, Dog Kennel Hill, SE22 0171-738 4900

East Ham, 2 Myrtle Rd, E6 0181-503 4997

Eltham, 1a Philpot Path, SE9 0181-859 8700

Forest Hill, 44 London Rd, SE23 0181-699 7977

Fulham, Townsmead Rd, SW6 0171-384 1606

Golders Green, 612 Finchley Rd, NW11 0181-458 6977

Haringay, Williamson Rd, N4 0181-809 6065

Hendon, The Hyde, NW9 0181-201 3078

Islington, 35 Liverpool Rd, N1 0171-278 1789

Kensal Green, Ladbroke Grove, W10 0181-960 4324

Kilburn, 90 Kilburn High Rd, NW6 0171-328 3536

Kingsbury, 632 Kingsbury Rd, NW9 0181-206 0929

Lee Green, Burnt Ash Rd, SE12 0181-318 5313

Lewisham Centre, 33 Riverside, SE13 0181-318 3042

Low Hall Chingford, Walthamstow Avenue, E4 0181-523 2617

Muswell Hill, 12 Fortis Green Rd, N10 0171-732 6433
New Cross Road, 263 New Cross Rd, SE14 0171-732 6433
Nine Elms, Wandsworth Rd, SW8 0171-622 9426
North Finchley, High Rd, N12 0181-446 2655
Putney, 2 Wenter Rd, SW15 0181-789 6286
South Norwood, 120 Whitehorse Lane, SE25 0181-653 7640
South Woodford, George Lane, E18 0181-989 8224
Stratford, 38 The Mall, E15 0181-534 7597
Streatham, 496 Streatham High Rd, SW16 0181-764 0435
Swiss Cottage, 177 Finchley Rd, NW3 0171-328 1444
Tottenham, 867 High Rd, N17 0181-801 6879
Victoria, 3 Kingsgate Parade, SW1 0171-834 3103
Walthamstow, 112 High St, E17 0181-521 6113
Wandsworth, 35 Garratt Lane, SW18 0181-871 9888
West Ealing, Melbourne Avenue, W13 0181-579 5593
Whitechapel, 1 Cambridge Heath Rd, E1 0171-247 2604
Wimbledon, 8 Worple Rd, SW19 0181-946 2210
Winchmore Hill, Green Lanes, N21 0181-364 1211
Wood Green, 2 Lymington Avenue, N22 0181-889 4668
Woolwich, Calderwood St, SE18 0181-317 8025

Tesco

Bermondsey, Old Kent Rd, SE1 0171-237 1866
Bethnal Green, 10 Punderson Gardens, E2 0171-729 4948
Brent Cross, Hendon Way, NW2 0181-201 9145
Brent Park Neasden, Great Central Way, NW10 0181-459 6591
Brixton, 13 Acre Lane, SW2 0171-441 9400
Bromley by Bow, Three Mills Lane, E3 0181-981 2427
Canary Wharf, Canada Square, E14 0171-513 0270
Catford, 18 Winslade Way, SE6 0181-258 9100
Colney Hatch Lane, N12 0181-368 1244
Covent Garden, 21 Bedford St, WC2 0171-853 7500
Edmonton Green, 34 North Mall, N9 0181-803 6931
Edmonton, Meridan Way, N18 0181-345 5895
Elephant & Castle Shopping Centre, SE1 0171-599 7500
Finchley, Ballards Lane, N3 0171-599 7400
Goodge Street, 10 Goodge St, W1 0171-599 7400
Hackney, 180 Well St, E9 0181-986 3010
Hammersmith, Broadway Shopping Centre, W6 0181-741 4345
Hendon, Sentinel Square, NW4 0181-210 7600
Lewisham, 290 Lewisham Rd, SE13 0181-463 0051
Leyton, 825 High Rd, E10 0181-558 2629

Notting Hill, 224 Portobello Rd, W11 0171-229 8743
Oxford Street, 311 Oxford St, W1 0171-493 2960
Paddington, 114 Church St, NW8 0171-853 7400
Palmers Green, 296 Green Lanes, N13 0181-886 4259
Palmers Green, 804 Green Lanes, N21 0181-360 7298
Rotherhithe, Surrey Quays, SE16 0171-237 5286
Shepherds Bush, 182 Shepherds Bush Road, W6 0171-603 1501
Stroud Green, 105 Stroud Green Road, N4 0171-281 2323
Tottenham, 222 High Rd, N15 0181-801 6673
Upton Park, 346 Green St, E13 0181-470 6446
Victoria, 18 Warwick Way, SW1 0171-834 4788
Walthamstow, 394 Hoe St, E17 0181-520 8554
Wandsworth, 67 The Arndale Centre, SW18 0181-258 7600

Waitrose

Brent Cross, Shopping Centre, NW4 0181-203 9711
East Sheen, 292 Upper Richmond Rd. West, SW14 0181-878 4792
Finchley, 273 Ballards Lane, N12 0181-343 7303
Holloway Road, 366 Holloway Road, N7 0171-700 3717
John Barnes, 199 Finchley Rd, NW3 0171-624 0453
King's Road, 196 King's Rd, SW3 0171-351 2775
Putney Shopping Centre, Putney High St, SW15 0181-246 6848
Temple Fortune, 33 Temple Fortune Parade, NW11 0181-458 6645
West Ealing, 2 Alexandria Rd, W13 0181-579 3379
Whetstone, 1301 High Rd, N20 0181-446 0323

PRODUCT INDEX

The number following each product indicates the shop where it can be found. Thus albongindas can be found at City Meats, SW10. The asterisk indicates an outlet specialising in this product.

Albongindas (Spanish Meat Balls): 103
Afro-Caribbean Groceries: 62*, 98, 135, 194*, 213, 367, 396
Afro-Caribbean Meat (See under Meat)
Alligator: 40(M/O), 295
Almonds; Fresh in season: 69, 364, 367, 457
American Muffins & Loaf Cakes: 49*, 376
Anchovies; fresh preserved: 10, 17, 25, 44, 50, 54, 57, 61, 84, 86, 132, 105, 110, 117, 133, 158, 169, 186, 203, 205, 226, 234, 254, 257, 273, 292, 297, 353, 393
Arboath Smokies: 25, 50, 54, 57, 61*, 84, 110, 117, 160, 203, 242, 393
Asparagus; Wild in season: 59, 203, 223, 424, 444
Bacon: 10, 24, 57*, 58*, 86, 93*, 132, 109*, 161*, 187*, 194, 235, 200, 217, 203*, 207(m/o)*, 205*, 238, 243, 250, 251, 264, 290, 292*, 295, 300, 304, 349, 331, 342*, 344, 347*, 361*, 372, 371, 377, 393*, 380, 410*, 420, 423*, 444*, 445*, 453
"Bacon"; Vegetarian: 440
Bass; Sea 17, 25, 50, 54, 55, 61, 66, 80, 82, 84, 110, 114, 117, 134, 158, 169, 189, 191, 194, 196, 201, 203, 206, 205, 216, 242, 226, 254, 257, 273, 279, 281, 325, 342, 353, 365, 388, 393, 414
Beef; Grass-fed: 8, 24*, 37*, 38, 43*, 48*, 51, 57*, 68, 72*, 73, 89, 107*, 112*, 120, 140, 141, 150, 151, 152, 168, 179, 187*, 193*, 200, 203*, 204, 207(M/O)*, 212, 205, 218, 237*, 239*, 250*, 264*, 276, 284, 290, 295*, 344*, 347*, 361*, 365, 377, 391, 393*, 410, 412, 420
Beef Mince; from grass-reared animals: 8, 24*, 37*, 43*, 48, 57*, 68, 73, 107*, 112*, 187*193*, 200, 203*, 204, 207(m/o)*, 237*, 239*, 250*, 264*, 284, 295*, 342*, 344*, 347, 361*, 377, 393*, 400*, 412, 420, 431*, 453*
Beef; Organic: 37, 73, 168, 204, 250, 264, 291, 295, 342, 344, 361, 393, 404, 410, 412, 423, 431, 447, 453
Beef; Salt: 8, 24, 132, 203, 264, 295, 361, 367, 393, 420
Biltong: 24, 93, 161, 167(m/o), 193, 203*, 244, 295, 372, 393*, 397*, 380*, 431
Biscuits; Sweet: 2, 10, 32*, 44, 56, 57, 65, 69, 74, 79, 93, 104*, 109, 125, 128, 133, 136, 137, 142, 154, 157, 161, 165, 166, 178, 181, 182, 184, 194, 195, 197, 217, 202*, 203, 205*, 232, 243*, 244, 251, 252, 262, 292, 297, 298, 299(m/o), 327, 330, 329, 334, 342, 343, 363, 370, 372, 382, 377, 378, 384, 383, 387, 393, 394, 401, 405, 419, 423, 429, 430, 438, 441*, 442, 444, 445, 447

Biscuits; for Cheese: 10, 44, 57, 65, 69, 71, 74, 79, 90, 91, 92, 104, 132, 133, 136, 142, 161, 171, 173, 181, 184, 235, 203, 208, 205*, 231*, 244, 292, 297, 304, 309, 349, 327, 336, 342, 362, 363, 371, 372, 377, 378, 387, 393, 394, 379, 419, 423, 426*, 430, 442, 444, 445, 446, 447

Biscuits; Gluten free: 35, 69, 71, 197, 306, 310, 339, 342, 346, 354, 363, 394, 440, 452, 454

Biscuits; Organic: 63, 69, 71, 197, 208, 171, 181, 297, 322, 342, 363, 372, 393, 394, 454, 454

Bison: 40(m/o), 167(m/o), 295

Black Pudding; see Sausages

Blini; ready made: 83, 378

Bloaters: 25, 54, 74, 80, 105, 110, 203, 206, 388, 393

Boar; Wild: 40(m/o), 110, 167(m/o), 203, 295, 393, 380

Bottarga: 78, 77, 253, 262, 297, 300, 349, 405, 438

Boudin Blanc; see Sausages

Bread, general: 2, 10, 11, 31, 32*, 33, 41, 49, 44*, 56, 57*, 58*, 63*, 65, 69*, 71, 74, 90, 97, 104*, 106, 132, 109, 119, 131*, 133, 137, 144, 153, 156, 161, 162, 166, 172*, 173*, 171, 180, 182, 184, 194*, 195, 197, 217*, 199, 202, 203*, 205*, 231, 232, 243*, 244, 261, 295, 300*, 251*, 252, 260*, 161, 272, 275, 268, 292, 293*, 297, 304, 308*, 309, 322, 327, 349, 330, 328I, 334, 337, 340, 342*, 346*, 352, 355, 357, 363, 363*, 367, 370, 371, 372, 376*, 394*, 393*, 401, 411, 379, 419*, 420, 426, 429, 433*, 435, 438, 440, 441*, 442, 444*, 445, 447, 454*, 457

Bread; Afro-Caribbean: 2, 62, 98, 135, 194, 213, 367, 396

Bread; French: 11, 12, 32*, 57*, 97, 104*, 128*, 153, 156, 173*, 194*, 235, 199, 203*, 266, 268*, 328, 330, 334, 74, 355, 430, 433*, 441, 442, 447

Bread; East European: 2, 197, 232, 244, 326, 350

Bread; Gluten free: 69, 71, 171, 197, 306, 310, 322, 338, 342, 346, 354, 363, 395, 432, 440, 452, 454

Bread; Indian Sub-Continent: 130, 146, 386, 439

Bread; Italian: 10, 14, 44, 56, 74, 58, 78, 77, 97, 91, 104, 131, 137*, 144, 161*, 166, 165, 171, 177, 181, 180, 182, 184*, 186*, 197, 203, 232, 251, 297*, 298, 300, 304, 327, 74, 357, 363, 372, 382, 383, 384, 387, 393, 394*, 405, 423, 429, 433*, 438, 444*, 445

Bread; Jewish: 44, 79*, 125*, 195*, 209, 343, 367, 370, 393

Bread; Middle-Eastern: 18*, 31, 272, 367, 411, 435, 457

Bread; Organic: 69, 71, 172, 194*, 197, 297, 310, 322, 342*, 346*, 363, 371, 393, 437, 454*

Bread; Portuguese & Spanish: 2, 176, 178, 255*, 329, 351

Bread; Rye: 10, 29*, 32, 44*, 56, 57, 58, 63*, 71, 74, 91, 104*, 106, 109, 125, 131*, 161*, 172, 173, 171, 194*, 197, 217, 203, 208, 209, 205, 232, 243*, 251, 300, 304, 306, 308*, 322, 326, 327, 328, 349, 346*, 350, 352, 357, 363, 363*, 370, 372, 376*, 393, 394*, 411, 423, 440, 441*, 442, 444, 454*

Bread; Soda: 44, 56, 58, 63, 71, 91, 97, 109, 161, 172, 171, 194*, 197, 203, 300, 349, 363*, 372, 394*, 393, 411, 440, 454*

Bread; Sour Dough: 32, 33, 56, 57, 58, 63, 69, 71, 91, 93, 109, 131, 161*, 172, 171, 184, 197, 217, 203, 205, 231, 232, 243, 251, 300, 304, 306, 308*, 322, 327, 349, 342, 343, 74, 346*, 350, 363, 393, 394*, 444*, 445, 447, 454*

Brill: 17, 25, 37, 50, 54, 55, 57, 61, 66, 82, 84, 86, 105, 111, 115(m/o), 114, 117, 170(d/s), 158, 189, 201, 203, 206, 242, 226, 229, 257, 281, 365, 366, 388, 414, 421

Buckling: 54, 74, 105, 110, 327, 343, 388, 393

Bulgur wheat: 35, 63, 69, 71, 133, 172, 85, 171, 172, 197, 300, 304, 306, 309, 310, 322, 349, 338, 342, 346, 339, 354, 363, 377, 378, 394, 430, 432, 435, 439, 440, 444, 447, 452

Butter: 41*, 67, 44, 57*, 58, 65, 77, 78, 90, 91*, 93, 104, 118, 132, 133, 136*, 137, 142, 154, 161, 180, 182, 194, 217, 199, 203*, 207(m/o)*, 205*, 231, 244, 251, 262, 295, 297, 298, 300, 304, 327, 349, 330*, 342, 363, 372, 377, 378, 384, 383, 393*, 394*, 426*, 429, 430, 433, 438, 444*, 445, 447, 454

Butter; Organic: 63, 71, 91, 172, 171, 197, 342, 378, 387, 394, 447, 454

Buttermilk; 63, 71, 172, 197, 363, 371, 378, 393, 394, 447, 454

Cakes, 10, 12*, 26*, 32*, 33, 56, 75*, 93, 104*, 106, 119, 128*, 156, 161, 184, 194*, 217, 203*, 205, 243*, 251, 260, 261, 267*, 268*, 298, 305*, 327, 328, 349, 330, 334*, 355*, 363, 372, 393, 405, 441, 444

Cakes; Healthy but still entertaining: 2, 63, 171, 197, 363, 454

Cakes, Christmas: 12, 32, 75, 106, 128, 161, 203, 205, 267, 268, 275, 334, 377, 378

Calves Kidney: 8, 24, 203, 250, 264, 295, 361

Calves Liver: 8, 24, 141, 203, 250, 264, 295, 347, 361, 393

Carp: 45, 54, 80, 134, 191, 216, 393

Carp; Live: 191, 455

Caul Fat; (always give the butcher advance warning): 8, 24, 43, 48, 57, 72, 107, 112, 151, 168, 187, 193, 217, 203, 212, 228, 237, 239, 250, 264, 284, 295, 344, 361, 400, 404, 412, 423, 431, 453

Caviar: 25, 32, 54, 57, 58, 74, 83*, 89, 93, 111, 161*, 160*, 217, 203*, 206, 205, 232, 244, 257, 262, 299, 327, 331, 336, 364, 372, 393*, 405, 427(m/o), 442

Charcuterie: 2, 10, 14, 24, 32*, 44, 57*, 65, 70, 78*, 77, 90, 93, 132, 109, 126, 133, 136, 137, 142, 154, 156, 161*, 166, 165, 177, 178, 179, 180, 182, 183, 184, 186, 203*, 217*, 199, 202, 217(m/o)*, 205*, 199, 202, 203*, 205*, 207*(m/o), 217*, 231*, 232, 234, 244, 251, 252, 253, 262, 292*, 295, 297*, 293, 304, 330, 336, 74, 300*, 320(m/o), 327, 329, 340, 342, 350, 352, 372*, 373, 381, 382, 383, 384, 382, 383, 387, 393, 380, 401, 405*, 379, 419, 429, 433*, 438, 442, 444*, 445*

207*(m/o), 205*, 231, 235, 243, 244, 247*, 248, 251, 280, 292, 296, 297, 298, 299*(m/o), 300, 304, 327, 328, 330, 349, 369*, 372, 379, 385*, 387, 393*, 394, 405, 423, 438, 442, 444, 445

Chocolate Coffee Beans: 296, 427(m/o)

Chocolate; Organic: 251, 300, 342, 363, 378, 387, 393, 394, 440, 454*

Chocolate; for diabetics: 3, 71, 95(m/o), 129(m/o), 161, 208, 243, 292, 306, 327, 330, 343, 363, 372, 378, 393, 440, 454

Christmas Pudding: 56, 57, 58, 63, 71, 74, 93, 132, 136, 144, 157, 161, 171, 172, 197, 203*, 205*, 217*, 232, 244, 275, 292, 280, 297, 298, 299(m/o), 300*, 304, 306, 327, 349, 363*, 372, 387, 393, 394*, 419, 423, 444*

Christmas Pudding; gluten free: 63, 171, 394

Chutney; Pickles & Relishes: 10, 41, 44, 57*, 65, 69, 70, 74, 90, 91, 93*, 104, 109, 122*, 130, 132, 133, 136, 142*, 146, 151, 157, 161*, 166, 171, 179, 182, 194*, 197*, 217, 199, 202, 203*, 205*, 208, 228, 231*, 232, 234, 235, 243, 250, 251*, 292*, 297, 298, 299*(m/o), 300*, 301*, 304, 309, 312, 327, 349, 333*, 336, 342, 352, 359*, 361, 363*, 372*, 378, 379, 393, 404, 406, 407*, 413, 423, 426, 430, 433, 438, 439, 444*, 445*, 447, 454

Clams; in season: 17, 50, 54, 57, 84, 86, 105, 117, 164, 189, 203, 206, 205, 242, 226, 254, 257, 325, 365, 388, 393

Cod; Salt: (see recipe for Brandade page 135): 110, 194, 255, 281, 367, 378, 384, 444

Coffee: 2, 7*, 10, 56, 57, 58, 70, 78, 76*, 77, 93, 104*, 132, 133, 136, 137, 154, 161, 166, 165, 181, 186, 235, 74, 217, 203*, 211*, 205*, 220*, 227*, 231, 243, 248, 251, 252, 280*, 280*, 292, 296*, 297, 300, 277*, 304, 327, 330, 349, 340, 346*, 352, 363*, 372, 378, 385, 387, 383, 393, 423, 429, 430, 433, 436, 438, 442, 444*, 445*, 447, 451

Coffee; Organic: 63, 69, 71, 172, 197, 342, 346, 363, 387, 394, 454

Coffee; Syrups for flavouring: 227

Confit of Duck; See under Duck

Cornish Pasties: 93, 136, 194, 203, 250, 304, 393

Crab; Cooked: 6, 17, 25, 34, 37, 50, 54, 55, 57, 61, 66, 74, 80, 82, 84, 86, 105, 110, 111, 117, 134, 159, 164, 169, 189, 191, 194, 196, 201, 203, 205, 206, 226, 242, 249, 254, 257, 273, 281, 325, 353, 365, 388, 393, 455, 458

Crab; Live by arrangement: 25, 37, 54, 55, 61, 66, 80, 82, 84, 86, 105, 110, 111, 117, 164, 169, 189, 191, 194, 196, 203, 216, 226, 242, 254, 257, 281, 325, 353, 388

Crayfish: 50, 54, 57, 74, 84, 117, 203, 242, 257, 325

Cream; Unpasteurised: 10, 161, 194, 217, 300, 309, 363, 378, 387, 423, 444

Cream; Organic: 57, 171, 197, 363, 371, 387, 423

Cream; Clotted: 93, 136, 161, 203, 205, 232, 378, 393

Cream; Soya: 69, 71, 171, 208, 428, 440, 454

Creme Fraiche: 57, 93, 132, 136, 203, 244, 205, 297, 342, 377, 378, 387, 393, 430, 447

Creme Fraiche; Unpasteurised: 231, 378

Crocodile: 40(m/o), 167(m/o), 325, 380

Croissant: 10, 12, 32*, 57*, 75*, 93, 104*, 106, 128*, 144, 156, 194*, 203, 205, 209, 243*, 244, 267*, 269*268*, 275*, 328, 330, 334, 337, 349*, 355, 372*, 376, 393, 444*, 445, 447

Curry Paste: 58, 93, 122*, 130*, 132*, 146, 161, 205, 244, 301*, 312*, 359*, 377, 378, 393, 406, 409, 430, 439*, 447

Delicatessen, general: 2, 4, 10, 13, 15, 32*, 44*, 57*, 65, 67, 69, 70, 74*, 77*, 78*, 93, 103, 104*, 109, 132, 133, 136, 137, 142*, 149, 154, 156, 161*, 162, 165, 166, 177, 178, 180, 182, 183, 184, 186, 199, 202, 203*, 205*, 217*, 232, 234, 235*, 243*, 244, 251*, 253*, 262, 275, 280, 292*, 293*, 297*, 298, 300*, 304, 321, 326, 327, 331, 340*, 342*, 343*, 349, 351, 352*, 363*, 370, 372*, 373, 377, 378*, 379, 381, 382, 383, 384, 387, 393*, 401, 405*, 419, 423, 429*, 430*, 433*, 438*, 442, 444*, 445*, 446, 447*

Dim Sum; Prepared: 190, 216*, 259*, 283, 312*, 421, 455*, 458

Dripping; Organic: 250

Dublin Bay Prawns: see Langoustines

Duck; Free-range Aylesbury-type: 8, 24, 37, 55, 73, 86, 203, 205, 250, 290, 295, 342, 344, 361, 393, 431, 447, 453

Duck; Confit: 58, 93, 132, 161, 203, 235, 217, 207*(m/o), 210*(m/o), 231, 264, 295, 299(m/o), 300, 361, 372, 387, 393, 445

Duck; Barbary: 203, 378, 293, 410

Duck; Gressingham/Lunesdale 8, 72, 203, 250, 264, 295, 344, 347, 361, 378

Duck; Hereford "Trelough": 207(m/o)

Ducks Legs for Confit: 8, 24, 73, 158, 207(m/o), 250, 264, 295, 344, 347, 361, 393

East European Groceries: 29, 232, 244*, 326, 350

Eels; Fresh: 54, 84, 86, 110, 117, 191, 196, 242

Eels; jellied: 54, 80, 86, 110, 169, 203, 205, 249, 353

Eels, smoked: see Smoked Eel

Eggs; Bantam: 20, 203

Eggs; Free-range: 10, 25, 24, 35*, 55*, 58*, 69*, 68*, 74, 84, 85*, 86, 93, 104, 110, 113*, 116*, 121*, 124*, 127*, 133, 136, 138*, 148*, 150, 161, 162*, 168*, 172*, 171*, 179*, 194, 197, 235, 203, 208*, 205, 242, 229*, 231, 243*, 249, 250*, 251*, 257, 264, 273, 284, 290, 292, 295, 298*, 300*, 304*, 306, 314*, 318*, 322*, 327, 349*, 342*, 344*, 346, 339*, 352*, 354*, 356*, 361*, 363, 371*, 372, 377, 378, 391*, 393*, 380, 404, 412*, 413*, 423, 426, 428*, 430, 431*, 432*, 437*, 438, 440*, 442, 444*, 446*, 447, 454*

Eggs; Hens, Organic Free-range: 20, 63, 71, 170(home delivery), 197, 260, 295, 342, 346, 347, 378, 394, 413, 423, 447, 454

Eggs, Duck: 20, 86, 110, 235, 203, 216, 250, 251, 264, 290, 292, 295, 344, 347, 361, 423

Eggs; Salted Duck: 216

Flour; Italian for pasta: 10, 57, 78, 104*, 132, 133, 137, 154, 165, 180, 181, 182, 184, 244, 251, 252, 262, 297, 300, 330, 363, 372, 373, 378, 382, 381, 383, 384, 387, 393, 405, 423, 429, 438, 442, 444, 445

Flour; Millet: 175, 359, 439, 454

Flour; Organic: 69, 194, 197*, 244, 310, 322, 338, 339, 342, 346, 372, 378, 394, 440, 444, 447, 454

Flour; Potato: 69, 359, 454

Flour; Rice: 359, 458

Flour; Rye: 69, 244, 346, 444, 454

Flour; Soya: 310, 346, 454

Flour; Spelt: 310, 346, 378, 394, 444

Flour; West African: 62, 135, 194, 367, 396

Flowers; Edible: 60, 17, 203 (**Elderfowers in season:** 424)

Foie Gras; Fresh: 8, 32, 58, 89, 132, 161, 235, 217, 203, 205, 262, 292(special order), 295, 298(special order), 304, 372, 393, 427(mail order)

Food as presents: 7, 49, 88, 143, 161*, 188*, 203*, 205*, 221, 247, 258(m/o), 268, 297, 320(mail order), 369, 385, 444, 451

French Groceries: 32, 44, 57, 58, 67, 74, 93, 132, 133, 142, 161, 162, 203, 205, 217, 235, 244, 292, 293, 300, 330, 331, 352, 372, 378, 393, 401, 430, 444, 445, 446, 447

Fruit; crystallized: 2, 10, 32, 58, 95*(m/o), 93, 203, 205, 231, 244, 297, 300, 330, 346, 363, 383, 393, 407, 440, 444

Fruit, fresh: 19, 34, 42, 45*, 46, 47, 59, 60*, 62*, 64, 67, 69, 87, 98, 99, 101, 135, 145, 147, 155, 170*(home delivery), 185, 194*, 203*, 205, 213, 222, 223, 233, 240, 249, 265, 270, 275*, 288*, 307, 311*, 315, 316, 317, 345, 344, 364, 367, 370, 375, 378*, 393, 396, 398, 415, 416, 417, 430, 434, 437, 444*, 447*, 448, 450*, 456, 457

Fruit; fresh Organic: 63, 69, 71, 170(home delivery), 197, 311*, 322, 342*, 367, 408, 452, 454

Fruit; dried: 2, 10, 69*, 93, 101, 197*, 205, 244, 280, 310, 322, 338, 339, 378, 393*, 418, 444, 447, 457*

Fruit Juices: 2, 10, 28, 44, 57, 63*, 69, 71*, 74, 93, 104*, 136, 149, 157, 171, 197, 208, 217, 232, 235, 244, 251, 275, 292, 297, 298, 300, 330, 338, 342, 346, 349, 371, 372, 378, 394, 426, 440, 444, 445, 454

Fruit Juices; Organic: 63*, 69, 71*, 171, 197, 208, 306, 342*, 346, 363*, 372, 394*, 426, 430, 445, 454*

Fudge: 10, 58, 70, 93, 136, 143, 157, 161, 203, 205, 217, 235, 243, 244, 251, 292, 297, 298*, 300, 304, 327, 349, 372, 393, 445

Game; general: 8*, 25*, 24, 37, 55, 72*, 80, 86*, 89, 110*, 117, 120, 140, 150, 158*, 187, 200, 203*, 205, 206, 226*, 228, 250*, 264, 273, 290, 295*, 303, 242, 344*, 347*, 361, 393*, 400*, 410, 427(m/o), 431

Goat's Meat; see Kid:

Geese; between Thanksgiving & Christmas: 25, 55, 37, 73, 80, 86, 112, 120, 141*, 151, 161, 192(m/o), 203, 205, 215(m/o), 250, 295, 344, 393, 400*, 431, 453

Geese; at Easter: 37, 192(m/o), 215(m/o), 344, 393, 400*

Goose Fat for Confit: 57, 72, 93, 132, 295, 393, 444

Gravadlax: 1*, 54*, 57, 58, 74, 83, 86, 157, 161, 160, 217, 203*, 205*, 226, 258*(m/o), 275, 292*, 300, 427(m/o), 304, 327*, 372, 393*

Greek Groceries: 4, 15, 28, 29, 289, 327, 335

Guinea Fowl: 24, 55, 86, 110, 158, 203, 205, 393

Haggis: 24, 72, 93, 136, 161, 179, 203, 250, 264, 295, 304, 344, 347, 361, 391, 410, 423

Haggis; Vegetarian: 71, 208, 346, 378, 393, 394, 440

Halibut; Real not Greenland: 17, 25, 50, 54*, 55, 37, 61, 66, 80, 82, 84, 86, 105, 111, 117, 160, 189, 203, 205, 206, 242, 254, 257, 273, 325, 365, 388, 393

Ham & Gammon: 8, 44, 57*, 58, 65*, 86, 93*, 132*, 133, 136, 152, 157, 161*, 162, 177, 179, 180, 181, 182, 183, 184, 187, 194, 203*, 205*, 207*(m/o), 212, 217*, 235*, 241, 250*, 251, 264, 290, 292, 293*, 295, 298, 300*, 304, 327, 331, 336, 342, 349, 352, 372, 393*, 420, 423, 433*, 442, 444*, 445*

Ham; Fresh Parma: 2, 8, 10, 14, 32, 44, 57*, 58, 65, 70, 77*, 78*, 93, 109, 132, 133, 137, 154, 161, 165*, 166, 177, 178, 180, 181, 182*, 183, 184, 186, 203, 205*, 217, 231, 234, 244, 250, 251, 252, 253*, 262, 264, 282, 292, 295, 297*, 298, 300, 304, 327, 330, 331, 336, 340, 343, 349, 352, 361, 372, 373, 379, 381, 382, 383, 384, 387, 393*, 405*, 423, 429, 433, 438, 442, 444*

Ham; Pata Negra: 161

Ham; Serrano: 2, 57, 74, 161, 178*, 181, 203, 205, 243, 292, 300, 329, 351*, 393, 444

Hampers; (all shops will need a little notice): 10, 78, 93, 132, 136, 161*, 199*, 202*, 203*, 205*, 231, 244, 275, 297, 327*, 330, 331, 372, 378, 387, 405, 430, 447

Health Food: 35, 63*, 69*, 71*, 85, 116, 124, 133, 171*, 172*, 197*, 208, 300, 304, 306, 310*, 322*, 338, 339, 342*, 346*, 349, 354, 363*, 394*, 413, 428, 432, 440, 452*, 454*

Herbs; fresh: 2, 198(m/o), 203, 205, 223, 230(m/o), 371, 378, 393, 419, 430, 423, 438, 444, 447

Herrings; Marinated: 17, 25, 44, 50, 54*, 57, 61, 70, 74, 80, 86, 105, 110, 117, 133, 158, 160, 169, 203, 205, 257*, 258*, 273, 287, 300, 326, 343, 353, 370*, 388, 393

Honey: 35, 41, 44, 57, 58, 63, 69*, 71*, 74, 77, 104, 116, 133, 136, 137, 154, 161*, 165, 172, 180, 194, 197, 217, 203, 205*, 208, 214*, 221, 224, 231, 234, 243, 244, 250, 251, 259, 262, 280, 292, 297, 298, 299(m/o),

300, 304, 306, 313, 327, 336, 342, 349, 363*, 372, 377, 378, 387, 393*, 394, 405, 407, 413*, 423, 430, 433, 438, 440, 442, 444*, 445*, 447, 454*

Honey; Organic: 63, 69, 71, 77, 116, 171, 172, 197, 214*, 232, 297, 342, 362, 383, 393, 394, 442, 454*

Houmus: 2, 10, 15*, 58, 74, 93, 136, 161, 166, 197, 217, 251, 275, 292, 297, 298, 330, 343, 349, 363, 371, 372, 377, 378, 387, 393, 394, 405, 430, 435, 440, 442, 447, 454, 457

Houmous; Organic: 63, 71, 300, 306, 342, 346, 394, 454

Huitlacoche (Fungus): 424

Ice Cream; 5, 10*, 20*, 32*, 57, 58, 63, 69, 71, 74, 104*, 132, 136*, 142*, 151*, 161, 162, 171, 172, 177, 184, 197, 203, 205, 208, 243, 251, 274, 292, 297, 298, 300, 304, 306, 309*, 327, 342*, 346, 349, 363*, 373, 384, 387, 394, 419, 433*, 438, 442, 445, 447, 454*

Ice Cream: non-dairy: 63, 71, 208, 306, 343, 346, 394, 444, 454

Indian Sub-Continental Basics: 4, 377, 378, 430, 447

Indian Sub-Continental Groceries: 98, 122*, 130*, 139, 146*, 175, 333*, 359*, 386, 398*, 439*

Italian Groceries: 10, 13, 14, 57, 77*, 78*, 133, 137, 154, 165*, 166, 177, 180, 181, 182, 183, 184, 186, 205, 244, 251, 252, 253*, 262, 292, 293, 297*, 340, 341, 373, 381, 382, 383, 384, 387, 393, 405*, 423, 429*, 438, 444

Jams & Preserves: 2, 10, 41, 44, 57*, 63, 65, 69, 70, 71, 74, 78, 93, 104*, 133, 136, 142*, 157, 161, 165, 171, 172, 180, 184, 194, 197, 199, 203, 205*, 208, 217, 224, 231, 232, 235, 243, 244, 251*, 252, 280, 292, 297, 298, 299(m/o), 300, 304, 321, 327, 342, 346, 349, 352, 363, 372, 377, 378, 380, 381, 382, 383, 384, 393, 394, 405, 413, 426, 429, 430, 433, 442, 444*, 445, 447, 454

Jam; Organic: 69, 208, 310, 342, 394, 440, 454*

Japanese Basics: 234, 454

Japanese Groceries: 22, 27, 205, 216, 225, 283, 294, 393, 458*

Kangaroo: 40(m/o), 167(m/o), 203, 295, 325, 344, 380

Keta; Salmon "Caviar": 83, 203, 205, 275, 393, 427(m/o), 458

Kid; (Goat): 34, 40*(m/o), 62, 135, 146, 194, 236, 358, 367, 400, 415, 434, 435, 457

Kippers; Undyed: 6, 17, 25, 37, 54*, 55, 61, 66, 80, 84, 86, 105*, 110, 111, 117*, 158, 160*, 161*, 189, 201, 203*, 205, 226, 242, 254, 257, 258*(m/o), 273, 299*(m/o), 300*, 343, 353, 365, 378, 388, 393*, 427(m/o)*, 444*, 445*

Kosher Baby Food: 346, 359

Kosher Groceries: 79, 171, 244, 327, 343, 359, 370, 393

Lamb: 8, 24, 37*, 38, 43, 48, 51, 57*, 68, 72, 73, 89, 107, 112, 120, 141, 150, 151, 152, 168, 187*, 193*, 200, 203, 204, 205, 207(m/o)*, 212, 218, 228*, 237, 239, 250, 264*, 276, 284, 290, 295, 344*, 347, 361*, 366, 377, 378, 391, 393, 410*, 412*, 420, 430, 447

Lamb; Organic: 37, 168, 193, 204, 250, 264, 290, 291, 295, 342, 361, 393, 404, 410, 412, 423, 453

Langoustines; Fresh: 50, 54*, 57, 61, 74, 86, 105, 110, 117, 203, 206, 254, 258*(m/o), 273, 283, 353, 365, 393

Lardo: 10, 77, 154, 173, 177, 181, 183, 244, 252, 262, 297, 321, 383, 429

Lemon Grass; Fresh: 4, 57, 60, 62, 69, 100, 104, 132, 161, 190, 203, 205, 216, 235, 251, 259, 312, 313, 349, 371, 377, 378, 392, 393, 430, 437, 445, 447, 449

Lobsters; Cooked: 17, 25, 37, 50, 54, 55, 57, 61, 66, 80, 82, 84, 86, 89, 105, 110, 111, 117, 134, 164, 169, 179, 189, 191, 201, 203, 205, 206, 226, 229, 242, 254, 257, 273, 353, 365, 378, 388, 393, 430, 447, 458

Lobsters; Live by arrangement: 17, 25, 37, 50, 54*, 55, 61, 66, 80, 82, 84, 86, 105, 110, 111, 117, 134, 164, 169, 189, 191, 201, 206, 216*, 226, 229, 242, 254, 257, 273, 325, 353, 366, 388, 402

Locust: 40(m/o), 295 (special order)

Macaroons: 10, 32, 166, 393

Maple Syrup; 7, 10, 70, 77, 93, 181, 203, 205, 208, 244, 278, 297, 299(m/o), 378, 393, 407, 442, 447

Marmalade: 57, 63, 65, 69, 70, 71, 74, 93, 104, 133, 136, 142, 157, 161, 199, 203, 205*, 208, 224, 231, 235, 243, 244, 251*, 260*, 280, 292, 297, 298, 299(m/o), 300, 304, 310, 327, 342, 346, 349, 352, 363, 371, 372, 377, 378, 393, 394, 406*, 413, 426, 430, 433, 438, 444*, 445, 447, 454

Marron Glacé; all year: 7, 93, 142, 181, 203, 205, 299(m/o), 320(m/o), 372, 393, 444

Marron Glacé; Christmas only: 10, 44, 70, 203, 205, 393

Meat; Cold from all countries: see Charcuterie

Meat; General: 8*, 24*, 34, 37*, 38, 43*, 47, 48*, 57*, 68*, 72*, 73, 89, 98, 103, 107*, 112*, 120, 121, 140, 141, 150, 151*, 152, 161, 168*, 170(m/o), 179, 187, 193*, 200, 203*, 204, 205*, 212*, 217*, 228*, 236, 237*, 238, 239*, 250*, 264*, 275, 276, 284*, 287, 290, 291, 295*, 303, 344*, 347, 356, 361*, 366, 377, 378, 391, 400*, 404*, 410, 412*, 420, 423, 430, 431*, 447, 453*, 456, 458

Meat; Organic & Additive Free: 37, 57, 120, 140, 151, 204, 250, 290, 291, 295, 342, 344, 347, 400*, 404*, 410*, 412*, 423, 431, 444, 453*

Meat; African & Caribbean Cuts: 62, 135, 194, 213, 236, 358, 396, 448

Meat; French Cuts: 73, 217

Meat; Halal: 34, 135, 146, 236, 287, 291*, 358*, 364, 367, 400*, 415, 435, 448, 457

Meat Pies: 24, 136, 140, 150, 161, 179, 203, 205, 250, 264, 295, 298, 352, 361, 393, 431, 442

Mexican Groceries: 377, 378, 430, 447

Meringues: 32, 75, 119, 156, 203, 205, 244, 267, 268, 275, 334

Middle Eastern Basics: 28, 93, 327, 377, 378, 430, 447

Middle Eastern Groceries: 2, 4, 21, 58, 123*, 364, 367, 417, 418, 435, 457

Milk; Organic Cow's: 63, 69, 71, 116, 172, 197, 304, 310, 322, 327, 342, 346, 363, 371, 378, 387, 394, 423, 437, 447, 454

Milk; Goat's: 63, 69, 172, 197, 203, 292, 306, 310, 346, 349, 363, 371, 372, 378, 393, 394, 413, 440, 447, 454

Milk; Organic Goat's: 69, 342, 454

Milk; Sheep: 292, 346, 394, 454

Milk; Organic Soya Milk: 63, 71, 197, 203, 208, 342, 372, 440

Mince Pies; at Christmas: 10, 93, 136, 194*, 203, 205, 275, 267*, 297, 378, 393*, 430,

Mostarda di frutta: 10, 70, 77, 78, 137, 165, 180, 203, 205, 262, 297, 330, 382, 387, 393, 423, 427(m/o), 429, 438

Muffins: 49*

Mulled Wine Sachets: 7, 70, 93, 244, 378, 447

Mullet; Grey: 25, 37, 54*, 55, 61, 66, 80, 82, 84, 86, 105, 117, 134, 158, 169, 164, 189, 201, 203, 206, 242, 226, 249, 254, 273, 325, 353, 365, 388, 393

Mullet; Red: 17, 25, 37, 50, 54*, 55, 57, 61, 66, 74, 80, 82, 84, 86, 105, 110, 111, 117, 158, 164, 169, 189, 201, 203, 205, 206, 226, 229, 242, 254, 273, 281, 325, 353, 366, 388, 393

Mushrooms; Fresh Wild in season: 2, 57*, 59*, 77, 78*, 173, 203, 205*, 217, 235, 244, 262, 265, 288, 295, 300*, 304, 327, 363, 371, 393, 423, 424*, 438, 444

Mushrooms; Dried: 10, 41, 57, 58, 59, 69, 70, 71, 74, 77, 78, 93, 132, 157, 161, 166, 177, 182, 183, 184, 199, 203, 205, 216, 217, 231, 232, 235, 244, 251, 262, 280, 292, 297, 298, 299(m/o), 300*, 304, 327, 330, 343, 349, 363, 371, 372, 382, 383, 384, 387, 393, 394, 407, 405, 423, 424*, 427(m/o), 429, 438, 442, 444, 445, 447, 454, 458

Mussels; Fresh in season: 6, 17, 25, 34, 37, 50, 54, 55, 57, 61, 74, 80, 84, 86, 105, 110, 111, 117, 134, 158, 159, 169, 189, 194, 201, 203, 205, 206, 242, 251, 254, 258(m/o), 273, 279, 281, 324, 325, 353, 365, 393

Mustard: 2, 10, 24, 44, 57*, 58, 74*, 78, 93, 104*, 132, 133, 136, 151, 157, 161, 194, 197, 203, 205*, 208, 217, 231, 235, 244, 250, 264, 292*, 295, 297, 298, 299(m/o), 300, 304, 309, 320(m/o), 327, 330, 342, 346, 361, 363, 372, 377, 378, 387, 393*, 394, 405, 413, 419, 426, 430, 433, 444*, 405*, 447*

Mutton: 24, 135, 236, 250, 264, 347, 358, 367, 434, 435, 457

Nougat: 2, 7, 10, 32, 58, 70, 93, 95*(m/o), 104*, 161, 177, 178, 181, 182, 184, 203*, 205, 217, 231, 244, 262, 298, 300, 327, 372, 382, 383, 393, 405, 429, 438, 444*

Nuts; Fresh: 2, 4, 69, 116, 122*, 130, 175, 185, 208, 311*, 310, 333*, 335, 338, 339, 418, 439, 440, 447, 457

Octopus: 27, 37, 54*, 62, 80, 164, 189, 191, 194, 226, 254, 281, 312, 313, 458

Oils:

    Almond: 320*(m/o)

Chili: 57, 74, 78, 161, 190, 205, 216, 235, 259, 283, 292, 293, 299(m/o), 300, 312, 313, 320(m/o), 393, 392, 409, 422, 449, 455

Grapeseed: 69, 320*(m/o), 377, 378, 454*

Hazelnut: 133, 203, 205, 320*(m/o), 299(m/o), 378, 454*

Macadamia Nut: 325, 454

Olive: 2, 4, 10, 14, 44, 57*, 58*, 69, 74*, 77*, 78*, 93, 103, 104*, 109, 131, 133, 136, 137, 149, 154, 157, 160, 161, 166, 165, 177, 178*, 180, 183, 184, 186, 203, 205*, 217, 231*, 232, 235*, 234, 244, 250, 251, 252, 253, 257, 262*, 289, 292*, 297*, 298, 299(m/o), 300*, 304, 310, 320*(m/o), 327, 330, 336, 340, 349, 352, 359, 363, 371, 372*, 373, 377, 378, 381, 382, 383, 384, 387*, 393*, 394, 401, 405*, 407, 419, 423, 426, 427(m/o), 429, 430, 433, 438*, 444*, 445*, 447, 454

Olive Oil; Organic: 10, 63, 69, 70, 71, 74, 77, 132, 171, 181, 182, 197*, 297, 306, 310, 342, 346, 387, 393*, 440, 454

Peanut (Groundnut): 133, 320*(m/o)

Pumpkinseed; roasted: 69, 320*(m/o), 427(m/o)

Sesame: 133, 203, 205, 216, 320*(m/o), 377, 378, 430, 447, 454*

Soya: 454*

Sunflower: 10, 69*, 320*(m/o), 377, 378, 387, 430, 447, 454*

Truffle Oil: 24, 77, 93, 132, 181, 183, 203, 205, 297, 320(m/o), 327, 363, 384, 387, 393, 423, 424, 427(m/o), 429, 444, 447

Walnut: 299(m/o), 320*(m/o), 371, 378, 427(m/o), 447, 454

Olives: 2*, 4, 10, 16, 41, 57, 58, 70, 77, 93, 104, 133, 161, 166, 173, 177, 178, 180, 181, 182, 183, 184, 186, 194, 217, 231, 232, 244, 251, 252, 262, 289*, 292, 297, 298, 300, 304, 320(m/o), 327, 330, 335, 340, 343, 349, 363, 372, 378, 381, 382, 383, 385, 387, 393*, 405, 419, 423, 429, 433, 435, 438*, 442, 444, 445, 457

Oriental Groceries; see Chinese & Far Eastern Groceries

Ostrich Meat: 40(m/o), 167(m/o), 295, 380

Oysters; Natives in season: 25, 37, 50, 54, 55, 57, 84, 74, 110, 111, 117, 203, 205, 206, 242, 254, 257, 258(m/o), 173, 393

Oysters; Rock: 17, 25, 37, 50, 54*, 55, 57, 61, 66, 74, 80, 82, 84, 86, 89, 105, 110, 111, 117, 134, 158*, 189, 201, 203, 205, 206, 226, 242, 254, 257, 258, 273, 325, 353, 365, 388, 393

Pancetta: 2, 10, 77, 78, 137, 154, 166, 180, 181, 182, 183, 184, 186, 203, 205, 262, 297, 327, 373, 378, 382, 383, 387, 393, 423, 429, 444

Panetone: 2, 7, 10, 74, 77, 78, 93, 104, 137, 154, 177, 178*, 181, 182, 183, 184*, 186, 203, 205, 217, 231, 232, 262*, 251, 252, 292, 297, 298, 300, 327, 330, 340, 343, 349, 371, 372, 373, 382, 383, 384, 387, 393, 405, 419, 423, 429, 438, 442, 444, 445

Panforte: 2, 7, 10, 58, 77, 78, 95*(m/o), 104, 177, 178, 181, 182, 184, 186, 232, 244, 262*, 297, 300, 327, 330, 372, 382, 383, 384, 387, 393, 405, 423, 427(m/o), 429, 438, 442, 444

Pasta; dried: 2, 4, 10, 13*, 14*, 44, 57, 58, 67, 69, 74, 77*, 78*, 93, 103, 126, 109, 131, 132, 133, 137, 142, 154, 161, 162, 165, 166, 173, 180, 181, 183, 184, 186, 203, 205*, 234, 244, 252*, 253*, 262, 289, 292, 297*, 329, 335, 340, 342, 352, 359, 363, 371, 372, 373, 377, 378, 381, 382, 383, 384*, 387*, 393*, 405, 423, 429, 430, 433, 435, 438, 442, 444, 447, 454

Pasta; fresh: 10, 70, 77*, 78, 102, 126*, 133, 136, 137, 165, 166, 180, 181, 182, 184*, 186, 203, 244, 252*, 253, 262, 292, 297, 332, 340, 373, 384, 387, 393*, 405*, 423, 429, 444

Pasta; gluten-Free: 69, 71, 171, 197, 306, 310, 338, 339, 346, 354, 363, 394, 432, 452, 454*

Pastry; puff: 243, 305

Patisserie: 10, 11, 12*, 26*, 32, 33, 56, 57*, 75*, 97, 106, 119, 128*, 156, 161, 203, 205, 209, 243*, 261, 266, 267*, 268*, 269*, 305*, 334*, 337, 355*, 393, 444

Patisserie; Jewish: 79*, 125, 367

Patisserie; Middle-Eastern: 18*, 31, 58, 203*, 232, 272, 364*, 393*, 435, 457*

Patisserie; Portuguese: 176, 256

Peacock: 40(m/o)

Pecan Pie: 49, 93, 97, 106, 181, 393, 411, 405*

Peppers; sun-dried: 41

Pike; in season: 25, 54*, 84, 117, 203(special order), 242, 254, 393

Pilchards; Salted: 54*, 115(m/o)

Pimenton: 2, 178, 194, 255, 328, 351

Pizza: 104, 340, 173, 332

Plastic Storage Containers: 245(m/o)

Polish Groceries; see East European Groceries

Pork; Free-range: 8, 24, 37, 43, 48, 51, 57, 68, 72, 73, 107, 112, 120, 140, 141, 151, 152, 168, 179, 187*, 193*, 200, 203, 205, 207(m/o)*, 212, 218, 228*, 237, 239, 250*, 264*, 276, 284, 295, 342, 344, 347, 361*, 366, 377, 378, 393, 404, 410*, 412*, 420, 423*, 430, 431*, 453*, 447

Pork; Eldon Blue: 40(m/o)

Pork; Organic: 204, 291, 378

Pork Pies: 161, 203, 205, 238, 342

Pork; Suckling Pig: 295(special order)

Porridge Oats; Course Natural: 35, 63, 69, 71, 85, 116, 197, 208, 215(m/o), 297, 306, 310, 322, 338, 339, 342, 346, 363, 393, 394, 428, 432, 440, 452, 454

Portuguese & Spanish Groceries: 2, 178*, 194, 255*, 328, 351*

Prawns; Fresh in season: 25, 37, 50, 54*, 57, 86, 117, 160, 203, 257, 273, 325

Prawns; King: 61, 189, 203, 216, 259, 312, 313, 378, 392, 402, 422, 430, 447, 449, 455

Pudding; Christmas: 26, 44, 57, 74, 93, 132, 203, 205, 243, 251, 275, 292, 293, 300, 331, 377, 378, 393, 442, 444, 445, 447

Pulses: 2, 4, 10, 28, 35, 44, 57, 58, 62, 63*, 69*, 71*, 77, 116, 122*, 130*, 132, 135, 175*, 178, 182, 184, 185, 194, 197, 205, 208*, 217, 235, 244, 251, 253, 286, 289*, 292, 297, 300, 304, 310, 322, 327, 330, 333*, 338, 339, 342*, 346, 349, 359*, 363*, 364, 367, 377, 378, 383, 387, 393*, 394, 396, 406, 417, 429, 430, 435*, 438, 439*, 440, 444*, 447, 452, 454*, 457

Pulses; organic: 58, 63, 69*, 71*, 116, 124, 171, 172, 184, 197, 208, 251, 304, 306, 310, 338, 342, 346, 349, 363*, 394, 440, 452*, 454*

Quail: 55, 203, 295, 377, 378, 393, 430, 447

Quinoa grain: 454

Red Herrings: 2, 50, 54*, 105, 117(special order), 343

Relishes (see Chutney, Pickles & Relishes)

Rice; Specialist: 10, 35, 44, 69*, 77, 93, 122*, 130, 132, 146*, 166, 175*, 181, 205, 244, 252, 271, 286, 297, 310, 312, 329, 333*, 338, 342, 359, 363, 377, 378, 382, 384, 387, 393*, 396, 423, 427(m/o), 430, 439*, 444, 447, 452, 454, 458

Rice; Organic: 10, 69, 116, 124, 310, 322, 342, 339, 387, 454

Rice Paper: 70, 244, 378, 387, 393, 447

Rillettes: 32, 57, 132, 161*, 203, 205, 299(m/o), 393

Saffron Cake: 393

Saffron Strands: 2, 4, 10, 44, 70, 77, 93, 122, 132, 146, 165, 181, 244, 257, 297, 333, 342, 351, 363, 367, 371, 377, 378, 387, 393, 423, 430, 444, 447, 454, 457

Salad leaves: 57*, 69, 170*(home delivery), 203, 275, 297, 300*, 311*, 378, 393, 424*, 430, 444*, 447

Salmon; Wild in season: 17, 25, 37, 50, 54*, 55, 57, 61, 66, 80, 84, 86, 105, 110, 111, 114, 117, 132, 158, 160, 203, 205, 206, 242, 254, 257, 258*(m/o), 273, 325, 342, 353, 365, 388, 393, 402, 414

Salt; Smoked: 285(m/o)

Samphire: 25, 54*, 55, 61, 66, 86, 93(special order), 353, 402, 424

Sardines; Fresh: 1, 17, 25, 37, 50, 54*, 55, 57, 61, 66, 80, 82, 84, 86, 105, 110, 111, 117, 134, 158, 159, 164, 169, 189, 194, 201, 203, 205, 206, 229, 242, 249, 254, 263, 273, 279, 324, 325, 342, 353, 365, 388, 393, 399, 402, 414

Sauces; Prepared Pasta: 57*, 67, 74, 77, 78*, 126, 133*, 180, 182, 184*, 186, 202, 203, 205*, 251, 252, 253*, 262*, 292, 299*(m/o), 320*(m/o), 332*, 340, 342, 352, 377, 378*, 381, 382, 384, 387, 401, 405*, 419, 429*, 430, 438, 444, 447

Sauces; Prepared Chinese: 100, 190, 216, 259, 313, 377, 378, 392, 430, 447, 455

Sauces; Prepared Curry: 122, 146, 193, 333, 377, 378, 393, 406, 430, 439, 447

Sauerkraut: 10, 93, 181, 244, 325, 349, 369*, 370, 393

Sausages: 8, 23*, 24, 40*(m/o), 48, 52*, 57*, 58, 121, 132, 161, 168, 187, 203, 205, 207*(m/o), 212, 218, 238, 244, 250*, 264, 290, 292, 295*, 298, 304, 323*, 344, 347, 348, 361, 380*393, 397*, 404, 410, 420, 423, 443, 453

Sausages; Black Pudding: 24, 32, 73, 74, 93, 161, 217, 203, 250, 290, 295, 330, 344, 347, 348, 361, 372, 380, 391, 393, 397*, 423, 445*

Sausages; Greek: 289

Sausages; Fresh Italian: 77, 442, 443, 448, 397

Sausages; Morcilla (Spanish/Portuguese Style Black Pudding): 103, 178, 351

Sausage Skins; natural: 8, 121, 187, 344, 361, 380, 397, 404, 420, 443

Sausages; White Pudding: 73, 217, 250, 344, 347, 361, 380, 443

Scallops; Fresh Bay: 17, 25, 37, 50, 54*, 55, 57, 61, 66, 80, 82, 84, 86, 105, 110, 111, 117, 158, 189, 191, 201, 203, 205, 206, 242, 254, 257, 258(m/o), 263, 273, 325, 353, 365, 393, 444, 458

Scallops; Fresh Queen: 17, 25, 50, 54, 117, 203, 254, 258(m/o), 279, 325, 365, 393

Scallops; Smoked: see Smoked Scallops

Sea Kale: 57, 424

Sea Trout; in season: 17, 25, 37, 50, 54*, 55, 57, 66, 84, 86, 105, 117, 158, 160, 203, 205, 206, 242, 325, 365, 388, 393, 421

Seaweed; Dried: 22, 27, 54, 205, 216, 225, 283, 294, 393, 424*, 454*, 458

Seaweed; Fresh: 430

Shrimps; fresh brown in season: 6, 17, 37, 50, 54*, 203, 393

Shrimps; potted 25, 54*, 55, 57, 58, 74, 93, 105, 161, 203, 205, 229, 235, 254, 279, 292, 298, 299(m/o), 300, 327, 331, 349, 372, 445

Skate: 6, 17, 25, 37, 50, 54*, 55, 57, 61, 66, 80, 82, 84, 86, 105, 110, 117, 158, 169, 189, 203, 205, 206, 242, 254, 273, 353, 365, 388, 393

Smoked; Cods Roe: 17, 25, 37, 54, 55, 61, 80, 86, 110, 117, 158, 160, 161, 189, 201, 203, 205*, 254, 258*(m/o), 353, 388, 393

Smoked Duck Breast: 57, 427(m/o)

Smoked Eel: 57, 86, 160, 161, 203, 205, 226, 258(m/o), 299(m/o), 393, 427(m/o)

Smoked Haddock; undyed: 17, 25, 37, 50, 54, 55, 61*, 66*, 80, 84, 86, 105*, 117, 158, 160, 196, 203, 205, 206, 229, 242, 254, 257, 258*(m/o), 279, 300*, 314, 365, 388, 393, 427(m/o)

Smoked Halibut: 54, 160, 203, 205, 226, 279, 393

Smoked Marlin: 54, 160

Smoked Ostrich: 203

Smoked Quails Eggs: 285(m/o), 292

Smoked Pheasant: 427(m/o)

Smoked Salmon: 6, 10, 25*, 32, 37, 44, 54*, 57*, 58, 61*, 66*, 70, 74*, 77, 79, 80, 83, 86*, 93, 105*, 110*, 134, 157, 161*, 160*, 189, 199, 203*, 205*, 226, 235, 244, 251, 254*, 257*, 258*(m/o), 262, 275, 287, 292, 298, 299*(m/o), 304, 327*, 330, 336, 342, 343, 349, 372, 377, 378, 387, 393*, 405*, 427*(m/o), 430, 438, 444*, 447

Smoked Salt: 285(m/o)

Smoked Scallops: 54, 258*(m/o)

Smoked Sprats: 54, 393

Smoked Sturgeon: 54, 161, 393

Smoked Swordfish: 86

Smoked Trout: 54, 161, 203, 205, 258*(m/o), 299(m/o), 378, 427(m/o)

Smoked Tuna: 54, 161, 393

Smoked Venison: 427(m/o)

Snails: 57, 70, 133, 205, 279, 299(m/o), 372, 378, 393

Snails; live: 289

Sole; Dover: 6, 17, 25, 37, 50, 54*, 55, 57, 61, 66, 80, 82, 84, 105, 114, 115*(home delivery)117, 134, 170(home delivery), 158, 169, 196, 201, 203, 205, 226, 206, 242, 254, 273, 342, 353, 365, 388, 393, 414, 421

South African Groceries: 380*

Spanish and Portuguese Groceries: See Portuguese & Spanish Groceries

Speck: 77, 78, 103, 154, 203, 205, 244, 262, 278, 382, 393, 405, 429

Spices; a good general selection: 2, 4, 10, 37, 44, 57*, 58, 63*, 69, 71, 74*, 77, 122*, 130*, 146*, 157, 163*(m/o), 171, 175*, 178, 194, 197, 198(m/o), 216, 232, 244, 251, 259, 280, 286, 289, 297, 298, 300, 304, 312, 313, 327, 333*, 346*, 359*, 363, 367, 371, 377, 378, 387, 393*, 394, 396, 406*, 407*, 422, 423, 430, 435, 438, 439*, 444, 447, 458

Spices; Organic: 69, 197, 342, 454*

Squab: 8, 158, 203, 205, 295(special order)

Squid; Fresh: 6, 17, 27, 37, 54*, 55, 61, 80, 82, 84, 105, 110, 169, 189, 191, 194, 203, 205, 206, 226, 229, 249, 254, 281, 294, 353, 365, 388, 402, 458

Squid Ink: 86, 169, 297

Star Anise: 57, 74, 100, 122, 139, 146, 163(m/o), 205, 216, 259, 283, 312, 313, 331, 359, 377, 378, 392, 393, 406, 407, 409, 422, 430, 439, 449, 455, 458

Sugar; organic: 342, 447, 454

Sugar; Perruche: 7, 205, 372, 393, 444, 447

Sugar; Unrefined: 342, 363, 372, 378, 447, 454

Swordfish; Fresh: 17, 37, 54*, 61, 80, 84, 86, 110, 134, 158, 169, 194, 203, 206, 242, 254, 273, 324, 353, 365, 388, 390

Taramasalata: 2, 10, 16, 54, 58, 77, 93, 136, 166, 181, 232, 235, 244, 262, 275, 298, 300, 327, 330, 349, 372, 382, 383, 387, 393, 447

Tea: 2, 7*, 10, 57, 70, 74, 83, 93, 104, 136, 157, 161*, 171, 197, 203*, 205*, 211*, 216*, 220, 227*, 244, 248, 251, 280*, 298, 299*(m/o), 300, 327, 346*, 349, 352, 363, 371, 372, 377, 378, 387, 393*, 394, 423, 425*, 430, 433, 436*, 440, 442, 444, 405*, 447, 451*, 458

Tea; Organic: 71, 171, 244, 342, 346, 363, 393, 451, 454

Thai Groceries (see Chinese & Far Eastern Groceries)

Tiramisu: 10, 166, 177, 186, 203, 253, 262, 297, 332, 373, 387, 393

213, 222, 223*, 233, 240, 249, 265, 270, 275, 288*, 289, 297, 304, 307*, 311*, 315, 316, 327, 335, 345, 364, 367, 370, 371*, 375, 378*, 393, 396, 398, 416, 417, 421, 423, 430, 434, 437*, 444*, 447*, 448, 450*, 456, 457, 458

Vegetables; Afro-Caribbean: 34, 62*, 63*, 64, 98, 101, 135, 194*, 213, 316, 367, 396, 415, 434, 448*

Vegetables; Indian sub-continent: 46*, 122, 146*, 155*, 286*, 306*, 367, 393, 398*, 434, 448, 450*

Vegetables; Far-Eastern: 259*, 271, 311*, 312, 313, 409, 422, 449, 455, 458

Vegetables; Organic: 63, 69, 71, 170(home delivery), 171, 172, 197, 289, 311*, 322, 342, 346, 363, 367, 371, 377, 378, 394, 408, 423, 437, 444*, 447, 452*, 454*

Vegetables; Preserved Char-grilled: 10, 14, 44, 57*, 71, 74*, 77, 78*, 93, 104, 106, 109, 132, 133, 161, 165, 180, 181, 182*, 183, 184*, 186, 197, 203, 205, 217, 231, 232, 235, 244, 251, 253, 262, 292, 293*, 297, 298, 299*(m/o), 300, 304, 320(m/o), 330, 340, 343, 349, 352, 363*, 372, 379, 382, 383, 384, 387, 393*, 394*, 405, 423, 427*(m/o), 429, 438*, 445, 447

Vietnamese Rice Wrappers: 259, 312, 313, 392, 409, 455, 458

Venison; Farmed: 8, 25, 37, 48, 72, 86, 110, 158, 203, 226, 250, 264, 284, 295, 344, 347, 378, 380, 393, 400

Venison; Wild: 8, 203, 264, 295, 377

Verjuice: 81(m/o), 235, 320(m/o), 444

Vinegars: 2, 10, 24, 44, 57*, 58, 63, 71, 74*, 77, 78, 93, 104*, 109, 131, 132, 133, 161, 162, 166, 177, 178, 180, 184, 186, 197, 203, 205*, 216, 217, 231, 234, 235, 251, 253, 262, 297*, 298, 299(m/o), 300, 304, 320*(m/o), 327, 331, 349, 359, 361, 363, 371, 372, 377, 378, 382, 384, 387, 393, 394, 401, 405, 407, 419, 423, 430, 433, 438, 442, 444*, 445*, 447, 454

Whitebait: 17, 25, 37, 54*, 55, 61, 80, 84, 86, 105, 110, 117, 134, 158, 159, 189, 201, 203, 205, 206, 242, 257, 273, 325, 353, 393, 402

Wild Boar; see Boar; Wild:

Yabbies: 324, 389

Yeast; fresh bakers: 33, 57, 77, 79, 137, 153, 195, 243, 256, 272, 293, 308, 328, 334, 337, 342, 357, 378, 411, 441, 444

Yoghurt; Cow's Milk: 2, 10, 57, 58, 63, 71, 74, 104, 161, 171, 174, 197*, 208, 217, 231, 251, 292, 300, 304, 309*, 327, , 363, 371, 372, 377, 378, 393, 394, 426*, 430, 435, 447, 454, 457

Yoghurt; Dairy Free: 63, 197, 208, 306, 346, 440, 454

Yoghurt; Organic: 10, 63, 69, 71, 93, 116, 124, 197, 251, 322, 342, 346, 363, 378, 393, 394, 454

Yoghurt; Goat's Milk: 10, 63, 71, 116, 172, 197, 342, 346, 363, 393, 394, 440, 454

Yoghurt; Sheep's: (Ewe's) Milk: 2, 10, 63, 71, 104, 197, 342, 349, 363, 393, 394, 426, 435, 454

Yoghurt; Soya: 63, 69, 71, 171, 428, 440, 454

Yugoslavian Groceries: 232

COMMENTS

Please use this page to recommend shops of outstanding quality within London or nearby, that you feel ought to be included in our next edition. Likewise, any complaints about shops included will be taken seriously.

Please post to:
Gray's Guide to London Food Shops,
1 Willoughby Mews, Wix's Lane, London SW4 OQH.
including your name and address.

COMMENTS

Please use this page to recommend shops of outstanding quality within London or nearby, that you feel ought to be included in our next edition. Likewise, any complaints about shops included will be taken seriously.

Please post to:

Gray's Guide to London Food Shops,

1 Willoughby Mews, Wix's Lane, London SW4 OQH.

including your name and address.

COMMENTS

Please use this page to recommend shops of outstanding quality within London or nearby, that you feel ought to be included in our next edition. Likewise, any complaints about shops included will be taken seriously.

Please post to:
Gray's Guide to London Food Shops,
1 Willoughby Mews, Wix's Lane, London SW4 OQH.
including your name and address.

COMMENTS

Please use this page to recommend shops of outstanding quality within London or nearby, that you feel ought to be included in our next edition. Likewise, any complaints about shops included will be taken seriously.

Please post to:
Gray's Guide to London Food Shops,
1 Willoughby Mews, Wix's Lane, London SW4 0QH.
including your name and address.

COMMENTS

Please use this page to recommend shops of outstanding quality within London or nearby, that you feel ought to be included in our next edition. Likewise, any complaints about shops included will be taken seriously.

Please post to:
Gray's Guide to London Food Shops,
1 Willoughby Mews, Wix's Lane, London SW4 OQH.
including your name and address.

COMMENTS

Please use this page to recommend shops of outstanding quality within London or nearby, that you feel ought to be included in our next edition. Likewise, any complaints about shops included will be taken seriously.

Please post to:
Gray's Guide to London Food Shops,
1 Willoughby Mews, Wix's Lane, London SW4 OQH.
including your name and address.

COMMENTS

Please use this page to recommend shops of outstanding quality within London or nearby, that you feel ought to be included in our next edition. Likewise, any complaints about shops included will be taken seriously.

Please post to:
Gray's Guide to London Food Shops,
1 Willoughby Mews, Wix's Lane, London SW4 OQH.
including your name and address.

COMMENTS

Please use this page to recommend shops of outstanding quality within London or nearby, that you feel ought to be included in our next edition. Likewise, any complaints about shops included will be taken seriously.

Please post to:
Gray's Guide to London Food Shops,
1 Willoughby Mews, Wix's Lane, London SW4 0QH.
including your name and address.